STORMJAMMERS

THE EXTRAORDINARY STORY OF ELECTRONIC
WARFARE OPERATIONS IN THE GULF WAR

BASED ON THE INSPIRING TRUE STORY

Robert Stanek

RP BOOKS
REAGENT PRESS

STORMJAMMERS
Copyright © 2006 by Robert Stanek.

All rights reserved, including the right to reproduce this book or portions thereof in any form. Printed in the United States of America.

Reagent Press
Published by Virtual Press, Inc.
Cover design & illustration by Reagent Press
ISBN 1-57545-084-4

Stanek, Robert.
Stormjammers: The Extraordinary story of Electronic Warfare operations in the Gulf War/Robert Stanek.
p.cm.
1. Persian Gulf War, 1991—Personal narratives, American.
2. United States. United States Air Force.
3. Stanek, Robert. Title.

About the Author: Robert Stanek

The author proudly served in the Persian Gulf War as a combat crewmember on an EC-130H, an Electronic Warfare aircraft. During the war he flew numerous combat missions and logged over two hundred combat flight hours. Additionally, he has nearly 1000 hours of EC-130H flight time.

In his military career, he has always been at the top of his class—a two-time distinguished graduate, honor graduate, and unit technician of the year. His civilian education includes a B. S. in Computer Science, magna cum laude, finalist for valedictorian, and a Master of Science Information Systems with distinction. His distinguished accomplishments during the Gulf War earned him nine medals, including our nation's highest flying honor, the Air Force Distinguished Flying Cross.

His last station while in the Air Force was at the 324th Intelligence Squadron, Wheeler Army Airfield, Hawaii. His initial training in the intelligence field was as a Russian linguist. His language background also includes Japanese, Korean, German and Spanish. As a writer, he has always preferred book-length fiction and non-fiction. One of his essays on military life won a writing contest, earning him a cash award and the George Washington Honor medal from the Freedom Foundation at Valley Forge.

His experiences in the Persian Gulf War changed his life and helped drive his successful career as a writer and entrepreneur. To date, he has written and had published over 50 books. His books are sold all over the world and have been translated into many languages.

Author's Notes

Times and dates are included to provide a sense of chronology and are not absolutes. The notes in my journal had times referenced in Greenwich Mean Time (Zulu), which were converted to local times dependent on location.

The events depicted in the story are taken from real accounts, my personal journal, and various other unclassified sources. Names have been changed to protect the privacy rights of those involved. Some aspects of the story have been dramatized to provide a more complete view of electronic warfare and the Gulf War in general.

The Air Players

Callsign	Aircraft type	Role
Gas Station	KC	Refueler.
Gypsy	AWACS	Airborne warning and control.
Paladin	F-15C Eagle	Air support. CAP. MiG Sweep.
Phantom	RC-135	Reconnaissance.
Shadow	EC-130	EW/Communications jammer.

The Package

Nickname	Aircraft type	Role
Buff	B-52	Heavy bomber.
Eagle	F-15C	Air superiority fighter/interceptor.
Falcon	F-16	Air-to-air, air-to-ground fighter.
Raven	EF-111	EW, primary radar jammer, attack.
Strike Eagle	F-15E	Deep interdiction; carries payload.
Thunderbolt	A-10	Ground attack aircraft.
Weasel	F-4G	EW radar jammer, attack, reconnaissance.

Note: A suffix indicates the aircraft's number as part of a group. Paladin-1 is the leader (Paladin Leader). Paladin-2 is his wingman. Paladin-3 is the next fighter. Paladin-4 is Paladin-3's wingman.

The Combat Crew

Normal crew load is 13 (this can vary)

Front Crew

Nickname	Full Name
AC	Aircraft Commander; the pilot
Co	Copilot
Eng	Engineer
Nav	Navigator
AMT	Air Maintenance Technician

Mission Crew

Nickname	Full Name
MCC	Mission Crew Commander
MCS (Pos. 5)	Mission Crew Supervisor
Positions 1, 2, 3, 4	Junior operators/ operators
Positions 6, 7	Senior operators

Inner Ship's Communications

Channel	Description
Flight Crew Hot	For emergencies. When pulled, it activates the headset microphone without having to key it. Also called Ship's Hot.
Listen	For listening to Flight Crew Hot comms.
PA	The ship's loudspeaker; only the front-end can talk on PA.
Private A	The mission crew commander's channel, used to pass targeted signals to the MCC.
Private B	The mission crew's channel, and for comms to the mission crew supervisor.
Select	Patch directly to other positions, like a dial-in telephone switching bank for general chatter.
Ship's Interphone	Cockpit comms and comms to the front-end.

July 1990

Summer in south-central Germany was calm and warm but not hot. Nevada, two weeks ago at the Green Flag exercise, had been hot. I powered down the windows, headed slowly down the kilometer-long stretch of road to the opposite side of the base. It was my first day back after a long operational exercise stateside. I was exhausted after the previous day's 18-hour flight, but exhaustion was the norm for flyers and combat crew.

Mustard fields separating the administration and flight line sides of the sleepy air base were in full yellow-green bloom. I stared out across the fields for a moment as I came to a solitary-looking stop sign. The stop sign, nearly a duplicate of the ones back in the U.S.A., was almost an oddity in this part of Europe. Most German road crossings sported yield signs—Germans didn't want to fuss with having to come to a complete stop when it wasn't absolutely necessary.

To me it seemed everything in Germany was about speed. The Autobahn had no speed limits in most places. The BMW 728i I drove could purr along comfortably at 200 kilometers per hour. But this wasn't the Autobahn and I came to a halt from a moderate forty-klicks.

A narrow two-lane road spread out before me. If I turned right and followed the road, I'd end up in a country village. Quaint and picturesque, the village was like a snapshot out of another time, a photo from an old postcard. Left would take me down Snake Hill, a treacherous stretch of road with many twists and turns. Snake Hill in winter had claimed more than a few lives, but this was not winter; and I only turned left so I could lean right and enter the flight-line side of the air base through the back gate.

A security police officer checked my identification card and waved me through. It was July the 25th. More than a thousand miles away, U.S. Ambassador Glaspie was visiting Iraq. Iraqi troops had been amassing on the Kuwait-Iraq border all month. Relations between the two countries were falling apart and the U.S. Ambassador was in Baghdad at Saddam Hussein's request. The official word given to Saddam Hussein that day helped direct history—a history that probably would have played on with or without the discussions though no one will ever know for sure.

I stuffed my flight cap into my left leg pocket and checked the zipper on my green nomex flight suit. I had to look good; I was entering the ops building, going straight to the director of operation's office. It was the first stop of many.

The director of operations, Major James Abernathy, was an old-school pilot who'd flown in Vietnam. He could be an S.O.B. when pushed but was well-liked and good at his job. I said my good mornings, trying not to interrupt the major's conversation with Chief Master Sergeant Dwight James Hancock, aka Old Jimmie, as I checked distribution. Checking distro was a part of the morning routine.

Remembering my flight helmet, which was getting fitted with a new mask, I backtracked to Life Support, which was closed. Heck, it was early, so the wasted stop didn't bother me too much. As I hurried down the long central hall of the ops building, I passed two large vaults that served as SCIFs. Mission planning and briefings were held in the SCIFs. No mission for me today, so the SCIF wasn't one of my stops.

I cut through the crew lounge, eyed the cases of Bischoff piled next to the cooler. Unlike some of the crewers who had come in several hours ago from a mission, I had the good sense to know that it was too early for beers.

I filled a thermos with coffee. Took a quick sip. It was strong. No cream. No sugar.

Outside the ops building was a long barbed-wire fence. Behind it were a group of buildings and the hardstands for the unit's aircraft. I showed my flightline badge to the SP inside the guard shack; displaying an access badge was a requirement inside the flightline. The guard buzzed me in.

A single four-engine turboprop, the great Herk, was parked on the second hardstand. The C-130 was one of the Air Force's truly great workhorses. During its lengthy tenure in service, it had done and seen it all.

It was a tactical aircraft that was readily modifiable to do any job. As an AC-130, it was the Gunship—one of the most deadly close-air support birds in the sky—and it had proved itself many times during attack, reconnaissance, and close-air support missions. As the KC-130, it was a capable aerial refueler. During Vietnam the C-130 had been used to drop the Daisy Cutter, a specially designed bomb used to clear landing zones for helicopters in dense jungle.

A payload of bombs was nothing compared to the payload delivered by the EC-130—the great Gray Lady. The EC-130 was one of the Air Force's most capable and trustworthy Electronic Warfare platforms.

The grace of the Gray Lady wasn't in her payload. She wasn't a B-52 or an F-15. She didn't deliver a payload of rockets or bombs. She was a silent killer and a giver of hope, just as powerful as the Mighty Buffs and just as lethal as a Screaming Eagle.

EC-130's had been in every major confrontation since Vietnam and were battle-proven in Beirut, Grenada, Panama, Nicaragua and elsewhere, but few knew they even existed. She was a modern marvel. As the EC-130H, she could cripple anti-aircraft artillery batteries, surface-to-air missile units, ground troop movements and fighter pilots by blocking their communications and signals emissions. As the EC-130E, she conducted psychological warfare on the enemy, delivering a payload of fear to our enemies and hope to mistreated peoples. She was the one aircraft fascists and dictators feared more than the B-52.

I glanced at the tail number of the EC-130 parked in the hardstand. It was the same specially configured bird I'd flown back from Nevada in after the combined exercises. In that bird, I was truly an airborne commando, combat crew through and through.

We had tested out her new capabilities in the Nevada desert and raised more than a few eyebrows, but the invitation by General Kingston to come play war games in the desert had a hidden agenda. Washington brass wanted to shut down the EC-

130 program in Europe. Modern warfare equipment was expensive; and the politicians didn't always understand the need for high-tech, high-cost platforms like the specially configured Gray Lady I looked at as I stepped on by.

The main question seemed to be what was an entire wing of air and support crew doing in Germany flying "training" missions. It was an excuse to close the base, save the Air Force and the good old U.S.A. millions each year. The Washington brass knew the "training" missions had little to do with training. Soviet fighters didn't react to "training" missions and I had seen more than my share of Soviet fighter pilots out the window.

My team had flown every day in Nevada during the exercise—sometimes jarringly, teeth rattlingly low to the deck as we raced into the mission zone, other times making the turboprops whine and screech as the pilot showed off countermeasures. By the time we made that final transatlantic dash I was more than ready to come home to Germany.

Even as I entered the plain green prefab building that I worked in, I could hear and feel the roar of engines. The sensation that I was soaring at 30,000 feet hadn't gone away. It was flyer's lag, the feeling that you are flying even when both feet are planted firmly on the ground. It'd go away in another day or two—if I was lucky.

All members of the group had day jobs that were different from their jobs in the air. My day job was to run Crew Scheduling. Key perk: I knew every flyer in the unit by name, grade and skill.

I sat down, went through the papers in my inbox. A few newbies had come in since I'd been gone. They'd have to come back through scheduling if they wanted to fly. No one flew until they had a sit-down with me—it was a policy requirement and not because I had big brass balls.

It was 09:00 by the time I got a chance to update the Big Board, a two-week planner that listed the unit's missions and the crews assigned to each mission.

A standard mission had five front-end and eight back-end crew. The front-end crew—pilot, copilot, navigator, engineer, and air maintenance technician—were responsible for the plane and its systems. The back-end crew—mission crew commander, mission crew supervisor, and six specialists—were responsible for executing the mission, whatever the mission might be.

The Big Board was decidedly low-tech but I preferred it to computerized tracking. Crew assignment changed often. Flying the zone was stressful and sustained high-levels of stress meant people got sick more often than was normal. When crewers got sick, mentally or physically, they were put on the Duty Not Including Flying (DNIF) list until a flight medic took them off of it. And DNIFs were only one of many reasons crew assignments changed, which meant being able to see the status of every crewer at a glance was not only valuable, it was often a requirement.

In the air I was part of the back-end crew. I worked as a mission crew supervisor or as a senior mission specialist, depending on the duty. On the Hot Sheet for the next week was a mobility exercise. Chief Hancock's handwritten note asked for me specifically. I scheduled a different mission crew supervisor for the mobex anyway. I'd just been away for 5 weeks. My wife wouldn't understand why I had to go off again, especially when I was the one running scheduling.

Then I got to thinking about the Washington brass and their small-minded view of Electronic Warfare. EW platforms were like stealth bombers. Bureaucrats recognized the value of planes that were invisible to radar but often couldn't justify the expense. And while they might be willing to pay for stealth fighters, stealth bombers at 2 billion and change each seemed way over the top—even if it meant the U.S.A. could get first strike.

I wasn't about to let them win. Like the chief, I had something to prove to the Washington brass. I penciled myself back in as the MCS for the mobex. No matter what Katie said, it'd be easier explaining to her why I had to go away for two weeks than trying to explain to Chief Master Sergeant Hancock why I shouldn't go.

The old chief was married to his job and the military. He didn't understand what it was like to be a newlywed; or if he did, his memories of those days some thirty years ago just weren't as clear as they once were.

"Absence makes the heart grow fonder," is what the chief would say, if he said anything at all. My usual response of "or indifferent" would get a chuckle but wouldn't really be heard. The chief wanted the best crewers on critical missions and I was one of the best—fortunately or unfortunately.

Ten hours later, I was home, sitting in front of an ever-filling screen, pounding away at the keyboard, waiting for my wife to come home. I had a box of manuscripts that I was consistently piling higher and higher. Tom Petty was playing on the radio, and I stopped pounding the keyboard briefly to jot down a few notes in my journal and sip at my beer, a Bischoff. Then I turned back to the computer screen.

Katie came home from work at 19:30. We made supper, made love, talked about the away mission—in that order—and the order of the events is what pissed Katie off.

It was a typical Wednesday, ending with Katie slamming the bedroom door in my face and my sleeping on the couch.

August 1990

04:00 came way too early. I showered, ate, and was out of the house by 05:00. I had an 05:45 show, 3 hours of pre-brief, 9 hours of flight time, and 2 hours of post-brief to look forward to. It was a Thursday. This was going to be an average day as fly days go.

Wednesday's flight had been a No-Go, so today's flight was a Gray Warrior—in-flight training for chemical warfare. I lugged my chemical protective gear out of the car, entered ops and went straight to Life Support. I dropped my gear next to the O2 station, then preflighted my oxygen mask and helmet.

At 05:29, I touched my thumb to the scanner on the secure vault door outside the flight briefing room. I remembered to slap on my green badge as the door closed behind me with a dull thud and a click.

Check-in went quick. I initialed the flight orders next to my typed name while looking over the info to make sure it was correct. Then I sat down for the short wait.

By 05:45, the pilot, copilot, navigator, and engineer were present as were the eight mission crewers. The only one missing was the air maintenance technician. The AMT, Sergeant Martin "Crow" Endwick, was prone to being late; and true to form he showed up flashing his hang-loose sign three minutes later. In crew time, late is late, whether it's seconds or minutes.

"You got beer after wheels down," I whispered into his ear, slapping him on the back. It was a crew dog rule: late to fly, first to pay.

Mission Planning for the flight, a standard training profile with the inclusion of chemical gear practice, didn't take long. We'd wear our plastic bags to and from the plane, all right.

We were waiting to fly when the messages started coming in. Iraq was invading Kuwait. At the time, the thirteen of us sitting in the ready room didn't think much of it. Our concerns were centered on the flight and the mission ahead.

The invasion of Kuwait progressed rapidly. Most of their units were caught in garrison, having been pulled back from defensive postures. No Arab nation believed an Arab would attack another Arab nation. In the end, Kuwait didn't mount much of a defense at all. Iraq would have its prize in less than three days. That day, the thirteen of us departed on time, plastic bags and all.

Five days later, early in the morning on Tuesday, August 7, some of us would be sitting in the same ready room waiting to fly. Over the weekend a lot had transpired. The fourth largest army in the world, the Iraqi war machine, had just stepped on a nuisance; and they had crushed it in less than three days.

King Fahd of Saudi Arabia feared the next step might take Iraqi forces into Saudi Arabia; and on Saturday, August 4, he had called for U.S. military advice. Our intelligence indications supported his fears; Iraqi forces were setting up in a defensive posture along the Kuwait-Saudi Arabia border. President Bush had already agreed to send forces to the Gulf; the only thing he needed to do it was to get the approval of King Fahd. The matter was a delicate one, handled aptly by a delegation headed by Secretary of Defense Dick Cheney that included a number of high-level VIPs and General H. Norman Schwarzkopf.

By Monday afternoon Germany time, the United States was committed to the defense of Saudi Arabia, which would lead to Operation Desert Shield and ultimately to Operation Desert Storm.

This day we didn't fly though we did follow the incoming messages rather closely.

U.S. and allied troops began arriving with regularity in Saudi Arabia. Within a week, five fighter squadrons and a brigade of the 82nd Airborne were poised for defense. For those of us at the tiny air base in Germany, the waiting game had begun only we didn't know it yet.

Over that next week, I watched three of our team go. They were Farsi and Arabic language specialists. Things were heating up in the Gulf; but for those of us that remained it was business as usual—well, almost business as usual. For a time we didn't fly. For a time afterward we flew less and less. I thought about those in the Gulf a lot. The desert sands seemed somewhat closer though still very far away.

September 1990

September was pretty uneventful. The days faded one into the other and are gone from my memory. Katie and I managed to get away for a few days, taking a long drive out into the German countryside. The castles along the Rhine River are strikingly beautiful and somewhat eerie in their majesty.

October 1990

Flight bag in hand, I entered ops and looked around. It was rather deserted for the middle of the morning.

"All flights have been cancelled for today," warned the Watch Officer from behind his desk, "you should check in with the chief."

"Check in with the chief?" I asked. The Watch Officer shrugged his shoulders. Needless to say, I double-timed it to the DO's office.

"Morning, Chief, what's up?" I asked.

"Ah shit, guess no one got hold of the crew that was flying today!" There was something about the way the old chief said it that made me chuckle. He was the only chief I knew who flew every chance he got. The major looked up from his desk. He didn't say anything; he just sort of smiled. To him, it was just old Jimmie being himself.

"Guess not." I replied.

"Get on down to Life Support and fit a chemical mask. Then head over for mobility processing at the hangar across the lot."

"Real world?" I asked.

"Real world. Mobex is just a prep; but you'll need your shot records, tags, and your gear. Should be in your bag anyway, right?" Old Jimmie looked up at me and I sort of nodded.

Just then, I noticed a brand-new bulletin board behind him with lists of names arranged by crews. My name was in position six on crew three. "Position 6?" I asked.

"We need the best ops on 6 and 7. You're it. Got it?"

I nodded agreement, didn't think much more of it at the time as I headed out the door posthaste.

In a few minutes I was sucking filtered air through a real-world chemical mask while the life support technician fitted it up and showed me how to use it properly—like I didn't already know how. But this one was different from the one I was used to; it wasn't stamped: TRAINING USE ONLY. I'd never really cared before if the seals fit just right. I did then.

By the time I got into the mobility processing line, it stretched all the way to the back of the hangar. Happy, Topper, Popcorn, Cowboy, and a few other crew dogs were also at the end of the line, mixed in with a large group of ground-support personnel. They had arrived a few minutes before me and under similar circumstances. We all would have preferred flying.

It didn't take long to get to the front of the line. We passed the time listening to Happy's anecdotes. By now a number of crewers had piled into the line behind us. I saw Able and Tommy. You couldn't miss them. Several others—who were all good friends—including Chris, PBJ, Mike and Captain Willie, were behind them.

Able was spouting off as usual. "You believe this f'ing shit," he was saying. Tommy wasn't helping to calm him down but was cheering him on.

All I heard of the remainder of their conversation was a string of f-words as I reached the front of the line. Personnel was first with emergency data cards. The cards covered whom to contact in case of emergency, next of kin, and what not. I had one typed. Then came the Security police with ID cards and dog tags. I got a new set made. Afterward the base legal team was there to make powers of attorney and wills. I didn't think I'd need either of those, so I moved on to the Chaplain and Finance. Immunization was through a door and across a hall. I got four shots. Two in each arm.

The mobex prep was a rather rude awakening; and about the time the fourth needle pushed into my arm, something I'd neglected to see the importance of clicked. I was on launch crew three and yet the official word was that our unit was still to remain in place. We would not be going to the Gulf, or so the buzz in the mobility line went.

After the mobility exercises, two weeks passed quietly, yet that morning when I entered the ops building at 07:15 it was buzzing. A crowd had gathered around the DO's office and there sitting in one of the chairs across from the chief was a man so tanned that I hardly recognized him. He looked like a sun-wrinkled prune. Lost weight, too, I could tell. One of our guys had come home. It was October 15th.

He was being bombarded by a never-ending onslaught of questions. "How was Saudi?" "Did you get to Riyadh?" "How was the desert?" "What was it like?" "Was it hot?" "What does the situation look like?"

He was a celebrity, our local expert. He'd been there; we hadn't. Yet the questions were all about the same thing. We all wanted to hear someone say it—anyone besides the newscasters and the second-guessers. It being the only question no one asked, "Do you think there'll be war?"

    I stood gawking for about fifteen minutes then went to work, business as usual—well almost business as usual. That day I went home for lunch and ate with my wife, Katie. We didn't have to talk about Saudi, the Gulf, or the possibilities. We had only to turn on CNN and it spoke for us.

November 1990

We didn't have the traditional Thanksgiving fare that year. It wasn't a well-roasted turkey we pulled steaming out of the oven. We had baked sweet potatoes, corn bread, pumpkin pie, and all the usual. But the main course was ham. Try something different, I had told Katie.

The neighbors from one floor up joined us. He was an air maintenance technician, a fellow crew dog, and his wife was a good friend of my wife.

The beer of choice after dinner, sitting on the couch watching the inevitable football game, was Bischoff, similar to the Budweiser I would have guzzled if I were at home in the good old U.S. of A.

Quite a few of our activities at work were directed at preparations for a probable deployment. The possible had become the probable although the official word was still a definitive no.

Some 250,000 allied troops had been deployed to the Gulf by then.

December 1990

At first glance the sleek gray-painted lady before me looked like any standard C-130 used for transport. But as you came closer, the rear antenna array told you she was different. She was unique.

I clambered up the entry way and went through the crew entrance door, taking care not to smack my head on the upper metal lip that was a few inches too low for me even as I hunched over. The interior lights were still off and the cabin was dark and silent.

I groped my way to position six and set my gear down beside the seat. Other than my normal gear, a helmet bag, and an A-bag, I had two extra bags this day. I waited for the external power hookups to kick in and for the AMT to turn on the interior lights. I was eager to get airborne, very eager.

Seconds later I heard the distant hum of the external power-set kick in. The overhead lights were brought up. The AMT opened the rear ramp and door, negating the need for the overhead lights.

I waited my turn to stow my extra bags in the rear behind the racks. As I did so, I took a long look up the belly of the Lady.

The cockpit was that of a standard C-130 with positions for pilot, copilot, navigator, and engineer. Behind the Nav's position was the forward bunk and above that the forward escape hatch.

It was behind station 245 that the Gray Lady really expressed her differences. Her belly was dissected by one main aisle that ran from aft to stern lined on both sides by an array of high-tech gear that filled her insides and weighed her down with thousands of extra pounds.

Behind the station 245 wall dividing the cockpit from the mission compartment was the emergency oxygen shut-off valve, a fire axe, and an extinguisher. Immediately behind that the tall racks housing the eight mission crew positions began. In front of the racks were eight high-backed flight chairs. The chairs swiveled to face the positions, but that's about all they did. They looked deceivingly comfortable, but all they were was cold steel and old foam cushions.

Each position within the two long racks that ran to the midsection, four to a side, had its array of high-tech gadgetry. On the starboard side near the center hatch, a single position stood all by itself. This was the air maintenance technician's position. Opposite it was an empty space where spare equipment was usually stowed. Also where most of the emergency medical kits were stored. Behind the AMT's position were two more rows of equipment, housed neatly in racks. This was the heart and soul of the great Lady. Yet with all her electronic gadgetry turned down, she still looked deceivingly innocent, at least to me.

I opened my flight crew checklist to the Preflight Checklist as I had a hundred times before. Following procedure, I ran my fingers across the equipment racks in front of me. I gave them the usual tugs then sat down. After wadding up a set of foam earplugs, I stuffed them into my ears. The whine of the four turboprop engines was unnerving, and in the long-term damaging. There were a few, though, that had been flying for a very long time. They didn't need the plugs anymore.

Headset on, I readied my communication panel, pulling out all the appropriate knobs from a seemingly daunting array of knobs and switches. The knobs were for listening to chatter on a particular channel. The channel selector let me talk on a given channel when I keyed my mike.

The knob marked PA was for the ship's loudspeaker; only the front-end could talk on PA. Ship's Interphone was for cockpit comms and comms to the front-end. Private A was the mission crew commander's channel. We used it to pass targeted signals to the MCC. Private B was the mission crew's channel and for comms to the mission crew supervisor. Listen let me hear Flight Crew Hot comms, which, when pulled, activated my microphone without my having to key it. It was used for emergencies. Select was like a dial-in telephone switching bank for general chatter. There were others for out-of-ship comms.

Mouthpiece in place, I called out, "One, Six, interphone checks." No reply. One was still busy with her oxygen regulator and helmet. "MCS, Six, interphone checks."

The mission crew supervisor's reply came into my headset loud and clear. We ran through the channel list: Flight Crew Hot; ship's Interphone; the Privates: A and B, Listen, and Select.

I gave the thumbs up sign to the MCS and waited for the others on the crew to check in and do the same.

A few minutes later the MCS called out, "MCC, MCS, preflight checks complete. Mission crew ready for Before Starting Engines Checklist."

"Roger, MCS," responded the MCC. He then relayed to the navigator that the mission crew was ready to go.

I could hear the front-end chatter in my ears amidst a chorus of other voices. They were just finishing up their preflight checks.

"Crew, Before Starting Engine Checklist. Loose articles stowed. Oxygen 100 percent." There were a number of responses, but by now I was only half listening. I was keying in on Tower, waiting for them to give us taxi and take-off clearance. "Crew, Before Starting Engine Checklist complete."

The copilot gave a quick brief, then the AMT pulled the chocks from under the wheels and tossed them in behind the racks. I knew this because they landed with a thunk just as the number three engine was whining to a start.

"Crew, four engines green." The engines whined a little louder as the pilot checked forward and reverse thrust and the brakes.

Taxi went quick. The gate was already open when we got to it, allowing us entrance to the runway. Once the pilot readied, he began the before takeoff checks.

"Crew ready for taxi and takeoff?" tweaked the MCC's voice into our headsets. We hoisted our thumbs high. "Pilot, MCC, mission crew ready for taxi and takeoff."

"Roger, MCC."

Finally we were ready to go. Strapped in, green nomex gloves on, seat facing forward, we listened to the pilot's voice announce the obvious. "Crew, we're rolling," he said and we prepared for takeoff.

Suddenly the eagerness to be airborne disappeared. A three-day TDY was before me and now all I could think of was what I was leaving behind. I imagined the rolling hills, the farmlands, and the thick green forests. Every German village I'd seen had been like the picture postcards of Europe I'd seen as a boy.

I'd pursued each and every one of those pictures. I'd followed the Rhine River by boat, admiring the medieval castles that frequented its shores. I'd walked castle bulwarks at night when torches lighted them and their walls reflected an ominous orange amidst thick shadows, imagining medieval knights defending the great walls against invading hordes. I'd been to the Black Forest, bought my cuckoo clock. I'd wandered about Bavarian vineyards. But I'd never been to England, which is where we were heading.

I had a full itinerary planned. Cambridge and London awaited if I got the chance to see them, and I hoped I would.

When clearance came after takeoff, I removed my gloves and turned to face position Six. I lowered the zipper on my flight suit so it was away from my neck and stared at the blackened screen before me while I waited for system power to be brought up. Today we'd just check out the equipment and make sure it was all working properly. Tomorrow, a mission.

My screen blinked. The AMT's voice tweaked into my headset, "The system's coming up. She looks good; no gremlins today."

I watched the blinking cursor and waited. The maintenance tech was busy bringing up the system, running around switching on boxes, cycling power on others.

Pressure changes as we climbed again made my ears crackle and pop. As I adjusted the foam earplugs, the roar of engines came in booming.

"AMT, MCC, system up yet?"

"Hold one!" came the reply.

I glanced at my watch; it was 09:15. So far we'd made good

time though the three hours of preflight had crawled by.

The system logo finally started scrawling across my screen. The system was almost up. The screen blanked out for a moment to be replaced by the log-in prompt.

"MCC, AMT, the system is yours!"

I looked left. Two positions down, the mission crew commander was logging in and checking out the system. A few minutes later, his voice coming across Private cleared us in.

Above the keyboard were three long rows of keys, all labeled and in different colors: green, red, yellow, white and black. Each key pulled up a separate action menu. I punched the appropriate key to give me access to the log-in prompt.

Once logged into the position, I performed the standard checks and waited for final clearance to the signal environment. I switched on the small spotlight above my position and aimed it at the now darkened keyboard as interior lighting had been brought down. I flicked through the settings on the displays above my position's display, ensuring they were set properly. Now as I glanced about the cabin, the Lady looked exceptionally extravagant; but she still flashed her true colors only when we threw her into jam. During Green Flag we had live-jammed, but ordinarily we didn't.

Before testing the system, the MCC ensured the system was in dummy load, which meant no jamming emitted from the plane. The AMT confirmed this.

We played around with the system for a time, but it just wasn't the same as a mission. On a regular mission, we'd be humping the buffer zone, busily working a live signal environment. All in preparation for wars we hoped would never come. But we were combat crew, and preparation for the real thing was our livelihood.

When we landed at Mildenhall, it was early afternoon and early evening before we settled into our rooms. The crew quarters, surprisingly, weren't bad. But none of us really cared about the rooms.

A group of us converted U.S. dollars to British pounds at an automatic teller machine. Then we set off for English fish and chips. Some sipped their first English ales before the fish and chips arrived. But that was about it for our big evening. Crew rest began at 22:00 and we had to return to our rooms. Crew rest meant twelve hours during which we were supposed to rest and weren't supposed to be disturbed. We also weren't supposed to consume alcohol in the eight hours immediately prior to flying, a rule that made good sense. Our lives depended on everyone's being able to do what we got paid to do.

Early the next morning we headed over to the Mildenhall operations center. The mission crew made the trek on foot because the crew van was nowhere to be found. Mildenhall ops was set up completely differently from Sembach ops. Here everything was crammed into tight quarters and buildings a hundred years older than any of us.

The schedule for the morning was pretty much set in concrete. We'd be flying as part of an integrated package in a mini-exercise. Planning the mission was the responsibility of the mission crew. The eight of us each had separate tasks to perform, which involved planning and mapping out our orbit box, orbit times, jam windows, simulated targets, and the times over target for the simulated packages we would be supporting. The front-end crew would go over the flight plan and the mission route then make sure our windows of opportunity and orbit times corresponded with the navigator's plans.

The final stage of mission planning was reviewing the communications plan. After that we were ready for an onslaught of briefings. During the preflight brief given by the members of the mission crew, we reviewed the mission plan and maps. The big map displaying all pertinent target information was our best visual aid—it told all. After the preflight brief, the aircraft commander gave his spiel. He told us the estimated length of the mission with transit times figured in, skimmed over emergency procedures, and detailed other significant factors. Today the mission would be over water; life preservers and poopy suits needed to be readied. I hated the poopy suits, the black rubber that stretched from head to toe was nearly impossible to get into and even worse to get out of.

The navigator briefed us on weather, which didn't look good. The runway was sopped in and the cloud deck was thickening. Weather was always a critical factor; and if it didn't clear, we wouldn't fly. It'd be a No-Go.

Next the MCC gave his briefing. He coordinated our windows of opportunity with the front-end once more. Planning and coordinating the jam windows was tricky business. We didn't want our orbit box to be too short, so we were constantly making turns. We didn't want it to be too long either. We didn't want to be in the middle of a turn when a package element was coming in over target. We also wanted to make sure we used our jamming array effectively, switching our jammers on when necessary and switching them off when unnecessary.

After the MCC brief we were ready to fly, but only if the weather improved. Flying a mission was always like that—planning, briefings, checklists and lots of waiting. When we were humping the zone, the adrenaline surging through our veins always compensated for all the fuss.

Fortunately or unfortunately, depending on how you looked at it, the weather worsened and the fog rolled in. It was then that we knew we were in England for sure. Four hours of waiting crept by. The weather didn't clear and eventually we were put on standby. We could go eat and whatnot but had to report back.

Fly days were normally long, but they were especially long when, after a long wait, you actually flew. There were limits to the length of the crew day, but we were still well within the window. 12:00 was our return time, so we hurried off on foot to grab a bite to eat.

I hated weather delays more than anything else. Some days you'd wait six or seven hours; then the weather would clear, and you'd go fly your full flight time. And a day that would have been twelve to fourteen hours turned into one that just wouldn't end.

Mildenhall was a base sprawled across the English countryside, and the side of the base we were on was a good clip away from the place where we were quartered. The trudge back to our rooms and to the exchange concessions was long and cold. Needless to say, we weren't the happiest bunch when we made the return trip after eating.

The weather stayed bad, but we returned for show time all the same. One crew got off the ground, but our crew never did fly that day. Evening found four of us racing down a narrow English highway in a tiny rented car. We were headed for the county seat of Cambridgeshire. Our first stop was Cambridge University.

We walked its hallowed halls and courtyards. Then for a time afterward we walked the streets of Cambridge itself, visiting shops and one pub along the way. English pubs were just as I'd always imagined them. Cambridge was a university town and so there was the usual university crowd gathered as well as those who appeared to be regulars. They were all having a grand time.

We ordered drinks and a light meal. I watched the gents playing darts and a group of college girls, obviously Americans, who thought they were among England's sophisticated elite. Everything seemed so rich in history and life.

The inevitable happened on the way home—we got lost. Our driver had been to England before and didn't seem too worried. Much to my dismay he stopped the car in the middle of the street and called out to one of the pedestrians. The passer-by was the typical English gentleman with an overcoat, plaid cap, and a thin black mustache.

We did as he told us, taking two lefts, then we asked for directions again. The English are polite to a fault.

At the Mildenhall operations center the next morning, it was back to business as usual. The skies were clear and our mission was a Go. We provided jamming support for the Falcons, Ravens and Eagles. The AWACS and others joined in the action and it was a sight to be seen.

After that flight, the remaining days passed quickly, and before we knew it we were on our way home from cheery old England. We had a few extra passengers, pax as we affectionately called them. With their planes already deployed to the desert, Mildenhall had aircrew that needed flight time—part of the reason we were in England in the first place—and so some of them came back with us primarily to get flight time.

They didn't know our plane or our systems, so we openly referred to them as "excess baggage" and "dead weight." Our

AMT threatened to dump them out over the North Sea to save fuel. Aircrew rivalries were common. We were EC and they were RC. We were all friends, but it was just the sort of thing aircrews did to torment each other.

On the way home, we had a special treat for our Mildenhall "buddies." We flew a mission in the buffer zone with an aerial refueling track thrown in. Crow, the AMT, kidded them that it was a puke tolerance test. And it was.

Christmas came and went a few weeks later. The holiday season just wasn't the same. I loved holidays. I was fanatical about holidays. Gloom on the horizon darkened my mood.

Katie and I exchanged our gifts, said our thanks, and not a whole lot more. It was a pretty somber occasion with the situation in the Gulf shuffling ever more into our everyday lives. Quite a few of my friends were in Saudi and elsewhere, waiting in the sand. We sent them care packages and thought about them, but things just weren't the same without them.

Across Europe, preparations were being made for possible terrorist activities. The flight line became a fortress. Traveling anywhere was a nightmare. We still hadn't received official word that we were deploying even though more and more of our daily activities were directed toward that end.

Family relations were being stretched to the limit. Mostly because everyone had been told that if hostilities started, dependents might be shipped back to the states for the duration to guard against expected terrorist activity. To make matters worse, we started working longer and longer days—dealing with a never-ending workload and then going home to a never-ending onslaught of questions to which we had no answers.

More aircrew arrived from Mildenhall. Our job was to train

them to use our jamming system. The real nature of their presence was apparent. They were expert Arabic linguists.

I'd already decided on my New Year's wishes and resolutions.

Friday, 11 January, 1991

It was my birthday. I was the big two-five. My birthday present to me was my last will and testament. I filled out the paper work for my will and a general power of attorney at the base legal office.

Katie threw me a birthday party complete with cake, presents, and friends. We celebrated, but it was clear that our thoughts were on other things.

Navy reservists had been arriving since the beginning of the week. One of the KCs out on the pad was named The City of Pensacola in honor of Pensacola, Florida.

Transport KCs were ferrying supplies and troops to the Gulf. They'd be the ones to bring back the body bags if the war really kicked off.

A great deal of uncertainty then. Every day, it looked more and more like we'd be going soon though I would always tell Katie I'd heard nothing.

For some time at work we had been studying Iraqi tactics and getting lessons in identifying the Iraqi dialect from the numerous Arabic dialects. Now we were studying key words, phrases, and their number system.

My journal that up until then I'd written in only sparingly was getting more-and-more frequent entries. All my other writing projects were on hold. I decided to pack away the book I was working on. There was just too much going on. I put it into a box with the others.

Work was different that day. It seemed as if everyone wished he were some place other than work. We moved up to forty-eight-hour standby. Now with as little as forty-eight hours' notice, our whole unit would be expected to pack up everything and deploy to the Gulf.

Uncertainties were rapidly diminishing. Our mission, should we deploy to the Gulf, was clear-cut. We'd jam Iraqi command and control communications and transmissions from ground and air targets. It was a mission we had been preparing for since early August. One we were more than ready to do.

The deadline for Iraqi forces' withdrawal from Kuwait was only four days away, yet Saddam Hussein didn't even want to meet with our Secretary of State to work this thing out with some level of civility. Saddam Hussein was still hedging his bets. The answer would most likely be war. Iraq had the fourth largest ground army in the world, an army tempered by the long Iran-Iraq war. The United States had the seventh.

We had an ace in the whole, though; Saddam Hussein didn't fully recognize the significance of air power though he had a sizable air force. Nor did he believe the United States was willing to commit to full-scale war. He firmly believed our current society could not accept the level of war casualties he was willing to make.

No matter how willing you were to serve and no matter how gung ho you were, there was always a level of uncertainty that prodded at the back of your mind—a thousand images of Vietnam played along with it all the time now.

I'd been putting off making that return trip to legal to pick up my will for several days. Eventually, I finalized it with little reservation. Afterward I put it in a locked box.

Katie saw it. She nearly came to tears. It's unexpected that a simple piece of paper signed and notarized means so much.

Monday 14, January 1991

The weekend was hardly a time for relaxation. Things at home were visibly tense though Katie and I pretended they weren't. She wanted to know for sure if I would go and I couldn't honestly tell her yes or no.

Arrival at work Monday morning brought the grim news of an upgrade to twenty-four-hour notice. Old Jimmie's advice was to get those things done you've been putting off. To find your A-bags and properly fill them. To spend some quality time with your family because there won't be any real soon.

The deadline was one day away. Saddam Hussein wasn't budging. His troops were digging in. They were prepared to wait or fight, prepared for the long haul. I could only pray we were, also. I could only wonder if all this could have been avoided somehow.

That day the deployment board said that I'd be on mission-planning cell if I did go, which meant I probably wouldn't fly right away. Yet the crews listed there one-by-one on the board were by no means final. The names were, in fact, being juggled on an hourly basis. In the course of a single day, my name was scattered all over the board along with everyone else's. Old Jimmie and the major were trying to get the best crew mix without sacrificing planning.

Countless phone calls came in from concerned friends and family. All had their opinions of the encroaching deadline and the possibility of war in the Gulf, to which I responded almost casually with "Uh-huh," finally ending with "I love you, too."

I wasn't at liberty to discuss anything and I didn't.

Tuesday, 15 January 1991

The deadline came and went. No one moved. Nothing happened. No one really knew what was going to happen, though officially we were told to go to minimal manning and again to spend time with our families. I knew for sure we were going though I hadn't been told.

We had known our deployment destination for some time, but we weren't at liberty to discuss it with anyone outside work. I called my mother and we talked for a long, long time.

She could tell something was wrong, but I said nothing. I wanted to tell her, "Mom, I'm leaving for the Gulf," but I couldn't. When she finally did ask if I were going, I told her, my voice clear and firm, "No, Mom, we're staying in place. My unit isn't going."

It was one of the hardest things I'd ever had to do.

Katie and I were in bed by 20:00. In her motherly way, Katie wanted to make sure I got enough sleep before anything happened.

The inevitable phone call came at 23:45. I heard the first ring. My eyes popped wide open, and I jumped out of bed. I knew what the phone call meant and ran to catch the phone before it rang again. I didn't want it to wake Katie.

The phone finished its second ring as I picked it up and spoke a timid, "Hello." I really hoped it was one of our relatives that had forgotten the time difference when calling to Germany again.

"Hello?" the receiver called out, "This is—" I didn't have to listen anymore. I knew the voice well enough. I'd heard it hundreds of times. It was Major James. "Pack your bags for the long term; you're going TDY. Report tomorrow morning at 10:45. Any questions?"

"No, sir!" I shouted into the mouthpiece, "I mean yes, sir. I'll report tomorrow morning!"

"Report tomorrow morning at 10:45," repeated the voice in my ear, "Bring all your gear!"

10:45? Wasn't that a bit late? "Ah, yes, sir!" I replied. I vaguely remember hanging up the phone. My heart felt as if it had stopped cold. In a weird way, I was relieved, elated, and sad, all at the same time. I hadn't said timid "yes sirs" or "no sirs." I'd said them loud and prominent. Here was my chance to defend freedom and American interests.

I turned around, ready to begin packing the A-bags I had never packed because I'd known all along that as soon as I packed them, I was really going to leave. Katie was standing behind me. I jumped back, startled. I didn't think the phone had wakened her. Then I put my hands on her shoulders and I told her what she already knew.

Katie's face went blank. Her eyes registered what could have been only shock or even horror as she looked up at me. She didn't want to believe what I'd said, so I had to tell her again.

"We are leaving tomorrow," I said, "the order finally came." My voice wavered. The tortured waiting and not knowing was over, or so I thought.

Tears began to stream down Katie's cheeks. We'd been married eighteen months and I'd never seen her cry. God, it stung me to see her cry. It was a strange and moving sight. I didn't know what to do. I just stood there, hands rigid on her shoulders until she pressed up against me, wet cheeks pushed up against my chest.

I held her for the longest time, staring blankly at the white wall behind me. The light was on in the bathroom. I had so much to do. Again I felt sad, relieved and strangely happy. I kind of wanted to go, had wanted to go, and this both upset and confused me. "Yes, sir!" I had told the major. "Yes, sir!" I had been excited; but then I turned to look down into those great liquid brown eyes, and I started to tremble.

Katie wrapped her arms tighter around me. I around her. Five, ten, perhaps fifteen minutes went by—it seemed both like hours and an instant.

After my heart stopped pounding in my ears and Katie had calmed, both of us knew it was time to begin packing. Frantically, I began stuffing my belongings into canvas aircrew bags. Katie helped by folding flight suits, BDU t-shirts, and underwear, placing them in my over-the-shoulder bag.

I was almost done packing when the significance of what had just transpired occurred to me. If we were deploying, the United States had plunged irrevocably toward war in the Persian Gulf.

Hours later I went to bed but didn't really get any sleep. I just lay there waiting for the impending doom tomorrow would surely bring, waiting for the alarm clock to ring, and waiting to walk out the door not knowing when I would be coming back—if I would be coming back. Somewhere along the course of those hours, I re-packed my bags, double-checked my will, and wrote Katie a letter.

Wednesday, 16 January 1991

"The United States is at war in the Persian Gulf!" the news announcer declared ominously as I clicked on the TV. I watched, enthralled by the images displayed, for the next thirty minutes. My face was bright red as emotion flowed over me. From the phone call last night, I'd known it was true, but it took the news announcer's declaration to really drive it home.

I stared out the window at the light snowfall as the newscaster announced again, "The United States is at war in the Persian Gulf. A massive air campaign was launched in the early morning hours. As elements of the first massive wave returned to their bases safely, many screamed shouts of joy. No American or allied losses are yet reported. U.S. warplanes continue their ceaseless assaults."

After another ten minutes, I finally clicked off the TV. I didn't know why, but this morning I had to fix the car. A distributor cap and rotor had been sitting next to the door for about a week. Suddenly it had to go in; I just couldn't leave it sitting there. I was determined to get it done. We owned a beat-up European green BMW with 280,000 kilometers on it. What the thing really needed was a tune-up, but I'd never gotten around to doing it.

The truth was that I really didn't know much about cars. I put the rotor in just fine. When I pulled the old distributor cap off, I unhooked everything. I slapped the new cap in place but hooked up the plug wires in the incorrect order. It was true that my thoughts were elsewhere and my subconscious kept telling me I might never be coming home again, but I messed up the most basic automobile repair job ever.

I'd started on the car at 06:30. It was now 08:30. Hands greasy, frustrated and tired, I cranked that old BMW until it ran dead as I tried to get the right plug order. The truth was simpler than I cared to admit. I didn't want to have to walk back up those stairs, stare into Katie's eyes, and tell her goodbye.

It wouldn't be like all those other times we'd said goodbye for a week, a day, or even a month. This time it was goodbye, I was going to war. I might not be coming home.

I recalled then the news announcer's message, "The United States is at war with Iraq." Dear Jesus. I'd hoped and prayed it wouldn't happen, but it had.

Katie coaxed me back up the long stairs that cut into the hillside to our first floor quarters. Her long brown hair was wet, though neatly pulled back into a braid. She looked radiant and more beautiful than ever. "The car won't start," I told her.

Katie looked at me and smiled. "I know," she replied, "I know. Why don't you eat some breakfast?"

A huge meal was cooling on the table. Katie's way of telling me she loved me and would miss me. I ate French toast, eggs, hash browns and bacon as if it were the Last Supper.

While I ate, Katie called Tom, the AMT that lived above us,

and asked if I could get a ride with him to the squadron. He said sure. Fifteen short minutes later, I was loading my bags into the back seat of his car.

I kissed Katie goodbye, presumably for good. How do you say a lifetime's worth in an instant? I didn't know. "I love you," I whispered, adding, "promise you'll wait for me no matter what?"

Katie answered in her sometimes poetic way, "My love, I'll wait for you until the last sunset." She whispered it in my ear in her quiet tone. The words were simple and beautiful and brought me to the verge of tears. Obviously, she'd spent a lot of time thinking about this moment.

I wondered why I couldn't think of anything more to say than "I love you" and "wait for me." It was all I could think of. I hoped it'd be enough.

When I arrived at ops, the squadron was a mess. People were scrambling everywhere. Some were sorting gear by type and last name—chemical protective, flight, and field. Some were loading the bags by crew onto trucks. Many others just stood idle, looking lost and confused.

I checked in with Jimmie. He put a check next to my name, present and accounted for. Captain Wilson was to be my MCC. Good old Captain Willie. The staggering news was that I was on airlift and on crew one. As crew number one, we were going to be the first to fly when we hit our destination running. This was the reason we were on airlift. Military regulations said we couldn't fly over as crewmembers on our plane then turn around and fly a full-blown combat mission. We could fly over on someone else's plane and then fly a combat mission. I guess even in the chaos of war there are rules. Crew 1? I wasn't supposed to be on the first crew. Now what?

Until it was time to go through the mobility processing line, I was tasked to help with the gear, making sure A-bags 1 and 2 and extra gear were in the correct places. I had an hour before crew number one was to report for processing. 14:00 was our Go time, still three hours away now yet edging ominously closer.

Able was in the vault double-checking bags for contents from a mountain of dark green canvas bags. "You believe this shit?" he asked me.

I shook my head. I did and didn't. "What do you need help with?"

Able explained what he was doing in his words and in his obnoxious way. I knew he was just being himself and venting steam with strings of expletives, so I didn't let it bother me. He was actually a good guy once you got to know him. He had a six-month-old baby at home and a stick shift Mazda 323 his wife didn't know how to drive. Worse still, he lived off post. He had a lot to be upset about.

"If you knew how my morning's gone so far, you wouldn't be so upset," I began, as I told him about my escapades with my car. He knew that old green BMW well. He'd been there when I bought it. His wife and my wife were also friends. I told him not to worry so much. "Those two will probably be visiting all the time. Katie can drive Debby to the commissary or wherever she needs to go.

"Providing, of course, the car gets fixed," I added with a chuckle.

The hour went fast as we talked and made our way through that mountain of green canvas bags. Before I knew it, it was time to head over for processing.

Mobility processing went smoother this time. I went through

personnel, security police, legal, chaplain, finance, and immunizations in record time. Finance had been authorized to pay advance money, so when I reached the end of the line I was stuffing a wad of twenties into my wallet just about the time a female Med Tech told me, "Unzip and drop 'em!"

By this time, I was in a room with three other guys and two other gals, part of crew number one. I dropped 'em and so did everyone else. One by one we got our gamma globulin shots. After that, rubbing our backsides, crew number one double-timed it back to the squadron. Go time was now an hour and thirty-five minutes away. Crew briefings were scheduled to begin in five minutes.

We were hurried to the ready room, now the war room. Since the thirteen of us were the last to enter, we sat down in the back. With Go time getting ever nearer, we were growing more nervous by the second. We heard the door open and close and then a familiar face passed by the center aisle to the podium.

"Congratulations, combat crew. Those of you seated in this room today were selected over all other members of the unit to deploy to the Persian Gulf!" screamed Jimmie. "The first thing we're going to do is to take roll and make sure everyone is here. I'll start off with the mission crews, one through three, reading the names down the list by crew. Afterward, Aircraft Commanders, if your crew is present or accounted for, just confirm that for me. Crew one."

The chief went through the list of names, thirty-nine primary aircrew members, of which I was one. The ACs responded, each in turn. Then the chief made his way through the long list of personnel on ground status: primary mission planners, intelligence analysts, intelligence briefers, duty drivers, medical technicians, other ground support specialists, and lastly, auxiliary aircrew members. From there the briefing progressed slowly through five additional briefers. Before we knew it, the chief was giving us a sending-off pep talk. "Remember, your destination remains classified. As you leave this room you are not at liberty to discuss it. You will all be met on the ground at your destination, where your first stop will be customs. The flight over, as you were told, is eight hours. Crew one, you'd better get some shut-eye on that transport ride over. You're going to have a long day. That's the end of the briefing, combat crew, support crews. Good luck to all of you!"

We came out of the ready room to find an ops building steadily filling with wives, husbands and children. The chief and the folks from IM had been busy calling families to give us an official sending off.

I knew Katie had to be somewhere in the crowd; and after getting Captain Willie's permission, I chased her down. I found her standing alone, holding lunch in a little brown bag. She was wearing a blue denim dress. Her long brown hair stretched neatly in long curly spans over her shoulders. If I had had a camera, I would have snapped a picture right then and cherished it forever. I hadn't expected to see her for a long, long time, and there she was.

We looked for a more secluded corner to sit down and talk quietly. Other families were doing much the same. Some seemed cheerful, others downright heartbroken. We didn't say much in those quiet, tense, and precious few minutes we had together. Soon I was saying goodbye.

Then I gathered my gear. I started to make my way out the door, when Captain Wilson found me.

"Stay here in ops," he advised, "looks like the time schedule might be pushed back."

I looked to Katie, and she looked at me. A delay just meant more tense minutes of waiting.

14:00 came and went. Nothing. The official word had not come as expected. At 14:30 a meeting was called and we were told that unfortunately we'd have to do this whole thing again tomorrow, but at least we could spend another evening with our families.

I had a few things to finish up, and then I went home. Unfortunately Katie had to work until 15:30 and couldn't get off, not that she didn't try; they just wouldn't let her. She was crying when she called work and afterwards when she hung up the phone. I told her it was okay, but really it wasn't. We spent fifteen short minutes together and then Katie left for work.

Afterward I packed a few more things, which included a framed picture of Katie that had stood on my computer table. I dinked around with the car some more, but I still couldn't get it to start.

Later I watched the news. CNN showed that NATO forces were landing in Turkey. The Turkish people didn't want NATO there and they were quite vocal about it. Turkey was our destination. The unrest added more doubt to the picture and was the obvious reason for the delay.

Thursday, 17 January 1991

I heard a knock on the door at 03:00, went back to bed afterward. One of the crews had been alerted, but not mine.

At 04:30, the phone rang. I was awake anyway. I had to report to squadron ops ASAP. Saying goodbye a second time wasn't any easier than the first. Seeing Katie cry again tore my heart into tiny little pieces. She wasn't as strong as she had been yesterday, and I didn't blame her.

I headed over to squadron ops. Captain Willie told me we had to "bag drag" to Ramstein. I never expected to go. After we arrived by crew bus at Ramstein, I called Katie and told her I didn't expect to be going today. That was at 10:00. At 11:00, one short hour later, I was boarding a C-5 bound for Turkey and war in the Persian Gulf.

We completed the journey without mishap. Our C-5 Galaxy touched down on a semi-busy airstrip in Turkey. Its cargo: war supplies, a small group of combat crewers and a number of ops support personnel. Sunset spread across the Turkish skyline in a myriad of oranges and reds. The earth raced flat and clean to distant mountains. The air was cool and a lot milder than any of us expected.

A support bus was waiting to take us to the airport complex where we would process through customs. In the middle of exiting the plane, we were greeted with one of the rudest welcomes a modern war zone can give: an Alarm Red.

None of us had our chem gear ready or close. We scrambled like mad dogs to the piles of gear half stacked in the rear of the aircraft and half strewn on the tarmac. My heart pounded in my ears as I searched frantically for my gear. The other crewers ran around the tarmac just as frantically. To make matters worse, the area was darkened during the alarm in case of incoming enemy fighters.

By the time I found my chem mask and donned my gear, I knew I was a walking dead man. You didn't have minutes when chems hit; you had mere seconds. The things neurotoxins and chemical agents do to a man no living person should ever have to see, but I had seen the aftermath of such attacks. It had been part of our briefings. Saddam Hussein's army had used chemical weapons extensively in the past and our intel said he would use them again.

When the All Clear sounded after what seemed an eternity of waiting, there was never a happier bunch of human beings kissing their own behinds in all the world. Needless to say, after that we clutched our chem masks in their pouches as if they were Bibles and we were repentant sinners bound for church.

At the airport complex, a lieutenant colonel, our deployed commander, greeted us. In later days, we'd come to call him Gentleman Bob, but for now he scared the hell out of most of us. When a lieutenant colonel greets you, shakes your hand, and tells you how happy he is you have arrived, you start to worry.

Gentleman Bob wasn't a little man. He was six foot four, give or take a bit, and broad shouldered. He was the commander of the 43rd—the front-end crew—and what little I knew of him at the time was from his cavalry call salutes on Monday mornings and Friday evenings. He directed us to the airport terminal where customs agents awaited.

Turkish Customs stamped our orders, told us about drugs, contraband, and their laws regarding females and then released us. Flashbacks from Midnight Express ran through my mind. The Turks with dark hair, the obligatory thick mustaches, and often thick dark beards that masked their faces and their dark-toned skin matched those images exactly. Their faces for the most part were expressionless except for the man in the long tan trench coat that just stared and scrutinized. I'm not sure who he was, but I know that when one of us tried to ask him a question, the custom's agent behind the counter who had been stamping our orders became frantic. At that moment, flashbacks from Midnight Express didn't seem so far fetched.

Turkey was a land rich in customs and traditions far different from any place I'd ever been. While largely Muslim, it was not entirely akin to its neighbors. The Turks were considered Ottomans and not Arabs. In fact, both Iraq and Kuwait were once part of the vast Ottoman Empire, a Turkish empire that thrived for six centuries and collapsed after World War I.

Outside, our A-bags were scattered everywhere and we had to sort through them to find our own. Afterward, our fellow ground support troopers took a bus to Tent City. I'd already heard about it, tents going up as fast as they could pound the stakes into the ground. In the coming weeks, Tent City would grow manyfold; and conditions that had once been bad would turn to near good.

We were fortunate to be aircrew, but not that fortunate. The need for crew rest and quiet hours mandated that we be quartered separately. With the air campaign ongoing, flyers were, after all, the reason everyone was here. We went off to quarters that would be quieter, or so we hoped.

The three females in our group were the fortunate ones. They were a combat minority and as members of another minority here, aircrew, they were given exceptional treatment—not that any of them wanted it or asked for it. They were dropped off at billeting, where they had private quarters, showers, televisions, microwaves, phones, and all the other amenities of life. Afterward, the crew van driver took those remaining to our new home. Two converted, freestanding one-room buildings that had once served as professional military education (PME) classrooms. All the desks had been stacked on the sides of the room and cots had been set up in their places.

Our fellow crew dogs were pleased and not pleased to see us, especially as we crowded extra cots into the already overfilled quarters. Two twenty-by-forty-foot buildings stuffed with thirty cots each didn't allow for much movement space. I barely got enough room to set up my cot so I wasn't kicking another guy in the head. Who were we to complain, though? There was a set of working toilets in the outhouse set back from the two PME classrooms and running water. Cold running water, which we weren't supposed to drink because it would most likely give us the shits, but at least it was working. Tent City didn't always have working water.

The one-day delay meant there was a rotation of the crews already under way and it was a relief to hear that we weren't going to be flying without being given time to sleep. It was 22:00 by the time the first of us new arrivals bedded down. We were told to expect an early alert and that we were on crew rest. "Get some sleep and soon," was the advice, and we did.

Friday, 18 January 1991

I awoke to the beam a flashlight on my face. It was 01:00.

"Captain Wilson's crew?" a voice called out. What if I wasn't?

Let's see, I'd gotten three hours of sleep, hadn't eaten since an early lunch yesterday. Was I? "I guess so," I finally replied after a moment of silence.

"Hey what's up? Good to have you with us. You got in yesterday, huh?"

I recognized the voice as that of a friend of mine but didn't say anything. At 01:00, even at home, I wasn't normally conversational. His name was Albert, but we all called him Happy after one of the Seven Dwarves. He didn't much like the nickname but there was an unwritten rule among crewers about the origin of nicknames: you can't pick it; someone else has to give it. If the name sticks, you're pretty much stuck with it. And so we called poor young Albert Happy—it was eerie the way the name fit him to perfection.

"Hey, man, I'll come back in thirty to make sure you're up. The step van will be out front at 02:00. You need all your flight gear and your chem gear. Don't forget to sanitize; and hey, cheer up!" He went on for a time, but I was no longer listening; all I heard was that he'd come back in thirty to make sure I was up and that was good enough. I still thought that maybe if I faded off to sleep, I'd wake up at home in bed next to Katie.

I did get up eventually, but only because I forced myself to. Sanitizing meant removing the insignia from my flight suit, emptying the pictures and IDs out of my wallet. Leaving behind anything that the enemy could try to use against me if our plane went down and I survived the crash.

At 02:00 I was sitting in the back of a SWAT-type panel van, helmet bag clutched in one hand, a death grip on the A-bag in my other hand. Captain Willie, Craig, Robert, Todd, Allen, Thomas, and I waited while Happy climbed into the driver's seat—it was 02:00 and he was already telling jokes. Craig, Robert, and Thomas were fellow crewers. Todd was the crew mission control supervisor. We called him PBJ because he always ate peanut butter and jelly sandwiches when he flew. Allen was one of the guys from England. Our pilot, copilot, Nav, Eng, and AMT were already at base ops.

At billeting, we picked up Charlotte—Charlotte, whose hair was blown dry. We razzed her no end about being housed in separate quarters only to find out that there was one whole crew that was also housed in billeting.

Base ops was a sight. There was a level of energy and intensity there that I'd never seen before. Happy, as our guide, walked us through the first few steps. Our first stop was intel to get our preflight intelligence briefing. Here we knew we would be briefed on the current situation of the battle, our theater of operations, and the mission. We didn't know exactly what to expect. I braced myself for grim realities as the intel briefer began.

"Good morning. Most of you know me and the lieutenant although I do see one or two unfamiliar faces. I am Sergeant Derrin Lorenz. This is Lieutenant Henry Albright. I'll be giving you your intelligence overview briefing and the L-T will go over mission specifics. You all look a little disoriented, so let's take a moment to catch our breaths.

"Okay, first of all, I want to apologize for running through this so quickly, but we're pushing the clock, combat crew. It's wakeup call time. Your uniforms should be sanitized. If they aren't, remove all insignia at this time. Remember to clean out your helmet bags and your wallets. Combat wallets should have only the bare essentials: dog tags, shot records, identification card, and little else. I know some of you have other items. You can leave them here and pick them up after the flight.

"On the desk behind you, you'll find a number of interesting items. You'll find a card depicting the articles of the code of conduct and the tap code. Take one, put it in your wallet. Getting shot down is a possibility, combat crew. We have nine aircrew members listed as MIA right now.

"Next, you'll find evasion maps and blood chits. You need to sign out one of each before you leave this room. Pay particular attention to the search and rescue codes listed on the board at the front of the room. Memorize them or write them down on your hand if you have too.

"As you all know, in the pre-dawn hours on the morning of January the 17th, the United States of America and its coalition forces' partners began offensive operations in the Persian Gulf. What you don't know is exactly what has taken place since then and this is what I am about to tell you."

Derrin paused to turn on an overhead projector.

"The Kuwaiti Theatre of Operations, 16 January. Take note of the placement of Iraqi forces, and of course the Republican Guard units. The next slide is more telling. The following scenario unfolded around 03:00 Baghdad time this morning. The massive strike force depicted here slowly made its way toward enemy territory. Their goals were 45 key strategic targets in and around Baghdad. The Baghdad electrical power grid was taken out in the first minutes after H-hour and the city fell to darkness. Command, control, communications, and intelligence (C3I) networks were another major objective.

"Many of these systems fell to precision bombing raids in the first minutes, effectively cutting off most of the primary means of communications to and from Baghdad. As you know, with the primary microwave and landline communication systems destroyed, the enemy will resort to radio comms usage, and this is where you come in. Disrupting, degrading, and denying enemy air and ground communications is vital to the success of our goals.

"By H-hour plus one, the Iraqi integrated air defense network has collapsed. Air Power, combat crew, there is nothing like it!"

Derrin paused, then switched off the projector while Lieutenant Albright moved to the fore. "Well, Derrin's pretty much laid it all out for us, but what he hasn't told you is the decisive role of Electronic Combat assets in all this. Our counterparts in the Gulf are doing one hell of a job. Without comms jammers, radar jammers, airborne command and control, and the rest of the gambit of EC assets, the tremendous success so far wouldn't have been possible. Command Control and Communications Countermeasures is the name of the game, combat crew."

Derrin turned the overhead projector back on and inserted a new transparency.

The LT continued, "Highlighted here is our theatre of operations, which is, of course, northern Iraq. Why northern Iraq, why not the KTO, I know some of you want to ask. But those of you who've done your homework understand why. These next slides will help you understand.

"Here you see the significant number of airfields in this region. There is a map similar to this one that'll be in your mission kits, along with a listing of best-guess ground and air assets for each. Review these as soon as possible. The more you know, the better prepared you'll be.

"Nonconventional warfare is a major threat. We expect to see the use of chemical, biological, and possibly even nuclear weapons before this thing is all over.

"Here you see the key installations suspected of these activities. Do you see anything that strikes you immediately? If the answer is no, you better take a long look again. Eradicating this nonconventional warfare threat will be one of our major goals.

"Next we'll review expected ground and air threats. We'll go through these slides kind of quick."

The LT paused as Derrin put in a new slide. "The Soviet-made MiG-29 Fulcrum depicted here is one of the deadliest fighter jets in the Iraqi inventory. Others include the MiG-25, the MiG-23, the Mig-21, the Su-25, and the F-1 Mirage." Derrin put in the appropriate slides.

"Expected ground threats. The Iraqis have a wide array of surface-to-air missiles, from hand-held stingers to the large SA-2 and SA-3 fixed sites. Anti-aircraft artillery ranges from short range 23 millimeter to long range 130 millimeter. We have seen a lot of SAM and AAA activity. AAA tends to be of the 57 millimeter variety.

"The critter you're looking at here is a Soviet-made ZSU 23-4. This particular piece of artillery is being used extensively. Pilot and copilot, have your evasive maneuver plans prepared in advance. You will see it, so prepare for it."

Derrin turned off the projector and the LT turned to the big map. "On the big map, you see your orbit box and those of other EC assets." The lieutenant paused to take a swig from a liter bottle of water, then proceeded to tell us about the missions we would be supporting and their targets, finally concluding with, "You have a little less than one hour. Good luck, combat crew, I hope to see you all when you return!"

We left intel with our hearts racing a hundred miles an hour. Security police was our next stop. We were issued .38s and given eighteen rounds in three numbered clear plastic bags—bullets and guns were always accountable. These we put in the holsters of our survival vests.

The pilot gave a pre-mission brief. We reviewed emergency procedures and contingencies. Our mission crew commander briefed us on the packages we would be supporting—primarily a strike package of B-52s. The Buffs would be going against airfields and aircraft while a contingent of Strike Eagles and Falcons departing from Turkey also went in. Our job would be to jam enemy communications using every and any means at our disposal.

Two hours after we entered base ops, our entire crew of thirteen was crowded into the back of a single step van and rolling down a darkened Turkish road. The Gray Lady waited for us somewhere along a dark and lonely runway.

I was able to see around the cabin for brief moments. Maybe it was my journalistic instincts or maybe it was because I was so emotionally wrought that I rationalized things by separating myself from them, but it was as if I were on the outside looking in as my life passed before my eyes. I did feel rather gung ho and eaten up. I wouldn't have admitted it, but I loved every minute.

This was, after all, why I had joined the Air Force. The military was a tradition in my family that stemmed from my grandfather on my mother's side to my own father. My grandfather had served in the last great war. My father had served, and now it was my turn. During my childhood, which hadn't been perfect, I'd heard it all. My father had told me stories of burying fallen comrades and much, much more. In a way, he had unknowingly prepared me for what I now faced.

So as I looked around, I saw the faces around me and understood their expressions. Captain Willie's eyes read unknowing; it was a relatively new concept for him. PBJ, a master sergeant and our MCS, looked scared to death. Charlotte was feeling rather motherly, protective. Robert, loud and booming and never at a loss for words, was quiet and tense. And Allen, whom I didn't know, was gritting his teeth.

The step van lurched to a halt and a few of us moved for the door. "FOD check," called out Happy, "lighten up. I have to check the wheels and the undercarriage for foreign objects. You'll know when we're there." This was his third day and he seemed the expert, so we all sort of listened. He reminded me of someone stuck in the seventies, listening to the sound of Saturday Night Fever playing over and over in his mind.

I'd find out real soon that in combat the people you thought you knew well you didn't; those you knew hardly at all, you'd come to know a little better; and that everyone copes with stress in different ways. PBJ, our MCS who was scared to death, would turn out to be one hell of a guy and a good friend—it'd be just those first couple of days that we'd find it hard to resist the urge to strangle him.

With one final lurch, the van came to a halt. We could see the plane out the window now, so we knew we'd arrived. The ten-minute ride out to the flight line had seemed a lifetime, and for some it had been.

A sense of closeness to fate triggered something and everyone started talking. Then the crew van door was sliding open and Happy was yelling, "Everyone out!"

We piled out as soldiers going to war, heads held high, scurrying with our bags, our survival vests fitted, the .38s holstered within, to the plane.

Up the stairs through the crew entrance door we went, filing into our assigned seats. I was on Six, my home away from home, away from home. We began the usual preflight checks, the checks most of us had done a hundred times before, except it wasn't the same. Our helmets would stay on for this flight. We wouldn't switch to headset as we would have under normal conditions. The parachutes in our seats needed to be fitted; that wasn't usual. The .38s in our holsters needed to be loaded; that wasn't usual.

Our AMT, John, and the newlywed, Craig, fitted their chutes. They didn't take them off for the entire flight. Those bottom straps are so snug they cut off the circulation to your privates after a time, and I could only imagine how that must have felt by wheels down.

Foam ear plugs stuffed into ears, aircrew helmets on, mikes in front of our mouths, and preflight checks completed, we strapped in. We were ready to go. The engines were roaring now and the front-end was finishing their checks.

"Crew attention to brief!" called out Captain Smily, the pilot.

I listened as he began a checklist I'd never heard before: the Before Combat Entry Checklist. That was about all it took for my thoughts to begin spiraling again. There was a song playing in my ears. "You're headed down to Vietnam," it rang and went on and on. I wasn't the only one who hoped this wouldn't be another Vietnam, but at the time no one knew what the future held. Now if we would have had our tarot cards spread out in front of us, maybe things would've been different. But they weren't.

The pilot reviewed the communications plan and double-checked radio settings then began to review procedures for lookout and threat calls. "MCC, Pilot, you have your spotter selected back there yet?"

"It'll be Four." replied Captain Willie.

"Four listen up closely. The rest of you as well, your turn will come soon enough. This isn't a drill, remember that; this is the real thing! I want everyone in the cockpit to be alert. Spotter, when we're on stations, stay faced toward the environment. Follow standard radio procedures for call up and then quickly give your traffic or threat call. Our direction of travel is always, always twelve o'clock. Give the traffic's position relative to ours and if possible, direction of travel, such as traffic at nine o'clock, low, moving to twelve o'clock. Be quick, I don't want anyone tying up intercoms too long!

"If you're making a threat call make it clear. Such as bogies at nine o'clock. Bandit at three o'clock. Bogies are unknowns and possibly hostile. Don't make a bandit call if it is not an enemy fighter that you see. But it is better to be safe than sorry.

"Crew, the briefing is complete. Interior and exterior lights checked. Radar altimeter is set. Co, you ready?" The rest of the front-end crew began to go through their checks, starting with the copilot.

Soon the pilot called out, "Crew, Before Takeoff Combat Entry Checks—Complete."

That was our cue to give the thumbs up sign that we were ready for takeoff. "Pilot, MCC, mission crew ready for takeoff, sir!"

Interphone tweaked and the pilot called out the obvious, "Crew, we're rolling!"

The Gray Lady rattled and hummed as we gained speed; then with a sluggish lurch, the wheels lifted from the runway. We were airborne. I gripped the armrests of my flight chair, eyes wide and staring straight ahead.

Once we reached our flight altitude, the system was brought up and we readied our positions. For me that meant logging onto the system when cleared and following a few other steps that I'd done a hundred times.

Private clicked and PBJ's voice hissed into my headset, "There are flight meals around if any of you are as hungry as me." Robert on One—we called him Bobby—unbuckled and attacked a nearby box of ready to eat meals (MREs), tossing them around to his fellow crewers.

MREs seemed to have improved tremendously since basic training or so I reckoned at the moment. I ate so fast that in a few minutes, nature was calling—that was another thing I hadn't done since departing Germany besides eat. Yet the unwritten law among veteran crewers, and I was a veteran crewer, was: no shitting on the plane. There were a lot of unwritten laws among crewers. "MCS, Six, clear to the rear?"

"Clear to the rear, Six," called back PBJ. As he was to my right, he shot me a knowing grin.

I immediately headed to the luxury powder room in the rear, a gray curtained open chemical toilet on a pedestal that needed to be manually lowered—I'd seen quite a few new troops hop up there without first lowering the platform. When a chemical shitter came crashing down with you on it, it wasn't a pretty sight. Most probably this was the origin of the unwritten law among crewers: no shitting on the airplane. There was also a funnel shaped thing that passed for a urinal. The right paratroop door was close enough to the toilet so I could glance out the window. The sky was still shrouded in darkness. The Buffs had a predawn strike, so I wasn't surprised to see darkness.

I had just plugged back up on headset when the MCC called out, "15 minutes to stations." The adrenaline was pumping, really pumping.

The moment of truth was near. We'd find out not only who had done their homework as they should have, but also who really understood it. If the military had taught us anything in our however short or long careers, it was how to adapt. I'd been through years of training to get into this hot seat that I sat in now. I wasn't about to blow it.

I took a deep breath and repeated to myself, "This is what it was all for."

The pilot began the Airborne Combat Entry Checklist and I knew this was finally it. In five minutes we'd be on orbit supporting the first package: Buffs as they bombarded Kirkuk, a key airfield in Northern Iraq. This would be our first combat sortie. The time to rise to the occasion was now or never. For some, the time simply would never come. For those of us who did rise to the occasion, we'd never be the same again.

Two minutes to orbit now. I heard the Spotter calling out the location of traffic. The AMT had been there before; but now we needed him to do his job, and that job was to keep the system up and running.

The pilot called out, "Combat stations," and the MCC relayed it. I punched off ship's Interphone and pulled out the out-of-ship radio buttons so I could back up the MCS on radio communications. Then I went to work. When I found that first target soon afterward and it was confirmed, I hit a new high—I'd climbed to the top of the world.

On radio, Gypsy was calling Shadow, and our navigator answered the call. Shadow was our call sign. Gypsy was the airborne warning and control aircraft (AWACS). They were passing an air advisory. I wasn't worried. We had our dedicated high-value air asset combat air patrol (HVAA CAP) of Eagles—F-15C—all-around air superiority fighters that could match any Soviet-made MiG any day of the week.

On a different radio channel, I heard chatter from Phantom. Phantom was passing the targets it had already acquired and I was writing them down as fast as I could. I passed the list to the MCS who was staring at the pencil trembling in his hand and a blank piece of paper. I wanted to slap him and scream, "Come on, PBJ, get with it!" but I didn't.

Phantom was the friendly folks on the RC-135; and after a short delay, PBJ relayed a greeting. His face flushed with a bit of color as a familiar voice tweaked back over headset. He knew their lead op. Afterward it was back to finding equitable targets, which meant searching the frequency spectrum and finding enemy communications wherever they might be. The operators on positions One to Four specialized in air communications, such as communications from Iraqi fighters, Iraqi air defense, and those communications between Iraqi fighters and Iraqi air defense. The senior operators on the other side of the plane took everything else and that meant the senior ops had walls of high tech gear to keep track of and manipulate.

On Position Six, I had three banks of electronic gizmos to contend with. On the left was a tower of RF spectrum analyzers that could be configured for automated or manual search in specific frequency ranges. In the center below my CRT was a line of hot button controls for the computer systems. Above the CRT was a specially configured wide spectrum analyzer. On the right, a tower of signal analyzers and other gear for locating the source or sources of origin, identifying and classifying signals.

As we found signals, we worked to verify them as either friendly or enemy. Enemy signals were quickly and closely analyzed to determine the type, origin, and more. It was important to know whether a signal was from an enemy facility, ground vehicle, or aircraft; whether the signal was being transmitted ground to ground, ground to air, air to air, or air to ground; and whether the communications were a possible threat to our operations. If an operator was unable to verify a possible enemy signal, he would pass it on to another operator, typically one with more experience. Once a signal was verified, it was passed on to the Mission Crew Supervisor or Mission Crew Commander who marked the signal for jamming and other possible countermeasures.

Time raced by as we worked the signal environment

feverishly. When we hit our jam window, Captain Willie slammed the Lady into jam, effectively blocking the targeted enemy communications channels. This not only confused the enemy but also prevented command and control communications for their air defense networks.

Soon the Buffs would be smacking the hell out of Kirkuk. Strike Eagles would follow. Behind them a dozen Fighting Falcons.

We were still on fast-forward when Captain Willie's voice tweaked Private and hissed into our headsets, "Crew, the packages have hit their targets. And they're successfully egressing!"

A tremendous uproar ensued. Emotions flowed. I know more than one of us had tears in our eyes. We'd done it; our first mission was accomplished. We had fifteen minutes of station's time left to ensure the last of the package made it out safe and then all we had to do was make it back to base.

That's when all hell broke loose and when Gypsy called out, "Bogies at your nine o'clock!"

No questions asked, the pilot did an evasive combat dive and our hearts jumped into our mouths. Everything that wasn't bolted down went flying and we learned our first important combat lesson: if you don't need it, don't put it on your position.

We were leveling off and about to turn back onto our orbit when Gypsy called out again, "Shadow, those bogies are bandits. Repeat, bandits nine o'clock high!" I'm not sure if anyone pissed in his pants, but I imagine some came close. The pilot took the Lady into another hard dive. Part of the MiG CAP sped off, chasing the Bandits. Gypsy was directing them hard—the crew in the AWACS were just as excited as we were.

We stayed on orbit, continuing our evasive maneuvers for fifteen tortured minutes. The radios were alive with screaming voices. Eagle Leader was advising that the Bandits were Soviet-made MiGs. And Gypsy was still directing the Eagle formation hard.

In the background I heard that Phantom was returning to base—bugging out as we called it.

Paladin-1, the Eagles' leader was screaming, but I couldn't discern his squawk from amidst all the other chatter. The radios were drowned in a clutter of excited voices.

The Eagles were doing their job, following Gypsy's advice, and some of us were praying. It's a good thing that during combat stations we were to remain strapped in and that no one had been in the rear except for the Spotter who was clinging to the starboard door for his life. Big John, the AMT, and Craig, who was supposed to sit Position Four but was spotting, were thanking the Almighty that they had their chutes on. Later that morning, someone would call Craig, the newly wed, Cosmo, and the name would stick.

"Gypsy, Paladin-3 advises Bandits are Mirages not MiGs," the voice of Paladin-1 squawked into my headset along with all the others.

The F-1 Mirage wasn't the deadliest fighter in the Iraqi inventory, but the F-1 crews were very skilled and had been tempered by the long Iran-Iraq war. I was sure the Eagles were taking the confrontation with deadly seriousness.

We continued to work, our hearts in our throats. I didn't have time to look about the cabin; but from the voices in my ears, I knew who was doing his job and who wasn't. PBJ to my right was still visibly shaken. He just sat there still as can be, his eyes glossed over. In combat you either rise or you fall, and PBJ was teetering on the edge of that bottomless pit.

Abruptly Captain Willie's voice tweaked in our ears, "Pilot, MCC, the packages have safely egressed. We're cleared off stations. Let's get out of here now!"

"Roger, MCC, breaking off," responded the pilot, relieved.

We headed home. The prospect of safety somewhere ahead snatched PBJ away from the endless fall. I could see in his eyes that he, like me, was a survivor. It had only taken him longer to realize it.

No one relaxed again until we were wheels down. In the end, the bandits got away, but we didn't care, our CAP of Eagles had done their job—in the confusion, that final bit of information had been lost. The incident prepared some of us for a day when the shit really would hit the fan, a day when the bandits would be coming after us hungry.

The adrenaline pump I felt wouldn't slip away until well after debrief. Debrief lasted about an hour.

Afterward, we turned in our weapons and the extra gear we had checked out. It was 13:00 before we left base ops and it was only then that I realized how exhausted I was; functioning on three hours of sleep just didn't cut it. In the PME, I fell asleep, flight suit and all. At the time, none of us knew it, but this would be our shortest and easiest day for days to come.

Monday, 21 January 1991

Saturday and Sunday had passed in a blur of activity and confusion. I had never fully realized how bizarre or wonderful our modern electronic age is. Here we were at war with Iraq and I was at an air base in Turkey.

I remembered an old black-and-white clip issued by the war department during World War II. It was a special on the Memphis Belle. The narrator described England as an air front. I guess that's what Turkey was, an air front.

In my mind, the Gray Lady stacked up to the Belle point for point; yet our missions can't be measured in payloads or tonnage dropped, but in lives saved and planes returned safely to base.

It seemed we were segregated from the war and that we only jumped in and out of it for short spurts. Then things happened that reminded us just how insecure we were even though we were hundreds of miles away from the war zone.

Iraq was again accusing Turkey of unprovoked aggression. They said that by allowing U.S. warplanes to attack Iraqi targets, Turkey was being drawn closer to war. Iraq threatened certain retaliation. Defenses around the air base had been bolstered, and reports said a Patriot missile battery was already here although I'd seen no reassuring signs.

We were directed to start taking our pyridostigmine tablets every eight hours for seventy-two hours. The powers that be believed Iraq would indeed attack Turkey. If the attack came, they believed it would come in the form of a chemical or biological attack. The experimental drug in the tablets was supposed to counter side effects that would otherwise cripple us in the battlefield.

Late in the afternoon, I awoke to the sound of screaming sirens. The sirens' wail, a wavering tone, told me attack was imminent or in progress. It signified Alarm Red.

Still exhausted from the early morning flight, it took me a few moments to orient myself. Shortly I remembered, as did everyone around me, words from our briefings on the unconventional warfare threat, "All attacks should be considered chemical until proven otherwise. Take immediate cover and don protective gear."

Real world chemical gear is carefully sealed in government plastic bags, each piece separate. The full chemical ensemble includes overpants, overjacket, plastic overboots, mask, hood, cotton glove inserts and plastic overgloves, all worn over the top of a standard uniform or flight suit. Over the top of all that went a protective helmet and a web belt with canteen, medical kit and a pouch containing nerve agent antidote: pyridostigmine tablets, three atropine auto-injectors, and three 2-pam chloride auto-injectors. In short, it was everything we needed to survive.

Plastic bags were being ripped apart all around the room. Many like me had already gone through a previous Alarm Red. We had our masks at the ready, our gear close by. Others who had arrived only recently were scrambling and tearing open bags.

Chemical hoods, part of the full ground-crew ensemble, are not only carefully packed in plastic but also packed with baby powder to preserve them. The filters for our particular type of masks, the full-face type, were packed in tin cans. There were about five or six people that were opening the tin cans and baby powder was everywhere.

I went for my mask first and messed with the ground-crew ensemble second. Then I huddled on the floor in the quasi-dark of that small room, waiting for the sirens' wail to end.

I glanced down at the pouch containing the irksome looking auto-injectors. I remembered from demonstrations and training that beneath the safety cap was a hidden needle over two inches long. The needle wasn't thin, but rather thick to prevent breakage and to allow the antidote to inject more quickly. To activate it you were supposed to slam the needle end of the injector hard against the side of your thigh until the needle triggered, then hold it there while the contents oozed into your leg. You did this first with the atropine then followed it with the 2-pam chloride. If symptoms persisted, you were supposed to do this again after ten minutes.

It could have been worse. The older auto-injectors required you to inject the antidote manually into your leg by squeezing and rolling the tube down the way you would a tube of toothpaste. I lay there in the quasi-darkness thinking about all of this. This was, indeed, war; and nowhere was truly safe.

The Alarm Red was followed ominously by Alarm Black, which meant imminent arrival or possible presence of nuclear, biological, or chemical contamination. This was a period of uncertainty. I was no longer just frightened but terrified by the very real possibility that there were weapons of mass destruction enroute to our location.

Seconds ticked by. The air outside was balmy and still. It became so hot inside the protective suit that sweat poured down my face and into my eyes. The suit clung to my body. All I wanted to do was close my eyes, thinking that maybe if I did, when I opened my eyes again I'd find it was all a bad dream.

As tends to happen in a bad dream, things got worse before they got better. One of the crewers started freaking out and running around the room. He was screaming something as he ran around the room. I don't know what he was saying, but I really didn't have to. He had let panic set it. Any thoughts running through his mind were surely worse than reality—at least that was my hope.

I couldn't help trying to remember if he were one of the newbies. Had he put on his suit and mask too late to prevent onset of chemical or biological agents that might be present in the air? Did he need to be injected with antidote? Was this just what it appeared to be—a panic attack?

I nodded to PBJ next to me and together we tackled the crewer to the ground. As I turned him around, I realized it was Big John. His eyes were wild and unfixed as we turned him about to face us.

It was then that the attack ended. The sirens stopped wailing. We couldn't be sure that NBC contaminants were not present. We knew it was a necessary safety precaution. Still, I couldn't help wondering and praying for the All Clear announcement.

The All Clear was long in the coming. I slapped Big John's shoulder reassuringly as I removed my mask.

Shouts of joy erupted from the silent and mostly dark chamber. We'd find out later that Scud missiles had been launched at Israel. The alarms had been safety precautions and nothing more. If the attack had been real this day, some of us would have been dead or worse, myself most likely included—I didn't dive for that mask as quickly as I should have.

No one spoke of what Big John had done. We all went back to what we were doing before the alarms sounded. The inevitable preflight alert came at 20:30. I never got back to sleep after the Alarm Red and I still hadn't eaten anything but an MRE the day before. I stuck my head in the faucet and turned on the cold water. The water was extremely cold due to the cool Turkish nights, but I needed it to wake me up and to clean the grime of a trying day.

In the first days of the war there was so much uncertainty, so very much uncertainty, and even more confusion. We never knew when we were going to fly next. We never knew what was going to happen next. It was sleep when you got time if you got time.

As the new day came, we were still sitting in intel getting the daily preflight intelligence briefing. The confusion we felt yesterday was gone, leaving a feeling of disorientation. We weren't at all accustomed to sitting in a war room with an intelligence planner telling us about real-world packages we were going to support.

Today the packages would be hitting enemy early warning radar sites, airfields, and aircraft, as well as chemical and biological storage facilities. The intent was to destroy Iraq's capability to conduct unconventional warfare, and this was one of the key goals of the forces in Turkey. Nearly all of these facilities were located in areas north of Baghdad. To complicate matters, large numbers of Iraqi fighter jets were withdrawing from the hot areas in the South to northern airfields.

From what I could tell, the air campaign was progressing well, but there was an evident threat from the powerful Iraqi machine. SAM sites, AAA sites and scores of Iraqi fighter jets were still intact and ready to knock us out of the skies. It was a threat that none of us took lightly—there was just too much unknown.

The items we'd been given on arrival and had simply accepted we found the good sense to start asking questions about. We knew about blood chits, SAR codes, and evasion maps, but we'd never had to put them to real use before. Blood chits were exactly what the name implied. They were written promises of reimbursement in Arabic should we be shot down over hostile territory. Basically our lives in exchange for reward. The blood chit had four corner tabs that could be torn off to give to a benefactor and each tab was specially numbered. SAR codes were used to aid search and rescue efforts. If we went down, we knew how and when to properly contact the rescue teams. The evasion map was a specially designed map of our region of operations. It also had a number of useful survival tips printed along its sides: various first aid procedures, how to find water sources, even pictures of edible plants. On one of its two exposed sides was a tiny replica of the gallant stars and stripes.

We took a closer look at our area of operations and the orbits depicted. The diagrams on the map were very familiar to us. We used them in our everyday operations and extensively during exercises. I'd planned scenarios that looked very similar to the ones scrawled across the map in different and coordinated colors many, many times. This was no longer a training mission or even a joint exercise we were looking at. It was a plan for a battle, a battle that was to be conducted solely from the air.

It was Allen who asked Lieutenant Albright to explain the plans. The LT cleared his throat then began. "Perhaps a review is in order. You all look like you could use it. It's been a tough few days."

He paused and looked at Allen. "Sergeant, I understand you are new to Combat Crew and EW, so I'll explain the best I know how. If I'm going too slow or too fast, don't hesitate to speak out."

Allen nodded and the LT continued, "Just like on the ground, where unit activities have to be closely coordinated, air space also has to be closely coordinated. Once in or near the enemy areas, air assets are given certain areas to stay within, called an orbit box. A typical orbit box could be 100 nautical miles long and 50nm deep.

"Depicted in blue is the orbit box for AWACS. Typically AWACS has a position farthest removed from enemy territory. This allows them to see the whole combat arena, which is essential to their effectiveness since they provide much needed coordination and threat warnings.

"The KCs' orbits are depicted in green; at least one KC will usually be on orbit. Their job of refueling air support fighters and deep interdiction fighters is absolutely critical. Without the KCs, you'll have no CAP.

"Depicted in blue are the members of the Electronic Warfare Triad. Each has its own orbit box, which is usually in the forward area along the borders of Iraq. RC is critical for reconnaissance. As you know, EC provides jam support, which is necessary to block enemy communications at critical times. Lastly, Ravens and Weasels jam enemy radars."

Lieutenant Albright touched the tip of his pointer to the map. "Here you see the High-Value Air Asset Combat Air Patrol, or HVAA CAP, assigned the protection of these vulnerable air assets. Two critical parts of this CAP are the MiG Sweep and the standard CAP. MiG Sweep has forward positions to intercept enemy fighters trying to destroy air assets. That's you, combat crew. Standard CAP maintains defensive positions and at least one is always refueling with the KCs.

"The packages you're supporting have air corridors for ingress and egress, but they aren't limited to a single entrance or exit corridor. These corridors are the thick black lines pockmarking the border of Iraq. Targets the packages are striking are circled in red."

We departed intel feeling prepared to do what needed to be done. I clutched at the survival vest I wore, examining its full contents. I knew it had a mirror, a compass, a whistle, a first aid kit, day and night flares, an emergency radio, and many other items. Right then, I needed to be reassured that they were there.

The gun holster was still empty, but our next stop was the SP section. We were each issued .38s and eighteen rounds in three clear plastic bags of six rounds each. Again, the guns were to remain unloaded until we hit the plane, but I couldn't help wondering how long it would take me to pop in six rounds and ready the damn thing if necessary. I figured about thirty seconds—probably about twenty-nine seconds too long. I figured Iraq would seek the retribution against Turkey that we had just been warned about in intel, which would probably be in the form of terrorist attacks—terrorist attacks that were not that far away.

Our operation's building housed KC ops, AWACS ops and EC ops. EC ops was our next stop. We checked the big board and signed the A-forms beside our typed names. Afterward, the AC gave his briefing. The last briefing, a more detailed outline of the packages we would be supporting, was later given by the

MCC, good old Captain Willie.

Finally we were each given a briefing folder to look over and study while the MCC reviewed it with us. The briefing folder contained every last detail of the mission. It was used both to reinforce the material we had already been instructed about and to ensure that no details had been missed. It also provided a means to check for conflicts in the schedule that hadn't already been worked out.

Captain Willie waited until we had reviewed the folders, then spoke, "I know things are going to be confused up there again tonight, so let's get our procedures in line ahead of time. Robert, you're on One."

Robert nodded. "Charlotte, Two. Thomas, Three. Craig, Four. That's the right side of the plane. You're general search." Captain Willie paused and eyed Allen. "You're our ace in the whole. You'll be sitting Seven."

Captain Willie turned back to face the rest of us. "In a critical situation, you pass the signal to me first. Give the specifics to Six or Seven second and let them take it from there.

"Senior crew, you know your positions. You're the left side and I'll depend on you. We jam someone, they're going to jump channels. Remember, you're the only ones with the capability to track them and lock them. Watch them closely." Captain Willie paused to take a sip of his coffee.

"If anyone has an important signal and I'm too bogged down to answer you, pass it to Todd on Five. As MCS, he'll also be helping to keep the jam list updated. That's all I have, gentlemen and lady. Unless someone has something they'd like to add."

No one spoke up, so all we had to do was wait in the lounge for the crew van. Life Support and the Med Techs had a room off the lounge where we could get earplugs and check our gear if need be.

The crew lounge was a cavernous room that the Turks had apparently used for a similar purpose: waiting. It had cushioned couches and cushioned chairs, most of which were only framework now since the ground support personnel and those flyers who were on permanent mission planning cell had scrounged the cushions to sleep on or to use as pillows. Their quarters were also in a room off the lounge.

Those who were living here were lucky. They had a shower in a bathroom down the hall with warm running water, a TV in the lounge, and even a microwave. Right about now I would have killed for anything cooked up in a microwave, yet I'd wait for the MRE I'd hopefully eat during the flight. At the moment, I was more tired than hungry.

We clustered a group of chairs around empty bookshelves, sitting rather quietly. Bobby stretched out on a couch and was soon near sleep. We didn't say much as we waited; rather, we just stared at one another. That feeling of impending doom returned. Yet along with it there was this undeniable adrenaline pump, feeding us along and sustaining us while time eked by.

We'd been here since 20:30 and it was now approaching 02:00.

Thirty minutes more seemed like a lifetime and the day was only beginning. I couldn't wait to hear words I knew I would later dread. Nonetheless, I wanted to hear Captain Smily's voice tweak into my headset.

"Crew, we're rolling," I knew he'd say.

Evening, Monday, 21 January 1991

The morning's flight went well. The crew was back at the PME by 14:00. We were all utterly exhausted. Big John was already snoring away. He had one loud snort! I didn't even think it would bother me one bit. I was writing my journal entry then because I doubted I'd have time later and because I was too wound up to sleep.

We knew for a fact that we would have another Go soon, but we had no idea when the alert would come. With lines flying round the clock, I was betting it would be soon. I was hoping for 20:00.

Patriot missile batteries had been set up after continued Iraqi threats against Turkey for allowing U.S. warplanes to stage bombing attacks against Iraq from there. I hoped Iraq would never launch against us, but I was glad the Patriots were there.

Gentleman Bob came by the PME to see how we were all getting along. He looked tired and worn, but he was still going strong. He promised that we'd get a recreation tent that we could put up soon and a much-heralded TV to watch CNN.

Tuesday, 22 January 1991

In the wee hours of the morning just after midnight, a dark panel van raced along a blackened Turkish road. Our driver stopped as he reached the flight line and performed the customary FOD checks, then climbed back onto a sweaty cushioned seat, driving away at flight line speed—a sedate pace.

Captain Smily, the pilot, was seated in the single passenger seat to the driver's right. In the back of the van, sitting on a bare and cold steel floor, twelve figures silently waited—Captain Willie, PBJ, Cosmo, Thomas, Charlotte, Allen, Bobby, Lt. Faber the copilot, Jerry the Eng, Captain Wilcox the Nav, Big John the AMT, and me. This would be our fifth wartime flight. I'd been here ninety-six hours and had gotten exactly fifteen hours' sleep since Friday night. Breakfast would be an MRE on the plane.

Happy wasn't our driver this night. His turn as duty driver was over. When I had seen him earlier, he was looking forward to his first flight sometime later that day. Gentleman Bob promised our crew that tomorrow we'd get some time off—tomorrow seemed so far away.

By the time the van pulled up in front of the Lady, the

ground support crews already had the external power equipment hooked up and humming. So far, they were doing one hell of a job of ensuring that the planes were ready to fly. More incredibly, for these past few days they'd been doing it with minimal manning. Back home more than 600 ground support personnel are needed for maintenance on a round-the-clock basis. Here we had roughly sixty.

The crew out there with our bird I knew on sight. I'd seen them dozens of times before. They are as proud and as true a group of silent heroes as any. Their rewards for a twelve-to sixteen-hour day oftentimes were only tired, time-hardened hands caked with dirt and grease so thick that it was nearly impossible to scrub away.

We were halfway to the crew entrance door when the warning sirens kicked in. From the warbling tone, we knew it was an Alarm Red. The scene that followed was one of mass frenzy. One of the ground crewmen appropriately raced across the tarmac to a nearby ditch. His only piece of ground gear was his mask, which he put on as an afterthought when he hit the ditch.

I dropped to one knee, pulled out my mask and hood, and slipped it on. Once the seals were clear, I raced across the tarmac to the ditch. Only two others followed.

Spread out across the flight line between the plane, the van, and the ditch, the rest of the crew were donning their ground crew ensembles. Some put the chem pants on first, others the charcoal insulated overcoat, while others had wisely chosen their masks and hoods.

PBJ, to my left, already had on his helmet, mask, and hood. Now he was lying on his back, struggling with the zipper of his chem pants. Charlotte was recognizable to my right only because of her small size. She was lacing up the plastic overboots, the proper final piece of her ground crew ensemble. Both had come a long way since that first awful night.

The sirens continued to wail as the rest of the crew scrambled for the safety of the ditch. A-bags were strewn all over the place. My helmet in place over my mask and hood, I hugged the ditch close while I finished tying my plastic boots.

At this point no one really knew what was going to happen. Silently we waited while the sirens screamed. Tel Aviv was probably taking a pounding again by Iraqi Scuds—Scuds that we were well within the range of, Scuds that we expected to hit Turkey.

The Iraqis were relying heavily on their mobile Scud launchers, which over the past days they had been using quite extensively. The Soviet-made Scud wasn't an effective weapon. Its aim was poor and even if its destination were precisely calculated and targeted, it could still miss its target by as much as a kilometer.

We lay in that wet ditch, our lives flashing before our eyes. We knew anything could happen. There were few rules in war. The All Clear eventually came, but not for many excruciating minutes.

Retaliatory fighters were immediately launched. Their job would be to help find the mobile launchers and destroy them before they got a chance to slip back into the night and strike again another day. Our Scud hunters had already done a tremendous job in helping to knock out numerous fixed Scud launch sites and quite a few mobile launch sites. We had faith in them as we watched them depart, afterburners lighting up the night sky.

Climbing from the ditch, we were angry, wet, and muddy. We marched as creatures possessed to the plane. The Alarm Red had wasted valuable time. We'd have to scramble hard to meet our station's window, or packages would arrive without jam support. And that would cost lives, American or allied lives.

In an incredible ten minutes, the Lady was racing down the runway. As soon as we climbed to an adequate altitude, Big John began the arduous chore of bringing up the system. We each did our part. Miraculously, the plane was turned onto orbit, the system was up, and we were logged in ready to go to work on time.

PBJ was on radios to Phantom while the copilot contacted Control and Gypsy. We had done it and it was a minor miracle. But the job had only begun. We still had to locate the enemy communications networks for their AAA, SAM, ground and air elements. It was a tall order in fifteen minutes.

The scene became tense as positions One through Six—I was sitting Six—madly searched the signal environment. The system could flag frequencies that had RF energy on them as well, but whether we jammed enemy signals or not when the MCC turned on the jammers was entirely up to how well we operators did. Our job was to sort through the tremendous amount of signals available in the RF spectrum and to use our years of analysis training to identify and target enemy signals.

Signals could emanate from the ground or air. They could be voice or data, encrypted or clear. We relied on our banks of equipment, the system, our ears, and sometimes our guts to help us make sense of it all. It was a difficult task even under the best of circumstances, made even more difficult by the number of variables. The airwaves were cluttered with friendly and hostile comms signals, not to mention comms from outside sources—those considered neither hostile nor neutral.

Both the MCC and MCS worked on updating the jam list, a list of targeted signals we operators had identified. Each signal was given a priority for jamming based on actual or expected activity for that particular signal. Again, it came down to the operators' telling the MCC and MCS what we'd identified.

Suddenly I heard Cosmo's voice hissing into my ears. He was the spotter on this mission. "Pilot, Spotter, traffic low moving twelve to six."

This was the first wave of the strike package heading in. They were five minutes early. To support them, we had to jam before our window came. I guessed they were eager to get in and see if they could spot any of those Scuds.

Cosmo would call in three more times and I'd only hear his voice among a discord of voices. I had too many other things to listen to at the time to worry about the status of the packages passing by. The only word I listened for was bandits.

It was a practiced skill to be able to listen to and follow two or three conversations at once, but between the three channels of outside ship chatter, ship's Interphone, two channels of Private, Select, and the live signals I was active on, I was listening to nine. I liked to know what was going on. More important, sitting Six, I had to be able to back up the MCS, who was to my right, on radios if necessary.

"Crew, MCC," hissed Captain Willie's voice into my headset from Private. "We're coming out of jam to take a good look around us for one minute. Tell me if you got anything that's hot and I'll throw her back into jam."

I punched out Interphone and switched off Select, which put

me down to seven channels, as I called out a target to the MCC. The target wasn't an immediate threat so the MCC didn't put the system back into jam.

Big John was headed up toward One when Two called out, "MCC, Two, target, immediate threat." My heart seemed to skip a beat as I keyed into Private A. "Sir, I have an Iraqi tower controller directing fighters to take off."

"Two, pass me the signal, give the specifics to Seven," responded the MCC.

"MCC, Two, you should have the signal and, sir, he's about to change frequencies."

"Two, I have the new signal. Crew, we're back in jam. Two, MCC, pass the fighter ID to Seven."

I switched the settings on my spectrum analyzer to the end of the spectrum I expected the fighter to switch to and watched for a new signal spike to appear. "MCC, Six, I got him up on air," I called out. "He just switched freqs."

All of a sudden, I heard it, the inevitable call I had been waiting to hear, "Bandits five o'clock low. They are a threat," warned Gypsy, "suggest evasive maneuvers. They're climbing fast!"

The AC cut the orbit short and turned the Lady hard. My heart jumped up into my throat as the blood rushed to my head. My hands and arms went heavy as I tried to type onto the keyboard in front of me and then was thrown into the chair as we began to climb. The Lady was by no stretch of the imagination as maneuverable as a fighter, but the pilot was taking her through all the evasive maneuvers she could manage. In this situation, it was prudent to remain a haphazardly moving target so the fighters couldn't get a missile lock if they were within range.

My heart was beating nonstop; and my fingers, glued to my keyboard, were trembling. It seemed as if the whole of the Gray Lady from front to aft was covered in silence. At Gypsy's direction, a two-ship of Eagles, our MiG Sweep, peeled off for intercept, afterburners aglow. The chase was on. The Bandits were coming in strong, and they were hungry.

Paladin Leader's remaining two-ship edged forward while Gypsy shifted as far back as possible. Phantom was far enough away today that he didn't much care. They had plenty in their own area to be concerned about.

Our packages weren't even outbound yet, and we still had more than an hour on orbit—Captain Willie was confirming this to the pilot. "Roger, Pilot, no one has called an abort yet. We'll do our best to get those fighters off our tail and to stay in jam. I don't know what good it'll do with us bouncing around like this. I really need you to hold her level for about a minute."

The pilot leveled the Lady off. "MCC, Pilot, the clock's ticking."

"Seven, MCC, are you ready? Six, MCC, are you ready? On my mark, you have twenty seconds. Mark!"

"MCC, Seven, I have their data comms, locking."

"MCC, Six, I have their voice comms, locking."

"MCC, Seven, sending the details. Ready for jam when you are."

"MCC, Six, sending the details for jam. Ready when you are."

Everything afterward was intense static as Captain Willie put the system back in jam. Allen continued to work his magic with the fighter's data signals, tracking and locking new signals. I continued to work on the voice signals, monitoring for the inevitable frequency hopping, tracking and locking as I went.

Elsewhere in the mission crew area, the other crewers were doing the same. Jammed targets switched to clear frequencies, so we had to constantly keep up with them. I searched as fast as I could. I wanted those enemy fighters to remain confused and without communications.

As we searched, no few of us were praying. Out of the corner of my eye, I saw Big John. He was visibly shaken. His face was pale; there was a look of terror in his eyes. Both he and Cosmo were hugging their chutes. Me, I was more worried about my .38—had I loaded it in all the excitement or not?—and freezing to death if we dropped down into the white caps I knew were below us.

Seconds ticked by with agonizing slowness as if time itself were nearly standing still. I was conscious of my own breathing and everything around me. I took in a breath. Let it out. I felt my fingers tap the keyboard. My eyes moved between the CRT in front of me and the banks of equipment to the left and right.

Captain Willie called out, a note of concern playing in his deep voice, "Pilot, MCC, first wave is egressing. Are we going to stay on orbit to support the second when they go in or not?"

"MCC, Pilot, what's their ETA to ingress?"

"Fifteen mike."

"Roger that, we'll drop back to the edge of box."

"Pilot, MCC, roger that."

"Did he follow?" Bobby called out, accidentally switched onto Interphone and not Select.

"We'll sure find out," I answered, keying Select to remind him what channel he was on.

"Thanks," he whispered, switching onto Select.

I said, "I think it's safe to say they're singing solo into their mikes if nothing else."

As the Lady turned, I glanced over my shoulder at Big John. He was sitting at his position with this blank, wide-eyed expression. His wide eyes made him look like a deer that'd just been caught in the beam of a flashlight. Cosmo, the newlywed, was in the back tossing up whatever he'd eaten in the hours since or before the flight. I knew this because Thomas pointed it out on Private B.

It took a few minutes after we leveled off for my thoughts to catch up with my racing heart, for the world to come back to normal. I flashed my eyes at PBJ and dialed into his station on Select. "MCS, Six, Select. Did they get him?"

"Gypsy's not saying anything; guess we'll find out in debrief."

What PBJ meant by "Gypsy wasn't saying anything," wasn't that Gypsy wasn't squawking, but that they were too busy to reply. She was screaming so loud I had punched off her station. Besides, on another channel I was trying to find out what Paladin Leader had to say.

I concentrated on finding signals. It seemed the second wave was over target forever. The adrenaline rush just wasn't lasting as long as it had in previous days, but there was no denying that the tension threshold was peaked. We still didn't know what had happened to the Bandits. We only knew they weren't an immediate threat to us at the moment.

My headset went through a high-low tone sequence, and I knew someone had dialed up Select and connected in with me. "I hope they got him," Allen said.

After a pause, I replied, "I bet they splashed that bandit. They'll owe us a MiG under those flags they're promising." I was referring to the painted on flags that symbolized the number of combat missions a particular plane had flown. The fighter symbolized an assist in a shoot-down.

I sighed and relaxed a bit in my chair as Captain Willie's voice tweaking into my headset told me it was almost over. "Crew, MCC, the second wave has successfully egressed. Excellent job today, way to stay on it!" He paused, and then switched to Interphone. "Pilot, MCC, stations. We're clear off orbit when you're ready, sir. Hell of a fly job."

"Roger. Crew, we're on our way home!"

There was silence again while we listened to the radios. Gas Station was headed home and so was Gypsy. Phantom was turning south.

"Who was that on Interphone earlier?" asked the navigator.

"Nav One, that was me," admitted Bobby.

"I guess bravos are on you. You know the rules: screw up on radio, you buy the bravos." It was another crew dog rule: don't screw up on radio, or you buy the beer, a case was the usual payment. "I only say this because tomorrow we're going to have time to catch some wind."

"Nav, One, I got the first case."

"Roger that, One."

A number of heads were nodding. Most of us could already taste that first icy cold beer. We were sure looking forward to some down time and an hour more than eight was all we needed to be able to drink a few beers.

The Nav's mike had just tweaked off Interphone when the wings began to rock back and forth. What the hell was going on? I twisted my seat around to face front and checked shoulder straps to make sure they were in the unlocked position, remembering then that I had pushed in Gypsy's squawk. I pulled it out just in time to hear Captain Smily's response, "Roger that, splash one confirmed."

Paladin-3 had confirmed a hit and a kill. We'd find out in tomorrow's tallies for sure. At the moment we were all elated, and none of us recalled how terrified we had been just a few short minutes ago.

I jumped out of the seat with the others and slapped out a round of high fives.

Time passed. We were thirty miles out from base. With the Iraqi border and the enemy behind us, we could all afford to relax in our seats.

The only channel I had pulled was ship's Interphone so I could hear the front-end chatter as we approached base. The pilot and the copilot were going back and forth about the air traffic and I listened in, "Co, we're bottlenecking here. I don't think we'll beat the KCs in today. Let me see if I can get clearance around them, or else we'll be stuck on the pad for an extra thirty. God knows it's been one hell of a long day already."

The copilot called Tower, and soon afterward I heard Tower's reply for the go-ahead. Accordingly, the pilot increased the throttle. I closed my tired eyes and rubbed them, then groped for my helmet bag and the bottled water within. I'd already finished one liter bottle, so I had to uncap a new one. Just as I popped the cap, a loud squeal came into my headset and then the plane banked hard to the left. Water went everywhere.

"What the hell was that?" I heard the pilot say on Interphone, "Did you see that explosion, Co?"

"I did. Holy shit," responded the Nav. "What was it?"

"I don't know; but whatever it was, it was aimed at us or that KC. Get the pilot on radio. I'll try Tower."

"It looked like a missile, but how the hell? We're within visual of Tower."

"Pilot, Co, Tower's redirecting us; they want us to circle wide and come in from the other side."

"Did you ask them what the hell's going on?"

"No, I didn't. Didn't have time to," responded the copilot.

Tower began re-directing all inbound traffic.

"As near as I can tell from all this chatter," began Captain Willie on Ship's Interphone, "that was a Patriot or at least that's what Gas Station said after the explosion."

Suddenly a look of extreme shock returned to our eyes. We all realized just how close we had come to death's door once again. Two close calls in one day were more than enough to bring us back into the dizzying spiral of confusion and frenzy. I swallowed my heart back down my throat along with a big gulp of water that I nearly choked on.

During debrief we found out that it had indeed been a Patriot missile. It had been accidentally triggered by an erroneous IFF transponder. We were just glad the missile had such an elaborate fail-safe system that it hadn't plucked us from the sky.

Evening,
Tuesday, 22 January 1991

In lieu of the promised recreation tent, six crew dogs crowded around a picnic table that stood between the two small buildings of the PME. We listened to a news broadcast on Allen's portable radio.

It was still early evening, but as the light drained from the sky, cold air began moving in. This time of year, the long Turkish nights were so cold you could see your breath. We huddled around the radio in our winter flight gear and thermals as if it could offer some extra warmth. Bad Boy was the exception; he had lived in Alaska for three years, and the cold didn't seem to affect him. Allen, Cosmo, and PBJ were part of the six, and we weren't sitting out in the cold for nothing; we were waiting for Bobby to return with the promised case of Budweiser.

There was a certain cohesiveness forming between members of the crews. You knew everyone else; you had your friends and associates, but your crew was your crew and you stuck with them. They'd been there with you when the shit had hit the fan. They'd been there with you when you'd seen the whole of your life flash before your eyes. They'd been there with you afterward while you waited the seemingly endless hours before you were to fly again.

I wolfed down a can of pork and beans straight out of the can and icy cold. It was supper, and it tasted exceptionally good. A group of us had headed across base earlier on a sort of "recon" mission. We found that the commissary two blocks up the street was finally open.

We discovered on our little sojourn that the air base, like us, seemed to be recovering from the mass confusion that had besieged it and us during those first few frantic days. Across the air base, though, there were still people housed in every possible nook and cranny. The base gym, the local YMCA, and the base rec center were all stuffed to overflowing with recent arrivals.

There were troops crowded into barracks hallways and day rooms, all sleeping on surplus cots as we were. There seemed to be an abundance of cots, which they were unloading by the truckload all around the base. Tent City had grown two-fold since our arrival and they filled each new tent just as fast as it went up. Back at the PME, we were quite thankful for the rooms we were packed into like sardines.

Happy, six-pack in hand, stepped outside and casually ambled to the picnic table. Where was Bobby with that case? I can't stay awake much longer. "That bravo looks great, Happy! I'd die for one right about now," I said.

Happy turned around and held the six-pack out.

"You shitting me?" I asked.

"No, take one."

I accepted, no questions asked. "You got an opener?"

"Nope."

I looked at the beer in my hand, "Where's the opener?"

Happy slapped me on the back, "You've been in Germany too long, my friend. It's a twist top."

"Twist top. Imagine that!" I twisted the top and was raising the beer to my lips when the crew van pulled up.

The duty driver called out my name and waved me over. I wondered whether if I pretended not to notice him, I'd be able to finish my beer. Deciding I wouldn't, I took one long sip before handing the beer back to Happy, who just sort of looked at me.

"Shit, I would've finished the bravo," he whispered after me. Good old Happy.

"What's up?" I asked the duty driver.

"You need to head down to ops ASAP!"

The duty driver put the van in reverse. "Hey, wait a minute. You going to give me a ride? Do I need my gear? Is something wrong?"

It became painfully obvious that either the duty driver didn't know or he didn't want to be the one to deliver bad news, so I hopped into the passenger seat without my gear.

We arrived to find a bustling ops center. One crew was leaving, another just coming in. I saw at once that the big board had changed. My name was now listed with a different crew, a crew that had an early morning alert. I tried to find out why the switch had been made. I asked the duty officer, but he didn't know or wasn't saying. I was certain I'd have to wait until pre-brief to discover exactly why the names had been swapped around.

Wednesday, 23 January 1991

Alert came all too early. It seemed my head had just touched my sleeping bag when I was awakened by a light shining in my eyes.

Some hours later I found myself in intel. Thankfully, the briefing was short, yet I couldn't help noticing that our orbit box was slowly pushing forward. We were scraping the edge of Iraq's northern border now, a grim thought with the AAA and SAM units pushing into that mountainous region. Mounted on top of any of those hills, heavy caliber anti-aircraft artillery and any surface-air missile could cause our great fears to be realized.

As we waited for a pre-brief from the pilot and the mission controller, we read through the various intelligence read files. When the pilot's briefing finally came, it was short and oddly energetic.

Tennessee Jim was my new mission crew commander. When he got up in front of the big map, his mouth full of chew and an almost filled spit cup in hand, I nearly broke into laughter. Spit dribbled down his chin as he spoke and described the myriad of scribbles spread across the map. To be honest, I never liked the guy; somehow, I'd always thought he'd be better off on that farm of his in Tennessee. He wasn't Captain Willie, but then again he wasn't anal retentive like some of the other MCCs I could've ended up with. I'd also find out real quick why the crews had been changed.

"Today, we'll be supporting the biggest package to date," Tennessee Jim said, spitting into his cup as he spoke, adding after a momentary pause, "we're stepping up the heat in that oven so to speak. Our mission remains the same: Command Communications and Control Counter Measures—C3CM. We'll jam until we just can't jam no more."

He went on and on in that Tennessee drawl of his, describing the missions of the Wild Weasels and the Ravens, the Screaming Eagles and the Fighting Falcons. When he finished, his spit cup was running over and dripping onto the floor. He seemed to notice it just then and he dumped it into a nearby trashcan. The wad of chew in his mouth followed the cup an instant later.

I quickly found out that when he flew, he was all professional. It was only afterward that I could have transplanted him to that farm of his in Tennessee where he would have been perfectly in character.

This new crew was a strange mix. The mission crew was three females and five males—Tammy, Ziggy, Sparrow, Chris, Mike, Popcorn, Tennessee Jim, and me. The front-end all males—Sammy, Bill, Ice, Crow, and Patrick.

With the exception of poor Ziggy who Happy would replace, this would be the crew I'd fly with for almost all of my remaining flights. They were one strange bunch. I fit in just fine.

Today was Ziggy's first flight. She was visibly trembling as she climbed into the seat on position three. She'd been working as a daytime duty driver since arrival. Chris was the mission crew supervisor and an old friend. My opinion of Tennessee Jim had wavered somewhat. Still, I wasn't sure if I'd like flying with him. I guessed I'd have to wait and see.

"Lock 'em and load 'em," called out Tennessee Jim, just after preflight checks. He was referring to our .38s. I loaded mine: one, two, three, four, five, six rounds, lickety-split.

Ziggy on Three dropped all six rounds onto the deck, not once but twice. "Just put the damn thing away," Tennessee Jim advised over Private A, which was a good suggestion.

Crow, the AMT, screamed out, "Righteous!" onto ship's Interphone, followed by, "Ready to rock and roll back here."

"Let's get this damn thing up in the air," Jim's voice hissed into my headset immediately afterward.

Bill, the Nav, responded with, "How many newbies you got back there?"

"Three, I'd imagine."

"That's three cases the way I see it," called out the pilot.

"Crew, MCC, you heard the pilot, bravos in my quarters after the flight. And you newbies know who you are."

It was right about then that I realized why the crew van had left the PME with only two people in it, the driver and me. This was the crew that was set up in billeting. They had been keeping a very low profile since then. I'd be glad on tomorrow's flight when Happy signed on; at least the two of us would be leaving the PME together.

"Crew, Before Engine Starting Checklist," tweaked the pilot's voice into my headset; and for a time, it was back to business.

I listened to the checks, to the engines start one by one, and before I knew it, I heard the pilot's voice advising, "Crew, we're rollin'."

I started thinking about the Weasels, the Eagles, the Falcons, and all the other players we'd be supporting today. Today's targets were especially important. We weren't turning up the heat in that oven for nothing.

I would have given anything to be in the back spotting when the packages came through although during the daylight you really couldn't see much. The night was when the real light show began.

I wasn't feeling too keen. My sinuses were congested. I couldn't get my ears to clear and the slow build-up of pain from changing pressures dulled my senses. The system wasn't operational yet, and as I glanced at my watch I knew we were getting close to the combat zone. I started to worry.

The Nav helped to confirm my fears a few minutes later. "MCC, Nav, fifteen minutes till we hit the zone. How's the system look back there?"

"Nav, MCC, it looks like the AMT is having some difficulties, but he hasn't said anything yet."

Crow looked up from his position. He was clearly flustered. "MCC, AMT, this system is FUBBed. You wouldn't believe all the gremlins I've found!" FUBBed meant fucked up beyond belief. "I'm going to have to take the system all the way down and back up again."

"Pull your dick out, AMT! We're fifteen minutes to orbit. You got ten minutes!" admonished Tennessee Jim.

Crow began to race around, powering down the system components.

"Damn it all to hell," muttered Jim as he tweaked Private. "MCS, MCC, get Phantom on the horn now! Have them give us everything they got. Get that list and pass the damn thing out."

Chris began his radio call to our buddies on Phantom. I was sitting Six. After tapping him on the shoulder and pointing, I got pen and paper ready to back him up.

"Crew, MCC, don't dick around when the system comes up, if it comes up. Get logged in and get ready to enter the list the MCS passes to you. Call them complete as soon as you're finished. I'm not going to acknowledge the damn thing, so press on afterward."

We gave a quick thumbs up acknowledgment.

Phantom was responding to our call now. I readied my pen, started writing down the list.

"MCC, AMT, this thing is still FUBBed I'm going to have to take it down again. There's no way I can do it in time."

"Four, MCC, unplug and help the AMT power back down. The rest of you get that damn list ready."

Popcorn unplugged from his position and raced back to the AMT's position. I was worried now. We were supposed to be supporting the largest package to date and we couldn't even get our system up. If we didn't get Iraqi ground and air communication systems jammed by the time the packages began to ingress, there were going to be losses. Today they might not be only Iraqi.

The pilot and MCC were faced with a dilemma. Worst-case scenario would be to call an abort for the majority of the inbound missions. In any situation we had to forewarn Gypsy of our problem. The package did have Ravens and Weasels, but they jammed radars.

"MCC, AMT, I'm going to pull the controller and replace it."

"Do it. How long's it going to take?"

"At least five minutes." I heard the AMT breathing into his

mike. He'd gone up on Flight Crew Hot so he didn't have to push the button anymore to tweak.

"You got three. Get on it."

After confirming the list, I tore my piece of paper into four parts and handed them out. The MCS gave me the thumbs up. He was busy on radios with other things.

"MCC, Nav, we're seven minutes to orbit. How's it looking back there?"

"AMT, MCC, you got that in yet?"

"Almost, give me a minute," hissed the AMT into his headset. He was breathing heavier as he ran back to his position. He looked on, waiting for the thumbs up from Popcorn. Popcorn was ferociously tightening the bolts on the controller box.

"System's coming back up," Crow advised, "let's see how it goes this time."

"MCC, Pilot, we're three minutes to orbit, we going to abort this thing or not? I got to tell Gypsy."

"AMT?" hissed the MCC. I didn't realize until then that the MCC had gone Hot also.

"MCC, Pilot?"

"MCC, Pilot, hold one."

We waited at the ready. If the system came up, positions One through Four would start entering Phantom's list. Mike and I sitting Seven and Six would start searching for other signals. The MCC and MCS would do everything they could to ensure that all the tracked signals were jammed as appropriate before the package ingressed.

With only minutes to spare, it'd be a minor miracle if we could pull it off. I crossed my fingers. I think a lot of us were praying. Praying seemed to be something you did much more in combat than any other time. Looking back, I can see how strange it was to pray to God above for such things. In that moment it didn't seem strange at all though.

"MCC, Pilot, it's now or never."

"AMT?" hissed the MCC.

"She's coming up! Prepare to log in, in five—four—"

"Pilot, MCC, that's a negative on that abort. We're going to be green in a moment."

"Shit," Crow hissed. "MCC, AMT, that didn't do it. We're going to have to try again."

"Stick a cork in it, AMT. Do whatever you got to do. You got two minutes."

"Hold on to that green light, Pilot. We're still tits up."

Crow was pointing at a box strapped down in the equipment storage area while he started winding out screws. Popcorn scrambled over to get it.

"What's the word back there, MCC? MCC? We got a green light or not? MCC?"

I looked left past Mike on Seven and saw Tennessee Jim staring at his blackened screen. He was up Hot, so he didn't have to push a button to respond; all he had to do was talk. It was fairly clear from the expression on his face that he wasn't responding just because he was stubborn.

"We're on orbit," called out the Nav. "Five minutes till first wave ingress." Bill had spoken up to calm Captain Sammy. Yes, we were on orbit, but we still had five precious minutes till package ingress began. The question was, was that enough time to get the system up and rolling?

Crow sighed and slumped down into his seat. Popcorn raced

back to position 4. "Cross your fingers!" tweaked Crow.

A moment later I heard Crow sigh again. "MCC, she's coming up."

We waited spellbound, fingers at our keyboards, ready to go as soon as we were cleared in.

"MCC, AMT, clear to log in!"

"You got that, Nav, the dick dance is over. We're coming online in three mike!"

"Crew, checking out the system. She looks good. Cleared in."

"MCS, Six, there's no spotter back there," I cautioned.

"Two, MCC, clear to the rear."

"Roger, MCC," responded Sparrow.

"Seven, MCC, I want you to be our data signal coordinator. Six, MCC, you're our voice signal coordinator. Your expertise will help you confirm signals faster. Crew, you got that?"

We gave a crew thumbs up.

"I'll take your list," Chris said over Private B. Sparrow gave it to him, and then raced to the rear. The seconds began to tick away as we worked on our assigned lists.

"MCC, Six, checks complete." I looked over to the MCS to see how he was progressing on Sparrow's list while working radios. He was coordinating with Gypsy, so I pointed and took the first list from him.

Mike called in next. "MCC, Seven, checks complete."

"MCC, Four, complete," called out Popcorn.

"MCC, Nav, is there a spotter in the window?"

"MCC, One, complete," said Tammy.

"Three, MCC?"

Ziggy was frozen in place. She keyed her mike but didn't speak right away. After a long pause, she finally said, "Three, complete."

"MCC, MCS, and Six, complete." I called out.

We all knew the list Phantom had passed was just the tip of the iceberg. We still had to make sure we had the key Iraqi communications networks targeted. I turned to my spectrum analyzers first while the others went to the system signal list.

As the data and voice experts, Mike and I became the coordination points for the time being. This helped speed up target confirmation. Positions One and Four passed potential targets to us as fast as they could. Position Three passed signals only sporadically. We worked to confirm the signals and pass them to the MCC.

"MCC, Nav, we've reached our window." The Nav's words seemed to hang in our ears. The package was coming in. We were supposed to be in jam to support them. If we didn't get the job done, the splashes today could be our own. We didn't stop madly searching the environment for additional targets, but we did listen closely for Jim's voice.

He didn't respond immediately. He was too busy pushing buttons. The wait was excruciating even though only a few seconds had passed.

"Crew, we're jammin'!" he called out, pushing in Hot and then keying his mike again, "The packages are ingressing now. Glory be, we did it!

"Crew, MCC, good work! Now get ready to bust some ass. This day is just beginning and far from over! Stay on top of those signal changes and find me more!"

"Pilot, Spotter, traffic low heading toward two o'clock. It's the first wave, sir. Afterburners and all! They sure do look magnificent," called out Sparrow.

For a fleeting moment before I went back to madly searching the environment I saw those afterburners in my mind's eye. My thoughts went to Katie in Germany. I knew she hated the loud roar of jet engines, but right then I imagined she'd think them as beautiful a sight as I did.

Thursday, 24 January 1991

Thursday morning. It seemed incredible that I'd been there seven days already. Later that day, I flew my seventh combat flight.

It was 22:00 when I returned to the PME after the flight the day before. I was not sure how many more of those never-ending days I could handle. The word was that things would only get worse before they got any better.

That day was fourteen hours of suspense and anxiety straight from the pits of hell. The flights were also strangely uplifting. There's no greater reward than knowing you're saving American lives.

Things on base continued to move toward normalcy. On Tuesday I discovered the nearby commissary. It was supposed to have reopened already, but Monday had been a holiday. Guess some people still got holidays off even in a war zone. Since we were officially TDY, it was just as expensive to eat at the open mess as it was to eat at the AAFES concession stands. With bills piling up at home, I couldn't afford either.

Still, I was doing quite well living off a stack of canned goods—pork and beans, beanies and weenies, canned peaches, and, of course, fig newtons, the strawberry kind—that I carried back along with a case of water. Happy and I were going to split the cost of the water. There was water at the squadron, but we were only supposed to take it when we flew. I guess I could have drunk tap water, but I didn't want to risk a case of the shits.

I discovered the base gym that had been serving as a shelter was open. It had hot showers! Guess the "O's" were hoping to keep this one to themselves for a day or so, because I caught old Captain Smily coming down the street with a towel in one hand and a shaving kit in the other. He told me where he'd been, but not very quickly.

I took my first real shower in eight days. The water was cold because by the time I got there dozens of other guys had made the same discovery. I didn't care. The shower felt good, cold or not.

Gentleman Bob came through on his promise of a rec tent. It was definitely a piece of work. It was probably a six-man tent, no larger, with a plywood platform forming the base. The one thing it had, though, that we all wanted was a television. We definitely owed Gentleman Bob for coming through on his promise of a TV!

The odd thing was that when I returned, the tent was deserted. I thought a bunch of guys would be watching CNN. No one was. I quickly found out why: we didn't have a heater and the tent was freezing at night. Alone, I watched the news for a time and unwound.

Today, we had a 13:00 alert. Good old Happy was flying with us, so now I wasn't the only one leaving the PME.

Ziggy was going back to duty driving. I don't think we gave her a fair shake. I don't think she gave herself a fair shake for that matter. I guess that's life in a war zone. Not everyone was born to fly into combat.

This not only applies to females but also to males. There are a number of people who simply prefer to keep both feet on the ground. Something about a fear of dying that, although I understand, I cannot accept as a viable excuse.

In the early afternoon I was eating peaches from a can, my eyes glued to the news, when I heard the crew van pull up. It wasn't 13:00 already, was it? I poked my head out of the tent flaps that had been unzipped to see Ziggy stepping out of the crew van. Her face was long, and she had deep bags under the eyes.

"Hey, Ziggy, what's up?" I called out in greeting.

She looked up and smiled then opened the van's back door. Four guys jumped up, clutching their A-bags and their masks with the newbie death grip. Jesus, did I look that scared the first day?

Happy, who had been sitting next to me watching the news, stepped out to greet them. I was sure glad he did.

We spent the next hour showing the new arrivals how to set up their cots and properly ready their chem gear. They were relentless with their questions, which we did our best to answer.

It was 12:45 when we finally told them we had to get ready to fly. I was looking forward to getting to base ops. They'd promised us that we could make a five-minute morale call home. It would be my first phone call home to Katie. I still hadn't got off a single letter that I had promised though three of them were stacked up beneath my cot. They weren't much more than I love you and I miss you, but at least they were written.

In the coming weeks, my letters would get longer and I'd tell

Katie about Turkey, the weather, and what I'd been up to. Everything but that which was the most important: flying and the war. I'd always sum that up in one or two sentences.

At 12:55 Ziggy returned to alert us. I was ready to go to base ops, so when she went back I went with her. She didn't say much during the short van ride, but I could tell things were eating at her. I tried to make polite conversation, but she wasn't in a conversational mood.

At ops, I went to the command center first. Gentleman Bob and Major James were engrossed in a discussion of mission progression. Major James was my direct commander and Gentleman Bob's second in command. He was one levelheaded individual. He put up with a lot of guff on a daily basis, plowing through it without hesitation. He was the action man and he got things done.

I stayed only long enough to check the big board and to make sure no serious changes had taken place then headed down to the ops support room to make my phone call.

"How do I make a morale call?" I asked Quincy, one of the ops support guys. He told me, and the next thing I knew, I was dialing. Suddenly, my heart was skipping faster than it had during yesterday's flight.

"Hello? Yes? Yes, I'd like to make a morale call to West Germany. Yes, I'll hold."

When the operator asked, I gave her the number. Again she told me to wait.

"I'm sorry, the number's busy. You'll have to try back later," she told me a moment later. My heart sank.

I moped around ops for about fifteen minutes. I checked Life Support and the read files in intel before I went back to try again.

"Yes, operator, I'd like to make a morale call to West Germany. The number?" I gave the operator the number. "Yes, I'll wait. Hello? Yes? Yes. Thank you. Katie? Is that you?"

My heart was pounding so fast, I had to sit down. I turned to look at Quincy who was still in the room. He didn't get the hint right away that I wanted him to leave though he finally did leave.

"How is everything at home? Did you get the car running? I miss you, too. I have an address for you so you can send me— Oh, the squadron already gave it to you."

We talked for five minutes. The operator cut in twice to remind us of how much time we had left, then to tell us the five minutes were up. The phone clicked and went dead before I got the chance to tell Katie I loved her more than anything else. I guessed she already knew, or at least I hoped she did.

It was right then that I realized her birthday had been on the seventeenth and that in all the confusion, I hadn't given her a card or even told her happy birthday. I felt like crying, but I didn't. I just sat in that empty, quiet room for a long, long time afterward. I didn't move from the chair or even look up. I stared at the floor and wondered when all this ended where it would leave Katie and me.

The rest of the crew arrived at 14:00. After a host of briefings, we were ready to go. I sat solemnly in the back of the crew van and watched the road fall away behind us—watched my thoughts fall away.

Friday, 25 January 1991

At the start of my second week I was on my way to my eighth wartime flight in eight days at a little after 05:00. The missions were gradually getting longer and bolder as allied forces gained domination over Iraqi skies. I feared we were getting a little too bold, but only time would tell.

Nearly 120,000 Turkish troops had amassed on the Turkish-Iraqi border after continued Iraqi threats. God help them if Saddam should choose to open up a second front.

If the flight went well, I would be back at the PME shortly after midnight. We seemed to be settling into a routine of fly, sleep, watch CNN, fly, sleep, watch CNN. Gentleman Bob told us we shouldn't expect a break any time soon. The plan was to turn up the heat on Iraq another notch.

The new crew was surprisingly energetic and a lot of fun. Although we were losing Mike to the MPC, I looked forward to flying with Cowboy. There would be three of us leaving the PME together now.

Allen, PBJ, and Cosmo came into ops as we were leaving. They were still flying with Captain Willie though the rest of the crew had been changed around. They looked like they were getting by.

My attention turned to Gentleman Bob as he began. "Today, gentlemen and ladies, we are supporting a very special mission package." Gentleman Bob liked to play things up so they seemed bigger than life. He let the words hang there ominously.

We'd been through the intel briefings already. For the most part, we knew what to expect. He began again, "Priority targets remain early warning and radar sites, airfields and aircraft. As you know, a substantial number of Iraqi fighter jets have fled north. More fighters in our area mean a substantially greater threat to our missions. Like you, I'd prefer that we destroyed every one of those damned fighters to make our job safer.

"However, as you know, special emphasis has been placed on completely eliminating the Iraqi chemical, biological, and nuclear threat. Toward this end, part of the package has a very special target." Gentleman Bob paused and Derrin from intel flicked on the overhead projector. "This picture is of a suspected Iraqi chemical warfare depot."

He began pointing with his pointer. "You can see from all the activity here that something is going on. Also, most of those fortifications are new. A contingent of Falcons will be striking those bunkers circled in red with smart missiles. The Buffs will follow and lay down a fine carpet.

"To support this package, we're going to have to be airborne longer than usual. I want you all at your best out there today. I know you're tired and it's been a damned long week. Together we can do it if we just hang tough," concluded Gentleman Bob. It was a nice close to an invigorating speech. It was clear he wanted us charged up when we were in the air that day. At the moment, we definitely were.

Tennessee Jim did his thing next. He wasn't good with words like Gentleman Bob. In fact he was rather blunt, but in his own way I guess it was endearing. Spit cup raised to his lips, he began, "I'm not sure if any of you looked at the big board or not, but it looks like we have an afternoon Go tomorrow. This being morning, war, and God willing, we should be finished by late afternoon. Crew beers in my quarters after the flight. I know that Cowboy has the first case."

Cowboy tried to argue that he wasn't buying, but it didn't work. He knew the rules. Tennessee continued, and somehow his mixed drawl moved us just as much as Gentleman Bob's pep speech.

Stress affects different people in different ways. For Crow, it was pushing him way beyond anything that could be considered normal even on the beaches of Oahu where he grew up and his mind seemed to be. The weird thing was that with Cowboy and Happy beside him, they seemed the perfect trio. Sparrow was the quiet type. She didn't say much. Tammy was quite the opposite. She spoke her mind, yet her youth was clear in her words.

Popcorn and I were also quiet, pensive types. We never said much while waiting in the crew lounge. It was always after a mission that we exploded to life.

Bobby was driving the crew van today. When he entered the lounge, we knew it was time to go even before Jim shouted, "Time to saddle up!"

We gathered up our things. I grabbed two bottles of water from Life Support on the way out. One I'd guzzle during the flight while I ate my pork and beans and fig newtons. The other I'd bring back to the PME with me.

The drive to the flight line seemed less forbidding than it had those first few days. I was beginning to get a good grasp of my surroundings now.

As the van turned onto the taxiway, through the back window of the crew van I saw the warplanes waiting on their pads. It was always inspiring to see Falcons and Eagles loaded to the teeth and ready to go. It was clear they had the tougher job of getting in and out of enemy territory unscathed, but every time we approached the Gray Lady and we clambered in through the crew entrance door, I always felt a little awed. The Gray Lady had her own mystique; and if we, the crew, treated her just right, she'd purr. That meant we'd be able to provide jam support when jam support was needed most.

I looked back on the week and envisioned all the close calls I'd had. I'd been as close to death as I ever wanted to come; but in the confusion of it all, I was caught up in the rapture that was war. War that was devastating, destructive, and even deadly.

Over the past days, a number of U.S. and allied planes had been shot down or had crash-landed in Iraqi territory. The Iraqis were using their first prisoners of war as propaganda tools. We all had our blood chits, our evasion plans, our .38s, our chemical gear, and our survival gear. To a man, we hoped we'd never have to use any of it.

As I climbed into the seat on position Six, I no longer thought about dying and returning home in a dark plastic bag. I thought about surviving, living to tell the story, and seeing Katie.

It's odd how little things mean so much, but on the back of the evasion plans there's a tiny American flag. When the time came, I'd set the stars and stripes beside me and go to work.

Before long we'd be humping the combat zone. The radios

would be singing in my ears. The Iraqis would be coming at us once again. For now, though, I had checks to complete.

I checked my position top to bottom, and then ran through the radio checks with Cowboy, who was sitting Seven. "MCS, Six, preflight checks complete," I called out afterward, and Tammy, Happy, Sparrow, Popcorn, and Cowboy followed suit.

"MCC, MCS, we're all ready to go back here," relayed Chris.

Crow and Happy were working on something feverishly as the pilot began the Before Takeoff Combat Entry Checklist. Soon afterward the engines were rising to a roar. We were almost ready for departure.

Crow ran back to his seat as we got clearance for taxi and takeoff. He was strapping in just as my headset tweaked. "Crew, we're rolling," Captain Sammy said.

I gripped the armrests of my chair as we rolled down the runway and lurched into the sky. The Gray Lady seemed exceptionally sluggish today.

We were climbing out of 5,000 feet when my headset tweaked. What followed sounded like a drum roll and I nearly shot out of my seat except the safety straps held me tight. Suddenly I heard music and Martha—Martha Reeves and the Vandellas. She was singing, "Nowhere to run."

The music was playing over Private A, so the front-end hadn't really heard it yet, except for the Nav, but old Bill didn't say a word. In fact I later heard that he tapped the pilot on the shoulder and told him to pull out Private. Later we switched the music to ship's PA, which we could punch on or off more easily.

As we were still thirty minutes or more from the sensitive area, music really caused no harm. It was just another channel of chatter we could push in or pull out if we wanted to. No one said anything though it was clear it'd be punched off prior to entering the sensitive area. A tradition began. Martha became our go-to-war chant. When she sang there's nowhere to run, I imagined she was telling it to Saddam Hussein himself.

Thirty minutes passed with surprising swiftness. The music was turned off. It was time to earn our pay.

"Stations, in ten mike," called out the MCC. "Four clear to the rear for spotting. AMT, any slugs in the system today?"

"She's hummin'," Crow replied.

"That's what I wanted to hear. Nav, MCC, ETA to package ingress?"

"On my mark, seventeen mike," Bill replied, "mark!"

"Crew, MCC, clear to log in and get ready to work. Prepare to give 'em hell. MCS, MCC, what's the word from Phantom?"

"Phantom's not airborne today. We're on our own on this one. What'd Gypsy just pass?"

I keyed Select and said, "Traffic advisory and two of the Eagles just pedaled off to juice up with Gas Station." Afterward, I completed my log in.

"Crew, Pilot, Before Combat Entry Checklist."

Crow blackened out the crew entrance portal and dimmed the interior lights from white to red. Staring at a darkened screen with red overhead lights put a definite strain on the eyes. I adjusted the little spotlight over my position so that it shone down on my position, ensuring that it, too, was properly dim.

"Crew, we're on orbit. Environment is left," hissed the pilot's voice into my headset, "Nav, ETA to package ingress?"

"Environment left," confirmed Jim.

"Seven mike."

"Roger, Nav, seven mike."

"Let's get those targets!" yelled Tennessee Jim.

As I started to work, I glanced at my watch. The first wave would be over Iraq for a long time. I knew that soon we'd be at the very edge of our box making sure we could support them one hundred percent as they went in deep. In fact, we probably would be over Iraqi airspace as we had been before but we'd still log our O-2s—combat support—as we had before. Our "official" O-1 flights over the heart of Iraq were only a few scant weeks away, but at the time none of us knew this.

Time rips by when one is working so intensely. We only registered its passing when the pilot whipped the Lady through a well-practiced combat turn. It was right then, when we felt our hearts leap into our mouths and we either clung to our seats or attempted to continue working through the turn, that we knew time had slipped by.

Then just as abruptly, the wings were level. We were facing the environment working up a frenzy, fingers pounding madly at the controls in front of us and giving it all we had, "giving it hell," as Jim said. It was a definite emotional high.

"MCC, MCS," Chris called out.

"Go ahead, MCS."

"Sir, I'm happy to report that the first wave has successfully reached its target and is, as we speak, working over target!"

A cheer went up from the mission crew, breaking the tension we'd all been feeling. I found myself screaming, "Yes!" into my headset.

"It's not over yet," cautioned Jim. "Let's make sure they get home safe."

"Roger that, MCC," Chris said.

I turned back to my keyboard and my displays. The inevitable emotional slump came when the first wave at long last began its egress, and we took that first real breath. The smell of jet fuel was all around us, clinging to everything as it tends to do in an EC-130. We sucked it in real slow, only to find that the second wave had started their ingress.

We could no longer think about that first wave or their special target. Now we had to focus on the second wave. They were bound for several Iraqi airfields; and so when we went back to work, the intensity level jumped back off the scale.

Minutes slipped away one by one. Hours followed. After we landed, we were tired and spent as he headed for debrief. Later, I could have easily gone back to the PME, crawled into my military issue sleeping bag, zipped it up tight and gone to sleep. But I would've awakened in the middle of the night again to find a darkened and cold room filled with sleeping crewers.

The big board said we were flying the afternoon line tomorrow with a 12:00 alert. We were all due for a little R&R, and we aimed to take it. Cowboy was, after all, buying the first case of bravos.

The rest of us did eventually chip in for two more. For thirteen tired crew dogs, that was just about right.

Saturday, 26 January 1991

I had my first real break since the start of the war. I blew off a lot of steam. It felt good.

During the festivities it was someone's bright idea that our crew all get "crew" cuts—well, marine high-and-tights, actually. We became Tennessee Jim's "crew" crew. Little did we know we would start a crew war. Captain Willie's crew raced out to the Base Exchange during their off time. Who would've guessed that they would've had a fresh supply of Dick Tracy dusters? They had their dusters, we had our crew cuts. Pretty corny, I know, but it was a way to clear the air. I wondered what the other crews would do now.

Although the air war was still going strong and the push was on to force Saddam to withdraw from Kuwait, everything seemed to slow down. Perhaps it was that the disorientation and newness of war were finally fading away. We'd certainly come a long way from those frightened souls who'd trembled in the darkness on the flight line in a wet ditch while an Alarm Red sounded.

In a war zone, things happen fast and always have a way of balancing out. The first suspected terrorist attacks on Turkey began as I feared. An explosion damaged a car outside the U.S. consulate in Adana. A second explosion blew out the doors of the Turkish-American Association also in Adana. Adana was the city right outside the gates of the air base.

We were alerted at 11:00 and entering ops not long afterward. Two hours later Cowboy was calling out in his Texas drawl, "Time to saddle up!" On his heels was the duty driver, Chubby, whom I hadn't seen in a long while. Earlier I'd been busy in the back of the van fussing with my bags. I hadn't paid much attention to who the driver was then.

Chubby was a good guy. I thought he was supposed to be on the recently formed crew four. At least that's what had been on the big board. "Hey, Chubby, aren't you supposed to be on crew four?"

"They're flying with an empty seat now. Three crewers are due in on the next C-5. I can't wait to fly."

I smiled a crooked smile and climbed into the back of the van.

As things were finally worked into a quasi-routine, today there were only eleven of us heading out to the flight line. The AMT and the Eng went out to the plane an hour early, as they normally did. Crow and Patrick were supposed to be ensuring that the systems were ready to go, but I had my doubts.

Seated so I had a good view out the rear window, I got a good look at the surroundings that it seemed I had only noticed yesterday. About a block away from base ops was the rear command center. It was housed in a tin-roofed building with several makeshift buildings around it. The complex was surrounded by rows of barbed wire and barriers. There was a gas station past it to my right. The same fortifications surrounded it.

After the gas station, there was a transportation depot. Further along, the area became somewhat barren.

Right then, I wanted to see the Lady more than anything else. When I climbed up the steps and went through the crew entrance door behind Cowboy, the interior lights were still off and we stumbled around in the half-dark trying to get to our positions. External power was hooked up, so I was able to switch on the little spotlight over my position, turning it from combat red to white so I could read by it. I slapped down my flight crew checklist on the tabletop beside position Six—the checklist I'd looked at a thousand times and had virtually memorized but was supposed to have open to follow procedure.

I opened it about midway to a page titled Normal Procedures and followed the list. After flicking on the O2, I attached my helmet to the appropriate hose and began sucking oxygen through my helmet mask to check it out.

Next, I began radio checks. One was already on headset, so I conducted radio checks with her. Setting the helmet down, I grabbed my headset and tweaked the mike, doing a similar radio check with it. Then I quick-fitted my parachute using the numbers that were penned onto the straps to adjust them.

"MCS, One and Six, stations and radio checks complete."

Chris gave a thumbs up, then replied, "Six, MCS, you got me on radios." I went through the headset checks again with Chris, noticing he didn't test out his helmet today as he had the previous days. He looked tired and worn. We all were.

A few minutes later, Chris called out, "MCC, MCS, all checks complete. We're ready for Before Starting Engines Checklist."

Tennessee Jim relayed the message to the AC.

The chocks were pulled and then I heard the engines begin to whine as the front-end went over the starting engines checklist.

Soon we were taxiing to the runway for takeoff. I turned to the dark blue inserts that were not normally a part of my checklist and to a page titled: Before Takeoff Combat Entry Checklist. By now, it seemed old hack.

"Checks complete," was repeated by the front-end and the MCC. We gave a quick thumbs-up, saying the mission crew was ready for takeoff, and the MCC relayed it. "Pilot, MCC, mission crew ready for takeoff."

"Roger, MCC. Crew, we're rolling."

I gripped my armrests less tensely than I had on previous days, never thinking that perhaps I was being lulled into a false sense of security. Still, today's flight was my ninth combat flight and the newness of it all was wearing off.

A short while later, as we leveled off, I heard Martha playing in the background. As Crow passed, I handed him a Bruce Springsteen tape. "I'll play it on the way home," his voice said in my ears through Private. "Damn system's not coming up again. It was working fine on the ground, but then it always works fine on the ground."

I watched him bring the system down and then up, working as fast as he could. When things went right there was little for the maintenance tech to do; but when things went wrong, he certainly earned his pay. It was still early, though, so he had plenty of time to fix things, unlike previous days.

Roger Daltry was singing, "Don't let the sun go down on me," on ship's PA. I relaxed a bit, taking the momentary reprieve in stride. Some days it seemed we were pushing the time envelope, racing to get on orbit to support the package. Other days like today, it seemed we had all the time in the world. On ship's Interphone, I heard the AC tell the Co, "Slow the pedals down," which meant to cut back the throttles.

The back of my head felt cold as wintry air from the overhead cooling and heating shafts hit me. This was especially so due to the lack of hair from my new crew cut. "AMT, Six, when you got a minute, could you turn up the heat?" I called out on Private.

"Yeah, give me a minute," he responded dryly. He was still having a hard time getting the system up and running.

"Thanks," I clicked in afterward.

I cracked open a can of ready-to-eat soup, which would have been more appropriately titled ready-to-heat soup. I ate it cold from the can despite the fact that the plane had an oven heated by hot air generated from the engines—the same hot air that could have been blowing out of the overhead ducts right now but wasn't.

I could always tell when we were nearing the mountains because the plane gradually grew colder and colder until the interior was thoroughly icy.

"System's yours, MCC," Crow finally called out.

Right afterward, Bill called out his orbit warning, "Ten mike to orbit."

"Crew, MCC, cleared to log onto the system." Happy on Four cut the music off as Jim finished up, "Clear to work after call in. Let's give them hell."

Phantom wasn't up at the moment, so we were on our own. Somewhere behind us, Gypsy was settling into her own orbit.

A few minutes later, we were all logged in and busily working. Radios were particularly cluttered. I vaguely heard the check-in with Gypsy. A two-ship of Eagles had just finished refueling with

Gas Station. Another pair was inbound to gas up.

We were on stations for a long while before the packages ingressed. A change of tactics, which were forever changing and never constant.

There was a better sense of unity among the crew today; and while I wasn't sure if it was due to our new hairstyle or not, I was sure that it was there. All we had to do now was to convince Sparrow and Tammy to get their hair cut similarly. Happy was already working on it.

"MCS, One, I got something odd here," Tammy called out on Private B.

"One, MCS, pass it to Seven."

Tammy passed the signal to Cowboy. Since he was to my left, I saw his face light up. "When are we going into jam?" Cowboy asked almost immediately.

Chris was just about to reply when Tennessee Jim cut in, "Is it hot?"

"Smokin'," Cowboy replied.

"MCS, MCC, Gypsy reported anything lately?"

"Not that I've heard."

I heard Jim sigh into his headset; it filtered quite loudly over Private. "Not that I've heard either. Get on the horn to Gypsy pronto."

Chris began calling Gypsy. On her other channel I already heard her squawking. She'd spotted a possible three-ship coming up. "Gypsy's got bogies climbing, possibly as many as three," I voiced.

"I don't think this shit's going to wait," Cowboy urged over Private.

"Pilot, MCC, we got a situation back here. We need jam

clearance prior to package ingress!" Tennessee Jim rolled out, rapid-fire.

"Gypsy's just identified them as bandits!" I warned. Chris was still trying to raise Gypsy on radios.

Sammy's response was quick, "Call Gypsy."

"Gypsy's tracking three Bandits. The radios are crowded. I don't think we have time to piss around!"

"Then jam!"

"Seven, MCC, you still got them?"

"You bet your ass."

"MCC, Six, Gypsy says Eagles are in chase. At least one bandit is on its way in."

"Crew, we're jammin'," Tennessee Jim screamed out. "Way to roll with it, crew. Let's hope they knock them out of the sky!"

Radios were getting hammered now, but we could still hear what was transpiring. A pair of Eagles was giving chase to a three-ship of Soviet-made MiG-23s. The fray was tangled and close in. We tried to keep our minds on our tasks, but it was hard knowing someone out there was about to die. We just hoped it wouldn't be us or one of the Eagle pilots.

"MCC, Six, threat. They just switched freqs. I'm passing the signal."

"I see it. It's on the list." Painful static filled my ears. I winced and quickly punched off the channel.

"MCC, Seven. I caught a bit of their conversation. One of the MiGs is engaging and firing!"

I turned up the volume on the Eagle's squawk. "This is Eagle Leader, I got a MiG." I heard the hiss of oxygen pouring into his mask. "He's engaging, firing. Shit! Shit! Shit! I'm breaking off! I'm breaking off! Coming round! Coming round hard! Eagle-2, you there?"

"I'm here, Eagle Leader. He broke off right."

"I got him. I got him. Go for the other two. Come on, just a little more. Come on. Lock on. Fire one. Fire two." A moment later, I heard Eagle Leader say, "Splash!"

"Splash one confirmed, Eagle Leader!"

I screamed out an uncontrolled, "Yes!" Just about everyone else on the crew did likewise.

The first MiG had fallen. Two others remained. Fortunately, only that one had seemed hell-bent on an aerial dogfight. The other two were speeding away, no doubt bound for Iranian airspace, which meant sanctuary.

The pair of Eagles was in hot pursuit, afterburners screaming. I couldn't help but key into the radios and pray for our guys. I matched a visual image to the voices in my ears as I tried to stay on top of the search for new targets.

Eagle Leader had his sites locked on the second MiG and was preparing to launch as the MiG made a hard banking turn. Eagle-2 was trying hard to get a fix on the final MiG. There was no doubt we had the enemy pilot's comms jammed. They were running scared. Gypsy was directing more fighters to intercept.

Eagle Leader launched then broke off left, turning a wide loop. An instant later an explosion rocked the sky. "Splash two! Sweet Jesus, splash two!"

Eagle Leader was still turning around when Eagle-2 locked and launched. The AIM missed as the MiG evaded. The MiG pilot was still running, thanking Allah for his good fortune.

Eagle Leader whipped around just as the MiG did an evasive maneuver. Eagle-2 launched again. "Fire two," his voice hissed. The improperly seated AIM dropped from the sky like a rock.

"Fire three!" Eagle-2 screamed, his voice filled with emotion as the MiG turned back to face him.

Eagle Leader was just leveling out of his turn. Eagle-2 had one AIM left. He was eye to eye with a fully capable MiG-23. While he was nearly within cannon range, he was going to make this one last missile count.

The MiG opened up with its two 23mm cannons; Eagle-2 countered, prayed, and then fired. "Fire four!"

We all knew it was Eagle-2's last AIM. It was this one or the MiG would surely get a piece of him. The lull that followed was no more than a single heartbeat, but it seemed an eternity. Blood was rushing in my ears. I gripped my armrests as tightly as I could and waited.

"Splash three! Splash three!" Eagle-2 screamed; the ensuing explosion rocked him as he broke off.

"Confirm splash. Confirm splash." Beautiful, just beautiful. "Gypsy, this is Eagle Leader. Splash three. Nothing more on radar. Is the area clear?"

"You're clear, Eagle Leader. Come on home!"

"Roger."

"Crew, we're coming out of jam," Tennessee Jim said as calmly as you please. "Get ready for package ingress in four mike."

My hands were still gripped to the armrests of the flight chair. For an instant, in my mind's eye, I saw a burst of red-orange flames, a smoldering hulk of mangled MiG crash into the desert below. I went back to work knowing the Gray Lady would eventually get three MiGs painted onto her side beneath the flags that would represent combat and combat-support missions.

Sunday, 27 January 1991

The flight went well. Cowboy was wearing a red bandanna on his head to keep warm. He started a new tradition.

We were airborne three hours after midnight. Eleven hours later, tired and worn thin, I was crawling into my cot. It was a miraculously short day and I was very thankful.

Another newbie came in early this afternoon; I know this because I awoke to a cot jabbing me in the head. Well, at least I was awake and would have time to go to the commissary before it closed. There were just too many people crowded into this tiny room. I stank like a pair of moldy socks.

The new guy's name was John. We called him Little John—as opposed to Big John the AMT. He'd been home in the states on emergency leave when we'd deployed. His mother was terminally ill. Since he was back, I assumed that that meant the funeral had already been conducted. Despite that, he seemed rather optimistic. He'd been bragging about his C-12 ride in some VIP's jet, and we let him.

I saw on the news that war protesters marched to the White House—an estimated 75,000. I had known about the protesters before, but this time it hit me hard, especially with all that had happened in the previous few days. Despite the hurt, I was somewhat relieved they made it clear that they supported the troops. I didn't want to go home to a Vietnam-style reception.

There was a lot of speculation as to why Saddam Hussein hadn't unleashed the full power of his air force. Personally I thought he was more afraid of losing mega-million-dollar machinery than losing human life. I also knew that our missions had been very effective in driving a hammer into the heart of his air force. You can't fly planes without parts, guidance, and weaponry. The ones that did fly, we saw fit to blow out of the sky. The war he was waging was very political and wrought with propaganda. I was sickened by the way the Iraqis were showing off allied POWs on TV.

We were hearing that the ground war was only a week away. I hoped not; I felt that it was too early.

It was almost 16:00, and I was waiting for Happy and Cowboy. They had awakened a few minutes ago, and we were going to make another run to the commissary if it were open. Yes, more beanies and weenies.

Gentleman Bob promised to scrounge up a barbecue grill. I was hoping that he would come through. The hair cut felt weird.

Later, standing by the picnic table, I heard the sound of CNN in the rec tent as I impatiently waited for the outhouse door to open. "You done in their yet, Cowboy?"

"Give me a minute."

"Hey, Happy, you know what time the commissary closes?"

Happy looked up from the TV just long enough to voice a "Nope."

Big John came out of the PME decked out in his Sunday

best. "Civvies!" I exclaimed, looking down at the flight suit I'd been wearing for three days straight. "Where'd you get civvies?"

"Brought them with me," Big John replied, taking a seat beside Happy.

"Where you headed?" asked Happy.

"PBJ, Allen, and I are going to church. You guys want to come?"

Just then I noticed the scripture book in John's hand—John was a Mormon. "This late?"

"Special service the base chapel set up."

"We'll go that way with you guys. We're going to get some eats. If Cowboy ever gets out of the head."

PBJ and Allen joined us a few minutes later clad in fresh flight suits. It struck me just then that PBJ was Catholic and that Allen was a Protestant. Only in a war zone could you find a Mormon, a Catholic, and a Protestant bound for the same Sunday service.

Cowboy stepped out of the head finally about five minutes later, a relieved look on his face. "My first shit since I been here; feels good!" he announced to the world while parading around for a moment like a proud peacock. "So you guys ready to go or what?"

"Just waiting for you," we responded.

We started off at a slow walk, PBJ, Allen, Big John, Cowboy, Happy and I. It was a fairly short walk up the street, about three blocks to the commissary. We arrived to find it closed. We were just about to head up base, when Happy spotted one of our crew vans. He flagged it down and good-natured Ziggy stopped. She had just alerted one of the other crews. The six of us piled into the back of the van.

"Can you stop by the base chapel?" Big John asked. Ziggy didn't know where it was, so he gave her directions.

I asked, "Ziggy, I thought you were working the evening shift?"

"No, days. Six to six." Ziggy replied glumly.

"Six to six!" Allen exclaimed, "I wish."

"Hey, did you guys know a C-5 came in from Sembach today?" Ziggy began, pausing momentarily as she turned a corner and prepared to stop in front of the base chapel. "They brought in a mail pouch; it's in ops."

"Mail? No, didn't know. Can you drop us back at the PME afterward?"

"Sure," Ziggy agreed.

Just before Big John got out, he turned to me and asked if I could check to see if he had any mail. "Sure. I'll check for all you guys." After all, it wouldn't hurt me to do a good deed.

When we arrived at base ops, we found that it was fairly empty for the middle of the day. The second line was airborne and the third line wouldn't come in for another hour. Expectantly, we hurried into the ops center. One of the ground support crew, Harmony, was in the process of separating the mail.

I glanced at the big board as I always did, noticed the newly formed fourth crew had a new name added to it. Little John's name was freshly marked in red. I didn't see Chubby's name and wondered if he knew he wasn't going to fly yet.

My office chief from Sembach was standing to Harmony's right; I hadn't seen Ray since arrival. He was roomed in ops, and at the present he wasn't flying either. At the same time, we shouted, "Hey what's up? Long time no see. How's everything going?"

He was a good PR man—public relations—and he had a tone of voice that was always warming. He meant the things he said. "You get a letter, Ray?" I asked.

"I'm still waiting to see, but I did see your name in there."

"You mind if I look through that stack?" I asked Harmony. She shrugged her shoulders. I snatched up the pile.

"Old Jimmie got ahold of most of the wives and gave them the address for down here right after we left," added Ray. "Chief's a good man."

"Definitely," I replied. "Hey, Big John's got a letter in here, the lucky SOB!"

A moment later, I handed two sweet-scented letters to Cowboy, who we all knew wasn't married. He snatched them up and disappeared. PBJ had a letter. I put it next to Big John's.

I was almost through the stack when I found a letter from Katie. It smelled heavily of perfume and far better than Cowboy's—at least to me. She'd sprayed it with Poison, my favorite scent—when she was wearing it.

I slapped Ray on the back and escaped to the crew lounge. I found a quiet corner and unsealed the letter. I could see Katie's face as I read the words. The scent of the perfume was overwhelming.

I read and reread the letter three times. That night I stuck it under my sleeping bag so her scent was near. In the letter she told me that someone from the squadron had come over and fixed the car, one less worry. I still don't know why I had to get that damn distributor cap and rotor in. I was glad to hear the car was fixed and that from what I understood the folks at the squadron were keeping the families updated.

Monday, 28 January 1991

Awakened in the manner I was slowly becoming accustomed to, a flashlight shining in my eyes, I lurched up.

"Alert," whispered a familiar voice, "I'll be back in an hour to pick you up. Which one is Allen?"

Allen who? I wasn't fully awake yet, and then I considered the question. "Third cot down, against the wall, but he's on Captain Willie's crew."

"I know," replied Mike.

"Wait a minute, you alerting Captain Willie's crew or what?" I asked, attempting to sit up.

"Two crews," Mike whispered back, while shining the flashlight at Allen, "Alert. I'll be back in one hour to pick you up. Which one is Todd?"

"If you weren't in Hotel California, you'd know," Allen said wryly.

"PBJ's in the other building," I answered before Allen said anything more. "What do you mean, two crews? We weren't supposed to be flying. I thought crew four was."

"Crew four had the O'dark-thirty."

"Why two crews?" I repeated.

"You'll have to wait. Is Happy in here?"

I reached out with my foot and kicked the cot kitty-corner to mine. Happy lurched up. "Alert, I'll be back in an hour," Mike said.

I put my feet onto the cold floor, reached for my flight suit just as Mike eased out the door. After fumbling around in the dark for my own flashlight, I grabbed my toothbrush and headed outside.

It was cold outside. I had the unfortunate luck of finding both bathrooms occupied. When I finally did get inside and splashed icy cold water onto my face, I was wide awake. My thoughts were running—two crews? Had something transpired during the night that we weren't aware of?

The rec tent was my next stop and since I was the only one in it, I turned the TV on. There was still no heater.

The news wasn't much different from any other day. After a few minutes I went back into the PME to gather my gear and find breakfast. Breakfast was a can of mixed fruit and a breakfast bar.

Shortly afterward, two crew vans pulled in front of ops and an unhappy gaggle of crewers piled out, me included. Inside the ops building everything was buzzing. It was readily apparent that something big was about to take place. As all of us tried to sign our flight orders and check the big board at the same time, the ops center quickly became overcrowded.

The intel briefing started well. The overview map depicting orbits was an absolute mess and among the mess two EC-130 orbits were scrawled in bright red. I keyed in as the briefer outlined the day's targets, but I wouldn't understand the big picture until after the pilot's briefing and during the MCC's briefing.

"Today will be one of the busiest days of the war to date for us as well as our counterparts to the south," began Tennessee Jim. "We're not only going to support one package group of multiple waves, but two package groups of multiple waves. This means our orbit time is essentially doubled. The first package group will sweep in in separate waves, engage their targets, come out, land, refuel and re-arm, then take off again for another entire round of bombardment."

Jim paused to spit into his ever-present cup. "A-group's target, the nuclear R&D facility here—" he slapped the big map with his pointer "—is a critical target. Part of our job and that of the package we'll be supporting is to divert Saddam's eye northward while an enormous strike force that includes an entire wing of Fighting Falcons closes in on Baghdad.

"The mission of the Fighting Falcons is to avert or destroy Iraqi fighters fleeing to Iran. Over the past week increasing numbers of Iraqi fighters have been fleeing to Iran for safekeeping. We simply cannot let Saddam Hussein keep those fighters from being destroyed."

I swallowed a lump in my throat. Jim continued, "Our mission in all this is to keep the Iraqi forces confused by jamming as many of their command and control, air defense, and other communications as we can find to ensure that our fighters have a clear way in and out. This means jamming enemy SAM, AAA, and other ground comms almost exclusively."

Jim paused, spit into his cup, and put down the pointer. "Our crew will be the primary crew. We'll stay on orbit throughout the entire engagement. Captain Willie's crew has what I'd call the quarterback fake. They'll go out an hour before us and set up on orbit with all the usual array of support aircraft, the full CAP and everything.

"We'll take off an hour after they do and while they pedal as fast as they can to the forward edge, we'll cut throttles and go in slow and low. Once our crew is set up on a low orbit, Captain Willie's crew will cut their jammers and drop way back. Afterward, they'll provide support only if necessary.

"At the appropriate time, we'll pop up and go to work slamming and jamming. The job only we do best!" Jim smiled. "If all goes according to plan, we'll lose no planes to enemy AAA nor to SAMs. And no Iraqi planes will escape to Iran."

Jim paused to catch his breath. My face was aglow with enthusiasm. "Today will be our longest combat mission to date. More than nine hours from wheels up to wheels down, a very long time to be airborne over any combat zone."

Right then I was thankful that I had a fair amount of sleep and that I had packed two cans of beanies and weenies.

"Needless to say, Captain Willie and I need everyone at their best out there today. Now unless Captain Willie has anything to add, this briefing is concluded."

There were a lot of anxious faces and a lot of anxious conversation as we waited for the appointed hour. CNN was playing loud in the background. Gentleman Bob and Major James were both present, looking on, though neither gave a pep speech that day.

I had almost expected to see Captain Willie's crew outfitted in their dusters, but it seemed none of them had the hats with them. Soon I watched them go and then settled in for another hour of waiting.

The hour passed slowly. Then, survival vests on and .38s strapped at our sides, we headed to the waiting van. I couldn't wait to get airborne. In the back of my mind, I saw a strike force sweeping in over Baghdad, a wing of F-16s with afterburners full aglow screaming across the skies.

The taxi call seemed to come belatedly as we were pushing a sluggish time schedule. Gloves on, headset on, seat facing forward, I waited for the AC to say, "Crew, we're rolling!"

Happy had his Walkman all ready to rock and roll, and though it wasn't playing, I could already hear Martha screaming, "There's nowhere to run."

Each of us had our red or blue bandannas fitted around our heads. Although the intent of it was to keep our heads warm, since with fresh and short haircuts the cold air at altitude had an especially biting sting to it, we started a new crew tradition.

We proceeded through the checklists slowly. Taxi and takeoff also went slowly. Afterward Martha was finally screaming as we climbed out of five thousand feet. Crow had brought in an oldies' tape and so for a short time we tuned into ship's PA.

Happy and Cowboy began playing solo air guitar. When Tammy and Sparrow joined in, Tennessee Jim looked up from his keyboard and smiled that silly Tennessee smile of his. He didn't say anything. It was all in good fun and it relieved a lot of stress.

Chris did a secure radio check with Shadow-1. We were Shadow-2 today. Afterward he contacted Gypsy.

Crow had the system up and running with surprising swiftness. We were logged in and ready to go to work well ahead of schedule. By now, Captain Willie's crew was set up and working the environment, going at it as if everything was the same as it always was. Periodically they kept us updated, passing us lists to ensure that when we popped up from our low orbit we were good to go.

They were jamming as if there were no tomorrow. Their reports said AAA sites were lit up and pulverizing empty sky. The Iraqis were expecting the package ingress we weren't going to give them.

It pleased me to know that the AAA sites were wasting precious bullets. I could only think back to a darkened night when I'd witnessed through a pair of NVG just how awesome that firepower was. 100mm artillery could really rip through the sky. The Iraqis had a whole array of anti-aircraft artillery in their arsenal, ranging from 23mm to 130mm. The SAMs that they were more and more often firing blindly when they spotted anything ranged from handheld Stingers to mobile systems that could instantly prove deadly without our jam support.

I glanced at my watch as the mission compartment became ominously silent. The interior lights turned red. The crew entrance portal was blacked out. All we had to do was wait for the go-ahead which would come from Gypsy if all were going according to plan.

The passage of time reverted from the ticking by of minutes to the agonizing passing of seconds. The radios were fairly quiet for the amount of traffic poised to strike. The only thing I could do as I waited was maintain a mental image in my mind of the progress of the packages. Ravens and Weasels were lining up, getting ready to blind enemy radars. Shadow-1 was preparing to withdraw. We were getting ready to pop up and jam Iraqi communications. The mood in the back grew more tense by the second.

"MCC, Nav, ten-minute warning," tweaked Bill on Private.

Tennessee Jim relayed what we had all heard. It only made time seem to slow down even more.

I glanced at my watch every few seconds while I stared at my terminal.

Unexpectedly, all displays blacked out. I heard Crow scream, "Shit, not now," as the system crashed. We had six minutes to go.

Suddenly I could hear both Jim and Crow breathing into their microphones. "Get on it!" hollered Jim, going up Hot at the same time Crow did.

I flashed four fingers at Chris, which was what Shadow-1 had just relayed. Four minutes till they left orbit.

"Status back there?" called out the Nav, "We going to be ready to go or not?"

"We're in reboot. Give me one more minute," Crow returned.

"Don't dick around setting back up. As soon as Crow says go, GO! And I don't want to hear anything but position and go when you're set up, you got it, crew? Clear to work as soon as you're ready," Jim cried out. "AMT? AMT, this thing up or not?"

Three was in the rear window spotting, and he was already calling out distant traffic marshalling. A short pause ensued. Everyone in the mission crew paused to hear Crow's response. "She's green, just a gremlin is all, better now than before."

"Save it. Nav, MCC, green light."

Chris was on radios to Shadow-1 as the front-end contacted Gypsy. Shadow-1 was pulling off orbit, seemingly turning for home. They reported AAA units had stopped their endless barrage, which was good. The fighters at the head of the wave would hit the AAA and SAM units that had set up in the open for the apparent ingress that had not come and were hopefully busily reloading ammo or preparing to move out. They would be easily knocked out before they realized what had occurred.

The green light came. We popped up just as Shadow-1 hit the back of their box. We came up jamming. Happy reported seeing explosions. The first package was headed in, in wave after endless wave. I couldn't help wondering about the strike force headed for Baghdad. Whether they were airborne yet I didn't know. I was working too feverishly at my terminal to calculate times.

Gypsy called out an air advisory. Captain Sammy took us into an evasive maneuver. We didn't know if anything was close enough to reach out and splash us but that had been the advisory. We weren't going to wait around to find out.

Captain Sammy dropped the nose hard. We dropped like a rock. My heart jumped into my throat. Minutes later, we climbed, leveled out, still jamming.

The first hour clicked by seemingly in a single heartbeat. It seemed I was only taking my second breath when the first part of the package began to egress. Happy, in the back window, was calling out groups of traffic coming out low and fast. At the same time, Chris was on radios to Shadow-1.

An emotional moment came as Gypsy reported that the entire package had safely egressed and were headed for base. For a time, the frenzy slowed, but we had to keep the Iraqi forces below thinking they were going to get hit again at any moment. We kept working.

At Jim's advice, Shadow-1 got back into the game, taking up a position in the forward half of our box. They'd turn a short orbit on one end. We'd turn a short orbit on the other. Both crews were periodically going in and out of jam. The Iraqi forces below were taking the bait.

When the AAA gunners couldn't see with their radars or couldn't communicate—most of the time—they kept on rattling off ammo. I didn't blame them. I'd be scared to death if I knew I was going to die, for our fighters would surely find the ones who had escaped the first onslaught during the next package ingress.

There was a definite sense of unity and performance as we waited. Gypsy reported the targets had been hit as planned and the skies were clear. We rejoiced.

I sucked at my water bottle during the brief lapse, cracked open one of the cans of beanies and weenies, wolfing it down in less than thirty seconds. Afterward, I was pumped up and ready to go again.

We cut our jamming ten minutes prior to the wave of Ravens and Weasels coming in, bringing it up and down again in two-minute intervals. The enemy AAA sites were still playing along with us nicely. They didn't understand the game, but we did—we had the rulebook. Our job was to tire them out, waste their ammo, and more.

We got the green light just as the initial wave swept inward and cut our jam. The Ravens and Weasels were on top of the enemy units, striking before the enemy knew what hit them. As the Ravens and Weasels did so, we went back to work. Far out in the Iraqi desert, the assault began. Part of the package would re-strike the nuclear R&D facility, while three other groups lashed out at key northern airfields.

Sweat had been pouring from my brow for a long while now and there were dark bands of moisture under my arms. While I was enjoying every terrifying minute, I never forgot for a moment that the same AAA and SAM sites we were jamming could reach out and pluck us from the sky in one swift and deadly instant.

For me, being on orbit was akin to riding a giant roller coaster that never stopped. It whipped around and around, around and around, up and down, up and down. When the ride was finally over, it left me emotionally and physically drained.

The second package was putting the ground forces below us through an hour of hell while the strike force swept toward Baghdad. The ride was almost over.

The initial wave was heading home. Soon others would follow, and then so would we. I was shaking with excitement, anticipation and anguish. We were at the top of the tallest hill on the ride. I was staring down the long inevitable fall. Once I started to fall, racing downward with my heart in my throat, I'd hit the bottom. The ride would finally stop. It would all be over.

I heard the AC relay the red light. I held my breath, waiting for Gypsy to say the package had come out clean. Happy called out the egress, groups of traffic low and fast.

Still holding my breath, I waited. Radios tweaked. I keyed in. "The last wave has safely egressed and is headed for base."

I released the breath and it came out in an elated rush. We'd done our job. The aircraft were safely on their way. The strike force was coming in over Baghdad. In the back of my mind I saw that wing of Fighting Falcons knocking Iraqi jets from the skies.

When we touched down, wheels slapping the runway, I was never so happy to find the ride was at an end. It was early evening when we returned to the barracks. By all accounts we should have been utterly exhausted, but we weren't. We'd promised Tennessee Jim that we'd come over for crew beers but weren't really sure we'd make it that far. First thing I needed was a shower, so I made the three-block trek to the base gym.

The showers were always crowded. Today, especially so. A group of soldiers had come in from the field. The floors were covered with bright Turkish mud; the showers were flooded because the drains were plugging up. I sloshed my way into the showers through cold, dirty water and found that there was still hot water. I must've stayed in that water for ten minutes—well, at least it seemed like ten minutes.

Afterward I went back to the PME to see if Cowboy and Happy were going to go over to Tennessee Jim's. There was a ruckus coming from the rec tent when I returned and that's where I found them. They were whooping it up with Captain Willie's crew. Charlotte had even come down from billeting, bringing her roommate Sandy with her—Sandy was on one of the other crews.

As soon as I came in, Captain Willie handed me a beer then hollered, "Close the tent flap! It's cold out there."

With me, there were now fifteen people crowded into a six-man tent, which still had no heater, so I did seal the tent's flaps to keep in the heat.

Charlotte started a round of the name game. The first name that popped into her mind happened to be the singer of the song playing in the background. Joe Walsh was singing, "Rocky Mountain Way."

"First names," she called out. Then turning to Cowboy she said, "Joe Walsh."

"Andrew Johnson," Cowboy replied.

Happy to his left had five seconds to think of a last name that began with 'A'. "Hank Aaron."

"Aretha Franklin," Bobby shouted out.

"Drink!" we shouted, "First names, not last names."

Bobby guzzled down his beer.

"Last names," Cosmo said starting the next round. "Al Stewart."

"Sam Perkins," said Captain Willie, another big sports fan.

"Sam Perkins?" PBJ to his right asked. Another rule of the game was that someone else had to recognize the name. The name couldn't be fictitious and it couldn't be a person anyone knew. In this case, Cowboy backed up Captain Willie, "NBA, Orlando."

"Peter Frampton," quickly voiced PBJ.

"Frank Sinatra," I said.

Sandy paused for a moment, "Scarlet O'Hara."

"Judges?" Happy shouted.

We gave her a thumbs down. "Drink, drink," we chanted, and Sandy bottomed out her beer. Happy gladly handed her a fresh one.

Thomas began a new round with last names and as the chain lasted around the whole room, we all drank. Now the name game played in moderation was fun, but when played to ever-changing crew-dog rules, it was even more fun.

The tent was finally getting warm or we were all getting a little drunk. We opened up the tent and annexed the picnic table.

We played at least a dozen more rounds of the name game, burning through a small stack of cassettes as we did so.

Around 21:00, things started to wind down. Both crews had a 10:00 alert in the morning and unfortunately, the twelve-hour crew rest rule said it was time to start thinking about breaking up the party.

Just when things should have been winding down, though, things began winding up. Sandy, feeling a sudden lack of inhibition jumped up on the picnic table and started dancing, Happy and Cowboy followed. The day had been stressful and we were sure relieving a good portion of the stress.

We were also blocking from our minds thoughts of tomorrow's impending flight. We had returned to base ops to find that two crews were waiting to launch and both crews were again flying the next line. Just when we had returned from our longest mission to date, we found out that tomorrow's line would stretch to ten full hours. Ten hours of flight time meant a minimum of a sixteen-hour day if things went exactly according to plan. Things never go exactly according to plan.

We whooped and hollered the way crew dogs do. At 21:59, the stereo quieted and the alcohol was put away. There was too much on the line if we couldn't perform our duties tomorrow. We also knew tomorrow's mission was of obvious importance though we'd have to wait for pre-brief to find out exactly why.

The festivities carried on for another hour though we slowly edged back into the tent. We never did make it to Tennessee Jim's quarters that evening, but we did have a lot of fun.

Tuesday, 29 January 1991

"Gentlemen and ladies," began Gentleman Bob, looking about the room the way he always did when giving in important speech. "Today's mission is a two-crew Go as you already know. Intel, the ACs and mission controllers have already briefed you on targets, so you understand the import of this mission.

"The game plan is again different from yesterday's. The ultimate success of the mission is in our hands. We have to do our job the best we possibly can to ensure that the packages get in and out safely." He demonstrated this graphically with his pointer.

"The mission will be a very long one. I know that as we near the third week of the war most of you are worn out from the seemingly relentless onslaught of fly-fly-fly. Stick with me through this one and I guarantee things will start to even out.

"Again, let me remind you the med techs are here. If you need something to make you stay awake, they can give you something. I don't want anyone falling asleep in their seats! Also, if anyone is feeling especially under the weather, this is the time to speak up. Anyone?"

Gentleman Bob paused to look about the room and take a sip of coffee. "Good. Now let's go get them!"

Already two crew vans were waiting. After gathering our gear from the hall, twenty-two crew dogs poured out of base ops with determination in our steps. The Eng and the AMT for both crews were already at the planes.

Captain Willie's crew piled into the first van. I noticed just then that they had a different copilot. Lieutenant Faber must have been switched out to MPC. Emily, their new Co, looked rather peaked; today was surely her first flight. There was always that look of uncertainty in people's eyes as they went out on their first combat flight. Emily had it plastered across her face as if it were written in indelible ink.

I climbed into the van behind Tennessee Jim, grabbing one of the wheel wells to rest my backside against. Our crew had one change too, but it wasn't Mike coming back as we had expected. Popcorn was replaced by Bad Boy. I could already see the impact this would have on our crew. Where Popcorn had been quiet and reserved, Bad Boy was anything but quiet and reserved. You wondered what color the sky was in his world. I was sure it wasn't blue. All in all, though, Bad Boy would fit in just fine with our motley crew.

A ten-hour mission meant we had eight hours of hugging the fringe of Iraqi territory to look forward to. Tennessee Jim had already told me that he wanted me in the window today spotting. I had eight hours of staring down into a potentially deadly storm of AAA to look forward to.

A ten-hour mission also meant we would be on orbit as night came. Darkness made everything seem that much grimmer.

Heading to the back of the plane, I passed position Six in the quasi-darkness of the Gray Lady's interior. First thing I did was to fit my chute, then I double-checked the pair of NVG I had and set them on the rear bunk.

As both paratroop doors were open, I stared out across the white of the hardstand to the black of the flight line. Everything looked deceivingly tranquil, but I knew that a short while after we departed, the flight line would be inundated by a host of aircraft readying for takeoff. Falcons, Eagles, Weasels, Ravens and many others would depart, afterburners screaming, in wave after wave.

I ambled back to Six, pre-flighted my helmet and headset, and then fitted a bandanna round my head. Bad Boy obliged with the radio checks.

The waiting began. I hated the waiting more than anything else. I listened to the radios and the bit of chatter coming from the members of the crew, yearning to hear Captain Sammy say, "Crew, we're rolling!"

Happy had Martha screaming way before we leveled off. Right afterward, he slapped in The Kinks. "You really got me," played in the background as I switched out to the window. Sammy seemed to like the tune, as he wiggled the wings to the beat of the music.

It didn't take Bad Boy long to adjust. He was out of his seat and grooving to the music with the others almost immediately. Hell, I even joined in for a while. Stress does crazy things to people who let it build up inside and eat at them. It's best just to let it all out sometimes. Somehow I imagined that that was Happy's gift in life. He had a way of making people do zany things. The funny thing was that if you joined in, you came out the better.

"Destroyer" was winding down and things were getting a

little out of hand. Tennessee Jim didn't say a word; rather, he just looked on as he always did. He wouldn't say anything until we neared the sensitive area if he said anything at all.

Crow was bustling, trying to bring the system up, but that didn't stop him from joining in briefly as he passed through. Happy and the others had their arms spread out like birds, running up and down the aisle between the positions. The Kinks were singing, "I Wish I Could Fly Like Superman."

I stared out at the white-capped peaks ahead in the distance. There was a light cloud deck around us but not enough to hamper the view. Outside the window it was a bright and sunny day, but all I could think about was the encroaching evening.

The air around me was growing colder by the minute. The window was chilly to the touch as I pressed close. "Pilot, Spotter," I called out. "Traffic high moving from one o'clock to three o'clock." It looked like Gas Station moving in.

The jagged peaks were below us; soon we'd be on orbit. The Nav gave his ten-minute warning. The crew dogs in the mission compartment became all business.

I heard Chris on radios to Shadow-2. He was coordinating the orbit box, which we would share with Shadow-2. Both planes on orbit at the same time meant a shorter orbit and that both would be jamming. This would require close coordination to avoid duplication of effort.

A shorter orbit also meant a lot more turns. I hugged the paratroop door as the AC brought us up on orbit. For an instant, the wing looked ominously perpendicular to the jagged and rock-strewn land below us. As we went into the steepest part of the turn, I was left staring nearly straight down at the ground below. It looked so close, too close.

"Stations," Jim called out.

I gave a forlorn backward glance into the darkness, wishing I was on position instead of in the window, and then concentrated on my search. "Pilot, Spotter, traffic low, moving nine to three. Inbound."

"Roger that, Spotter," tweaked Captain Sammy's voice into my headset.

Even in the bright daylight with shadows reflected across the land, I could see the outline of the group of fighters low to the horizon. They swept inward in two three-ship formations. It was the beginning of the first wave. I didn't watch them long. It was more important that I watch for things coming out and not going in.

The Lady swung hard as we came around again. I had to switch windows. As I swung back around to head toward the other paratroop door, I stumbled, temporarily blinded by the darkness of the cabin's interior. The outside was so bright and the inside so dark that it was as if I were momentarily snow blinded.

I rubbed my eyes and stared back across the rough landscape. In the daytime AAA was difficult to spot; but if we were close enough, it would look like a thick black rain pouring up into the heavens.

"Pilot, Spotter, two groups of traffic, low. Inbound and moving toward three o'clock."

"Roger that, Spotter."

We swung around sharp. My heart jumped into my throat as I stared down.

Before changing windows I called out, "Pilot, Spotter, traffic parallel, moving six to twelve. Two-ship." Must be part of our CAP.

Soon the unnerving shadows of dusk were at hand. The NVG didn't work at dusk and as I couldn't see much in the shadowed land, I keyed in to Gypsy's advisories closer than ever. The first package was already out. We had come to the inevitable lull between packages. To make matters worse, we didn't leave orbit or even back away.

I counted time to the beat of combat turns, marking time as my face was pressed against cold plexiglass. I waited for nightfall so I could break out the NVG and for the second package to begin its ingress.

As darkness finally shrouded the land, the portentous lines of AAA formed in the view port of the NVG. "Pilot, Spotter, AAA to our two, five and seven," I called out sweeping my view left to right. The AAA had probably been there all day but it only became crystal clear in the NVG. "No danger to our present position."

They were firing blindly due to our jamming. It was ominous the way the AAA gunners responded to our jam, turning on and off as we did. Yet I imagined they were pretty ruffled after the first package had swept through. With our help the second package would get in and out without a hitch. Hopefully they would even take out most of the enemy sites I was now watching.

The NVG filled with a sudden green glow: afterburners. They showed as fiery green globes and I saw the vague outline of inbound fighters amidst the glow. It was surely the first wave of the second package group.

The fighters swept in easily, avoiding the barrages of anti-aircraft artillery fired blindly by gunner crews. They started to pour into Iraq, in wave after endless wave. I called out inbound traffic nonstop for a couple of minutes—this was one colossal strike force going in.

Gypsy was giving an air advisory; and as usual, I keyed in. What the hell? That didn't sound right. Only when I heard Tennessee Jim repeat to the crew and the AC what I just heard, did I believe it. "Gypsy's bent. They're trying to get back up, but aren't having any luck. They advise we pull off orbit." Pull off orbit? What was Jim saying? The second package was just going in. He needed to be standing here watching these fighters go in.

"MCC, Nav, isn't the second package just inbound?"

"That's an affirmative. Let's hope Gypsy doesn't bug out. We can't just leave."

Jesus, without Gypsy, we had no air picture, no warnings or advisories. We might as well have a bull's eye painted on our underside.

"Gypsy, Shadow-1," Chris called out. "Your status, please?"

I gripped the NVG tight and waited for the reply while diligently staring out into the night sky. "MCC, Spotter, we have another pair of NVG back here," I relayed anxiously.

"Three, MCC, get to the rear and grab that other pair of NVG," Jim ordered.

"Gypsy, Shadow-1, your status?" Chris repeated. Shadow-2 was also trying to raise them.

"Shadow-1, Shadow-2, this is Gypsy, the system isn't coming back up," came the reply into my headset. "We're going to have to head home."

Happy tapped me on the shoulder. I pointed to the other pair of goggles. In the interim I missed the pilot's response, but I heard Gypsy clear. "CAP and Sweep will stick with you. Advise you to drop to back of orbit until prior to egress. Good luck."

Good luck? What the hell did that mean?

I watched as the lines of ground fire became slightly more distant. Red-orange explosions pockmarked the horizon. I saw these without the aid of the NVG. As I looked on, a sudden ball of hellish fire erupted into the night sky. A missile must have struck a POL storage tank; there was no other explanation for the intensity of the red-orange ball of fire I saw.

More explosions followed only seconds later. The secondary explosions were even more terrifying and magnificent than the original red-orange ball. As I reported the explosion, my face pressed against cold plexiglass, Captain Sammy brought the Lady into a sharply-executed combat turn. Shortly afterward, Happy began whooping and hollering into his microphone.

Turned away from the environment, things seemed mundane. I could only listen to my headset as Happy had done and watch vigilantly. I wondered if I were the only one to realize what the lack of an air picture meant; but then as I listened up on radios, I heard the evident strain in the voices of the crew. Tension surrounded not only me but also everyone on the ship.

I glanced over my shoulder at Happy. He was glued to the window and his NVG as if they were his lifelines and he was sinking into the sea of darkness below. Crow was drumming his fingers nervously at his position; and while I couldn't hear the tapping of his fingers, I could see it. He was impatiently waiting and maintaining a hawkish watch on the system stats that I'd never before seen. In the reddish haze of the cabin's interior I couldn't see much farther, but I did see Tennessee Jim. He was sitting with his back arched over the keyboard, his jaw tight. His left hand was propped up on his position and his left thumb was nervously caressing his microphone on/off button.

Quickly, I turned back to the window, waiting to see the

green glow of afterburners from more inbound fighters. I didn't realize it right then, but I was nervously tapping at my microphone button too. Then just as suddenly as I had turned back to the window and the darkness, Captain Sammy brought the Lady around, which left me staring at the still-burning fires of an entire row of destroyed POL tanks.

I noticed that without Gypsy's squawk the radios seemed eerily calm. Shadow-2 was quiet. Paladin's group was busy scouring the skies. Gas Station had dropped back to a protective orbit. Phantom had bugged out south. It seemed that we were alone, hanging in the air on a fragile thread. Our only lifeline was our ability to detect the presence of the enemy through communications or visual observation.

Gravity thrust me into the port window as the Lady turned sharply then leveled out. I saw a barely visible object in the distance that should have been Gas Station, but I called out the location of the traffic just the same. I would make no assumptions. My life and that of my crew depended on it.

Hugging the paratroop door close, I gradually combed the skies for any signs of activity. Finally, oblivious to the icy cold of the door's metal, I searched through a turn. The bridge of my nose stung where the frame of my glasses dug in with a vengeance as I pressed the night-vision goggles closer and closer to my face. I caught what appeared to be movement low and distant. "Traffic low and distant at two thirty. Looks like a multiple ship formation."

The Nav and the MCC conferred on package egress times—still five minutes to go. "Maintain a close vigil on that movement, Spotter," tweaked Sammy, "Nav, try to raise Paladin, see if they have those bogies on radios."

"Spotter, Pilot, current position on those bogies?"

I squinted my eyes to the distance to ensure that what I was looking at still seemed to be moving. "Pilot, Spotter, low to the deck at two o'clock moving to twelve. Looks like a three-ship."

Suddenly, split-second decisions were being made. Paladin Leader was getting no response from his inquiries. Tennessee Jim's first reaction was to throw the system into jam; if the approaching group were enemy aircraft, we'd be knocking out their communications. If they were friendly we'd be ensuring their safe egress.

After quick consultation with Shadow-2, Captain Willie's crew opted to bug out.

"Roger, Shadow-2," Chris replied, "there is no reason we should give them two easy targets. Have a safe trip home."

"We wish you luck, Shadow-1. Shadow-2, out."

It came our time to make the decision to stay or go. A two-ship of Eagles moved into a guarded stance. A second two-ship continued MiG Sweep, preparing to engage the approaching bogies if necessary. Still, without Gypsy, no one would have blamed us for bugging out or backing off orbit to a safe distance. If we backed off with package egress so close, it would be the same thing as bugging out.

We knew Gypsy was gone and Shadow-2 was heading home. We couldn't forget that the package was still in-country. We couldn't leave them.

"Crew, MCC, I want to see thumbs. Stay on orbit or go, now which is it?"

As a crew, we'd either opt to stay on orbit or return to base. Happy and I voiced, "We'll stay!" not moving from our positions.

I could only guess that the rest of the crew gave unanimous

thumbs up because Tennessee Jim was on radios to the pilot telling him words that made me proud to be combat crew. "Pilot, MCC, the mission crew is willing to stay. We're jamming. The decision is ultimately yours."

Captain Sammy's response was to take the Lady into another sharp combat turn. After we had leveled out, the copilot quickly reviewed emergency procedures with us. I heard Paladin's group trying to raise the incoming group on radios. Still there was no response.

Seconds crawled painstakingly by with the mounting uncertainty. I nervously fidgeted back and forth in front of the window. If I survived this tour without getting ulcers, it'd be a miracle.

With our renewed jamming, the enemy AAA sites sliced up the heavens in ever-thickening torrents. I was sure they also heard the distant hum of jet engines. Firing blindly as they were, they'd try to knock anything out of the sky that sought to overfly them, friend or foe.

Friend or foe, I thought to myself. Suddenly I had an idea. "Pilot, Spotter, anyone tied to hail on emergency? Maybe they're keyed wrong?"

"That's a good call, Spotter. I'll check it out."

I watched as the green glow of afterburner trails formed behind the approaching fighters. They were getting closer. It was, indeed, a three-ship formation. MiG Sweep was prepared to move in. Somewhere above us, a two-ship CAP anxiously waited.

Out in the distance beyond one of the AAA sites, I saw what appeared to be movement again. As I re-centered on them, closer movement caught my eye. "Pilot, Spotter, traffic low four o'clock distant. And three o'clock approaching." It had to be the package egressing, or so I hoped.

I heard Paladin Leader's voice tweaking in my ears, "Shadow, Paladin, good call. Comms channels are correct now. Package egress confirmed. All sightings confirmed as friendlies. Repeat, incoming are friendlies."

I sighed, relaxed slightly. I watched as the second package came out in wave after wave, safely detouring around the pockets of enemy AAA. What remained of my anxiety trickled away with the remaining minutes on orbit.

As we made the homeward trek, it was clear Tennessee Jim and Captain Sammy were proud of their crew. We had stuck together admirably in the face of uncertainty and adversity. We also had a newfound respect for the guidance from Gypsy that we had started to take for granted.

In the coming days lurked a mission when we would lose Gypsy's support again. This time we would be over the heart of Iraq and it would cost much more than anxiety.

Wednesday, 30 January 1991

We had an early morning alert, which came with distressing news. During the night Iraq had begun their first major ground offensive.

Yet this news was also strangely releasing. We had all been waiting for Iraq to make some sort of move, a show of force, anything at all. The first attack came an hour before midnight. Iraqis entered positions held by the Marines forty miles inland from the banks of the Persian Gulf. Countering, the Marine regiment pounded the incoming Iraqi mechanized column.

Shortly after this attack, a larger force consisting of an infantry battalion mounted in armored personnel carriers along with a company of tanks and a platoon of armored cars rolled toward the small border town of Khafji. The advanced guard of this force took the mostly deserted town several hours later.

Before daylight came to the Saudi desert, another attack was mounted against the Marine positions by a battalion of Iraqi tanks and infantry. Through what remained of the hours of darkness, the Marines fought gallantly aided by AH-1 Cobra Gunships and Harrier jets. As daylight finally came to the desert,

A-10 tank killers joined the fray.

Seated in the crew lounge at base ops, my eyes were glued to the television and CNN just like everyone else as we waited to fly. We had heard the news first from our preflight intel briefing, but now the news was catching up. We all had friends in Saudi and we anxiously listened to the news and the reports.

Although his spit cup was in hand and his typical partial grin was spread out on his lips, Tennessee Jim didn't seem himself today. None of us did, for it seemed that the long wait for the ground war to begin was perhaps over. I already knew what the mood during today's flight would be, it would be somber—and that's exactly how it was.

All in all, the mission went well, though. The flight was much shorter than the previous day's and early afternoon found us back in the crew lounge. The faces fixed to CNN were particularly haggard, and more than a few were ashen. The flu was making its rounds through the PME and it was slowly spreading through the ranks. We all needed a rest. This was my thirteenth flight in as many days, probably the same number as for my fellow crew dogs. Although we had been here less than two weeks, it seemed like two years.

I know I wasn't the only one who had had trouble clearing his ears on the flight. Pressure built up in my sinuses had become an unbearable burning pain by the time we were wheels down. My head felt as if it were going to explode, but I shrugged this off as I stared at the TV.

The reports were grim. Heavy ground fighting was under way. The Iraqis attempted a deceptive ploy near Khafji that involved a mechanized infantry battalion and a tank battalion. At first the two enemy battalions appeared to be surrendering.

Under such terms, they pushed into Allied positions without resistance. The battle that unfolded afterward was tangled and confused.

As we watched the news and read the reports, the remnants of the Iraqi battalions were withdrawing. The Iraqis held Khafji despite heavy Allied counterattacks.

Eventually we did leave base ops. Part of the crew, the lucky ones, went back to separate rooms, showers, and warm beds. Four of us—Cowboy, Happy, Bad Boy and I—went back to the unheated PME and our cold cots. The PME was developing a particular odor about it that was slowly progressing from mildly noticeable to overpowering, a smell much like the inside of a sweaty leather boot.

The flight suit I had on had been clean days ago, but now it wreaked of JP-4 and sweat. My plan for what little remained of the afternoon was to use one of the washing machines in the barracks across the street. I borrowed laundry soap from Happy and then headed over.

Even though the laundry room was centrally located on the first floor, it took me a moment to find it—I was more tired than I knew—and of course, I found that the machines that weren't broken were all in use. While I waited, I had a great deal of time to think. I listened to the spinning of the machines, the gentle swishing of water, and fought to stay awake.

I hadn't had much downtime or alone time to really think of home and how much I missed it. I missed Katie most of all, but I couldn't deny I missed the creature comforts that I had taken for granted so many times.

I missed hot meals and a warm bed. I missed watching old movies and reading a good book while sitting on a soft cushioned couch sipping a frothy beer. I missed my favorite pair of blue jeans with worn knees and my old gray sweatshirt. Things that all seemed so petty with war raging not so far away.

When my clothes finished drying, I walked back to the PME. "You need to sleep," I told myself, and that was my last real thought before I awoke to bright daylight streaming in through shielded windows. Looking at my watch that read 08:00, I scratched my eyes and looked again. I pushed the date button and looked again. 1-31. 08:00.

I couldn't have slept twelve straight hours. I would have had to be comatose. I unzipped my sleeping bag, braced myself for the cold floor. The floor was cool, not cold. The air outside the sleeping bag was also cool, not cold.

Had I been alerted? No.

Was it really 08:00?

I put my feet back into the sleeping bag and lay back down. I closed my eyes and thought that it seemed I'd finally hit the lull after the storm.

A familiar voice and a pillow being thrown in my face awoke me some time later, "You still sleeping? It's 10:15. We're heading over to base ops to see what's up. You want to come?"

"Shit, Happy. I was having the best—" I paused and worked my way out of the sleeping bag, "Sure, give me five." I looked at my watch. 10:15. Had I really slept fourteen hours? Fourteen hours was more sleep than the total sleep I'd had in the previous three days. More sleep than I'd gotten that entire first week.

I groped around for my shaving kit then headed for the outhouse. After turning on the faucet, I stuck my clean-cut head into the icy cold tap water. After toweling off I began shaving.

As I shaved, I stared into the mirror. It was almost as if a totally different person were staring back. I hadn't really taken the time to look during the past days. I'd always been in a rush. I did look now. There were thick lines of stubble coming in along the sides of my head where it had been clean-shaven. My cheeks were pale, but the deep dark circles under my eyes were mostly gone.

I flexed my biceps and looked into the mirror; the cut was gone. I couldn't wait to find a gym and hit the weights. I told myself that I'd start eating better. Where was that damned grill we'd been promised anyway? Just the thought of a well-grilled steak with a baked potato and corn on the cob made my mouth water. I was saving a ten-dollar bill in my wallet for the occasion.

Thinking of money made me remember I was going to ask Major James about going to finance, hopefully to get another advance. Except for that ten-dollar bill, I was virtually broke.

I flexed my biceps one last time in the mirror then turned away. As I rinsed my face with cold water, my thoughts quickly returned to my surroundings and the war. What had happened at Khafji? Was the ground war under way?

As I emerged from the bathroom I shouted, "What's the news?" to the guys in the rec tent who were watching CNN.

"The Allies have taken back most of Khafji, but the fighting is still underway," shot back Bad Boy.

"No shit? What are the losses?" I asked grimly, expectantly.

"Light so far. It looks like the Iraqis took a pounding, though." We all smiled, not a happy smile, rather a proud smile.

"You guys still heading up to ops?" I got three nods in response, and we started the long trudge on foot across base.

Happy, Cowboy, Bad Boy, and I made the walk to ops at a quick pace. The ops building and the ops center itself were fairly deserted even though the big board said one crew should be returning and one crew was enroute to the zone.

I noticed then that of the three lines listed our crew wasn't one of the three, also that Captain Willie's crew was listed last which meant we'd be the next line after that. We'd have an early morning flight the next day.

I talked to Major James about the money situation. It turned out I wasn't the only one caught in a financial bind. He already had plans in the works for getting advances for us and was, in fact, waiting for a return call for the final go-ahead from the folks at accounting and finance. His advice was to wait, and so we did.

More news came in about the battles in and around Khafji. We thanked God that so far it was all good. Despite heavy Iraqi losses, Allied losses remained light. We hoped they would stay that way.

Several hours later, we piled into a crew van that took us to accounting and finance to get much-needed advances. I was never so glad to see a stack of twenty-dollar bills in my life. Happy and I made a run to the commissary immediately afterward to restock our supplies. I bought a loaf of fresh-baked bread. I hadn't had a slice of bread, especially fresh-baked bread, in what seemed a lifetime.

Yet all through the day, my thoughts remained with the Saudis, the Qataris, and the Marines that were in the process of liberating Khafji. What should have been a day of relaxation from an exhaustingly long stretch of endlessly long days wasn't.

Thursday, 31 January 1991
Germany

Snow covered the now sleepy air base at Sembach in a thick white blanket that stretched as far as the eye could see out into the countryside. Dressed in a thick woolen sweater, Katie made the two-block walk from the commissary where she worked to an empty and silent apartment. She flicked on the TV, tuned in to the Armed Forces Network as she had every day for the past two weeks.

After performing the usual after-work things like changing clothes and preparing supper, she curled up on the couch in front of the TV. Abruptly the phone rang and she ran across the room, snatching up the receiver before it finished the first ring. "Hello?"

"This is Mrs. Kuntz from the base legal."

Katie paused and then replied weakly, "Yes?" Images flashed through her mind. Had something happened?

"Is your husband there?"

"No, he's in the Gulf."

Another long pause. "The claim your husband filed for

damage done to your property when your household goods were shipped to Germany has been approved. When can we pick up the furniture?" Our furniture had been damaged during the move to Germany. Our fine, silver-colored couch set had been water-damaged and soiled so badly that it was now a dull and dirty gray.

"Pick up the furniture?" Katie cried, "What do you mean? The couch and loveseat only need to be reupholstered."

"The cost of reupholstering the couch and loveseat comes to more than the cost to replace them. They're government property once we make payment. You need to deliver them to the Defense Reutilization and Maintenance Organization."

Katie looked at the couch and the loveseat that filled the living room, then cut Mrs. Kuntz off, "What do you mean? My husband is deployed to the Gulf. I can't move this furniture. What would I do without a couch?"

"That's policy, ma'am. We have to recover the property within so many days."

Katie was near tears now. "What do you mean, that's policy?"

"I guess I could make an exception. What if I arrange pick-up? Will that work?"

"No, I still won't have a couch."

"You should have thought of that when you filed the paperwork."

"It was a brand new couch set when we left the states," countered Katie, her voice heavy with emotion and oriental accent.

"That's policy, ma'am. What if I could get someone over there by next Friday?" asked Mrs. Kuntz.

"Are you listening to me? My husband is deployed to the Gulf. Can't this wait until he returns?"

"Afraid not, ma'am. I'll call back on Monday the 4th to confirm. Is that all right?"

Katie started to say something when the phone clicked and then went dead. She looked at the couch and the loveseat in the gradually dimming light—dusk was at hand. She was frustrated as she turned up the volume on the TV. She ate dinner in front of the TV while listening to the news as she had every night for two weeks.

She couldn't help thinking then that she'd been married for only eighteen months, that she'd never wanted to come to Germany in the first place, that this was the third long separation in eighteen months.

The first had been when I changed stations to Sembach; due to housing shortages I had needed to find an apartment prior to her arrival. It had taken almost two months to find an apartment and finalize all the paperwork—an eternity to newlyweds. The second separation was when I deployed to Nevada for the Green Flag exercise. The third now.

Of course, there were a number of shorter separations in between it all, three days here, four days there—the life of a military member who was a flyer. It seemed to her that we'd been apart more than we'd been together. More so this final time when her husband of only eighteen months departed for a war zone. Still, she'd braved it all and taken it in stride. She had a strong heart, a special charisma, and boundless love.

Still upset over the phone call, she sat on the edge of the couch and watched the news until a programmed show came on. "We take you to a regularly scheduled program. As of today, AFN has reversed its all-news policy. We will resume our normal weekly programming, bringing you highlights from the Gulf as they come in."

Katie crossed to the TV and clicked it off. During the moment of silence that followed, she stared into the darkness of the living room. She paused a moment more. Thinking perhaps she might still see more from the Gulf, she turned the TV back on.

Afterward, she went into the kitchen. She had just started washing the dishes when a special news bulletin interrupted. It was an update from the Gulf. "We interrupt our programming to bring you a special bulletin," the announcer stated.

Katie had a dishtowel in her hand and was in the process of drying a dinner plate as she crossed into the living room. "This news just in from the Persian Gulf," began the AFN reporter. "Tragedy has struck again. An EC-130 was apparently shot down during intense fighting. All fourteen crew members are reportedly missing behind enemy lines at this time."

The plate fell from Katie's trembling hands and crashed to the floor as the announcer repeated the message, adding, "We will do our best to keep you updated on the situation as more information comes in."

Katie sat numbly on the couch. She watched the TV for the rest of the evening and late into the night, hoping more news about the incident would be broadcast, hoping the phone would ring and knowing she would dread the moment either happened.

Friday, 1 February 1991

The evening flight of the day before had gone well, and I was beginning my third week. It seemed that I had truly been there forever. The second week had ups and down, highs and lows that equaled or rivaled those of my first week. So much had happened. Sometimes I just wondered when it all would end. Where would it leave me? Where would it leave the hundreds of thousands of deployed troops?

Six hundred German air defense troops were to arrive soon to bolster our air defenses with German-built Roland systems. Everyone was taking the threats from Saddam Hussein against Turkey seriously. I'd seen increased numbers of patrols on base. More and more Turkish troops were moving about.

Low-flying cruise missiles flew over Baghdad—what an eerie sight it must have been for those below. Iran warned against Israel's entering the war. Sometimes I wondered what would happen if Israel did enter the war. They could only take so many poundings by Iraqi Scuds before they sought retribution.

The stress level peaked that day. We were all told to make phone calls home as soon as possible. Katie didn't sound too good on the phone. In fact she was sobbing through most of the conversation. I'm not too sure what happened, but it sounded like the initial reports on the AC-130 Gunship crash said it was an EC-130, at least in the reports on AFN broadcast from Sembach. I hoped to God they would find the missing crewmembers soon.

It seemed that the fighting in and around Khafji was over. It didn't look like the ground war would come after all, which was actually a good thing. I could only hope that it would not come for some weeks yet. The longer we pounded the Iraqi fighting machine, the easier it would be to claim the final victory.

It wasn't all bad news that day. We finally got that heater for the rec tent. No more cold nights—well, as long as we could find some kerosene to fill it, that is.

Strangely, I was looking forward to our combat flights more and more. The previous three days had seemed monotonous despite the happenings. It truly seemed that we had hit a slump when we should have hit a high.

Bad Boy bought a couple of sets of poker chips. I'd been warned that he would cheat. I looked forward to "poker with the boys" all day. I needed something to get my mind off home and Katie.

We started out with a five-handed poker game that slowly progressed and changed. The rules we played by were crew dog rules, meaning anything went as long as you spelled out all the rules before dealing the first card.

Fabulous sat across from me, smoking a long, fat cigar, decked out in a long-sleeved cotton shirt, looking exactly like the sort of person you'd expect to see gathered around a poker table looking extremely haggard as the sun came up after a long night of hard cards. He preferred no wild cards, just straight-up poker.

Every time it was his turn to deal, that's exactly the way he dealt them, five-card draw, nothing wild, nothing special.

To his left sat Rollin, almost as smooth as the man himself. He preferred his game full of wild cards. During the night he introduced such games as twenty-nine and unlucky lady where queens were wild except for the queen of spades.

"Ante up," went the call. I slapped down my fifty cents, just like everyone else. The chips that had sparked the idea of the game sat on the edge of the table. They were there. We knew they were there. But it was a lot more fun to play with money—there was no substitute for money.

Bill the Nav began to set down a game of seven-card stud— two cards face down, one card face up. We quickly discovered he liked to slap his money down on the table quick and without thought. He was an officer. He had a lot of money to slap down, so we weren't complaining.

"Bad Boy, you going to ante?" I asked. He was to my right. He liked to play. He just never liked to pay. He'd hold the two quarters in the palm of his hand right until the cards were in front of him. I think some hard-core poker players would have kicked him out of the game after the first hand, but the cards were his and so were the chips that we weren't using. Luckily, Bill was a slow dealer and so he hadn't started to deal out the face up cards yet.

"Yeah, yeah," Bad Boy said slapping down his two bits.

Fabulous grinned ear-to-ear momentarily as the ace of hearts was laid before him, but then his usual smooth poker face returned. I knew this was going to be a costly hand as I watched the cards go out. A, K, K, 6, A.

"Your bet, Fab," Bill called out.

Fabulous tossed in a folded dollar bill. Bad Boy, with the six up, folded right then. The rest of us anted up.

"Pretty quick to jump out, aren't we?" Bill accused.

"Yeah, like a rat jumping a sinking ship," Rollin added.

Bad Boy unwrapped the bandanna that had been covering his head and busied himself with re-wrapping it.

"Wrap it tight," I added.

Bill called out the cards as they went down, "Seven of spades and no help. Three of clubs and no help. Ace of diamonds and looking good. Eight of clubs."

Since I had the best hand, I quickly tossed in fifty cents.

"I raise you," Fabulous called out, tossing in another crisp one-dollar bill.

Bill raised it another buck and finally called.

"Ace of spades, a pair of aces—king of diamonds, a pair of kings—queen of hearts, look at that straight—eight of hearts, pair."

Fabulous led with a buck; Bill raised it to two and Rollin called. The kitty full of change and bills looked exceptionally good. I glanced at my down cards again. "You guys keep betting like this, I'll be in bed wiped out in an hour."

"That is the point, isn't it?" retorted Fabulous. I don't think he meant it the way it sounded. He seemed to be playing Bill to his right, had been playing him for the last five or six hands. Bill kept reaching into his wallet.

"Seven of hearts, two pair showing," began Bill as he started the deal again. "Three of diamonds, two pair showing. Nine of hearts and no help. Yes! Eight of spades, three of a kind showing."

Bill began the bidding with two one-dollar bills, our pre-game limit. Fabulous bumped it up two to four and Rollin did the same. Suddenly, it was six bills to me. I laid down a stack of quarters, then sat back and watched as the game progressed; one last down card.

The final ante to me was quickly six dollars again. Sticking to my guns, I put it in. Bad Boy to my left was eyeing the pot. I could see he was glad he got out. I wished I had.

By the time Fabulous turned up his cards, the large pot had attracted two potential players. He had but two pair. Eventually, with a straight, I took that first big kitty. But then Rollin started playing games like Butcher and Blind Tiger.

Butcher was one wild game and when he first introduced it, it nearly started a fight among friends. All cards were dealt face up. When a player received a card of the same rank as one already dealt, it was transferred to the player holding that card. Four of a kind took the pot and low-hand split it with him. After a while we came to like the game. Except for Bill the Nav who had absolutely no luck.

Saturday, 2 February 1991

At 11:55 I had my gear in hand, a helmet, flight gear, chem gear, a can of beanies and weenies, and a newly-acquired bag of sour-cream-and-onion potato chips. I took one last quick glance at the PME as I waited for the crew van. Today was the first day in a long time that I'd seen the windows open and the shades drawn though the stagnant air still hadn't cleared.

On the far side of the room, Fabulous was pressing a suit, of all things. He even had an ironing board. Fabulous was smooth. Big John was fussing with his bags. I didn't know what he was all worked up about but he didn't seem to be in a good mood.

I heard the crew van pull up. My heart began to beat a little faster as I stepped outside. The driver was Mike from the crew. "Where's your flat top?" I called out. His reply was sort of a snarl. Mike had a way of doing that. "You here to alert us?"

"No. Didn't you hear, you've been bumped back two hours."

"Two hours? Shit. What am I supposed to do for two hours?"

Mike snarled again. "You seen Big John?"

"Yeah, he's fussing with his bags." I was about to head for

the rec tent to tell Happy and Cowboy about the delay when the glare in Mike's eye stopped me cold. I knew him fairly well, so I knew something was wrong. "What's up?"

"Big John's going home today. You want to tell him I'll be back in forty-five to pick him up?"

I glanced at my watch. "At 12:45?"

"Yeah, thanks," replied Mike. Before I could say anything, he hopped back into the crew van and started off.

I almost headed back into the PME, but then I remembered Happy and Cowboy waiting in the rec tent. They must've had CNN blaring to not hear the crew van pull up.

"We've been bumped back two hours," I yelled, ducking my head into the tent as I unzipped it. "Hey, Happy. Man, you want to come talk to Big John with me? Something's up. I don't know what, but they're sending him home. He doesn't look too good."

Happy may have been obnoxiously perky, but he understood people. He knew what made them tick, or so it seemed. "Sure, no sweat," he answered.

Big John was still fussing with his bags. His face was bright red. It was strange because he was otherwise the most mild-mannered individual I knew. It was only his size that threw people off. Most figured anyone that big had to be an animal, but he wasn't. He was a teddy bear.

"Hey, Big John, Mike said he'd be back at 12:45 to pick you up. You look like you need some help. You packing?" Big John didn't answer; I nudged Happy.

"Shit, Big John, you look bad," Happy said in his usual jocular manner. "What's wrong, someone die?" I could tell he didn't mean for the words to come that way, they just did.

Big John stopped fussing with his bags and tears came into

his eyes. "I'm going home," he said. "They're sending me home. Can you believe it?"

Fabulous was still ironing his suit, doing a good job of acting as if he didn't hear a thing. He might not have because of the music playing in his ears from his Walkman, but I was fairly certain he was listening. Our training made us preternatural curious types; listening was part of the job.

Happy and I helped Big John disassemble his cot. He didn't say anything for the longest time. Neither did we. Happy had that usual dumb smile on his face—I imagined he'd probably die with that same grin on his face some day.

We were in the middle of stacking Big John's bags outside, chem gear, flight gear, and A-bags, when Big John unfolded two pictures from his wallet.

"These are my kids." He handed the pictures to me. Right then I expected him to tell us that one of them had died. But he didn't.

"They're cute," I said handing the pictures to Happy. Big John didn't even break a smile.

Happy looked at the picture for a moment as if he was remembering something he had been trying to forget. "How old are they?"

"John junior is seven. Samuel there is five."

Happy handed John back the pictures.

"Cute kids," I repeated.

Big John stood there a moment rather glumly, and then he took two folded up drawings from his flight suit chest pocket. "I received these in the mail along with a letter two days ago. My wife Anna isn't doing too well. You know, when I first looked at those pictures, I saw only our plane and the mountains. That second picture there looked rather like a forest, till I put on my glasses. I don't much care for wearing my glasses, you know, only when I fly."

I stuttered, trying to say something in response but stopped instead. I was glad I didn't say anything, because as Happy handed me the drawings I saw shock on his face—and here I'd just thought about that dumb smile glued to his lips until the day he died.

"She told me things were fine but that John junior was having troubles in school with his teachers. Then I get this letter. See there, I thought those were gray clouds at first, and then I looked closer. It's smoke. There's fire. That second picture there my youngest drew. Where do they come up with these things?"

"I wish I knew," I replied. The second drawing wasn't of a forest but row after row of crosses. It was a cemetery and under one of them was a little sign that read, "Daddy." That's about all it took to bring me near tears.

"My wife's not taking this separation too well," began John after a long awkward silence. "She's been telling my sons that Daddy will never be coming home unless, of course, it's in a canvas bag. You know, I was fine until Thursday. I told her nothing like that could ever happen, and then it did happen. I don't know anymore."

Big John paused. There were tears in his eyes now. "I got a phone call late last night. That's when I heard the news about Anna." He continued in a barely audible whisper, "I'm glad I'm going home or otherwise I would've had a breakdown like Anna. I nearly did. I lost complete control yesterday. That's never happened to me before."

"Kids are a lot tougher than you think, Big John. You go

home and things'll turn out all right."

"I don't want things to turn out all right. I want them back the way they were before. What am I going to do without Anna?"

"They're cute kids, John," began Happy. "They're young. You go home and you tell them you love them. Spend a few days concentrating on nothing but them. You're leaving, John. Good God, the war's behind you. With the stress gone, Anna will bounce back. You'll see."

Silence followed. Big John, Happy, and I stood awkwardly waiting for Mike to return, which he did at exactly 12:45. Happy and I put Big John's bags into the back of the van, and then we said a quick goodbye. That was the last time I saw Big John. He caught a transport headed to Germany just as we were entering ops to go fly. He never came back.

Sunday, 3 February 1991

The mission of the previous day had gone well. We supported a full mission package with one significant change. We also supported a group of fighters whose payload was hundreds of thousands of psy-ops leaflets. Baghdad radio was running a propaganda campaign to the Iraqi people and the neighboring states; the Allies were countering with their own.

The leaflets were dispersed over Iraqi troop concentrations. Winds scattered them far and near. The ultimate aim of the leaflets was to inform Iraqi soldiers that if they would surrender they would be treated fairly and given food, water, and medical treatment.

We had one other surprise on the flight. Gentleman Bob was our AC. He even shared crew beers with us in Tennessee Jim's quarters after the flight.

At a little after 20:00, our crew was alerted, and I received great news. A C-5 transport had come in from Sembach. I went to ops expecting a letter; I was elated to find a package. Inside I found civvies. Finally civvies. My old blue jeans, not the ones with the holes in the knees, but a pair that would do just as well.

Sweat shirts, t-shirts, a jogging outfit.

Yes, Katie made me a tape too. Her voice sounded so sweet. Underneath it all was a loaf of homemade, mouth watering, banana-nut bread. I shared some with the guys; the rest I put away.

One last thing—we had a brand new grill sitting next to the picnic table. I remembered those conversations with Big John about a thick, juicy steak. He was probably home eating one right then. I was still dreaming about it and hoping I wouldn't have to dream much longer. So many good things happening in one day made me wonder what was lurking around the corner that I just couldn't see.

Shortly after midnight, I was clinging to the right side paratroop door looking out the portal when the wing dipped and left me staring straight down into the grim desert floor. Anti-aircraft artillery was so clear in my night-vision goggles it looked as if it could reach out and touch me—us. We were just finishing a very long communication jamming sortie. There in the background, far out to my right, the last of the secondary explosions caused by the Buffs' heavy bombing raid was lighting up Mosul airfield. It was both the most spectacular thing I'd ever seen and the most spine-chilling. A familiar voice was tweaking in my ears, mixing in with Gypsy's airborne warning. For a brief moment I tuned in.

"Thank you for listening to K-J-A-M radio," Crow cried out over ship's Private. "We're AM, FM, and all the way across the dial. We hope you're enjoyed our programming today and that you'll join us again soon, real soon. This final selection, Born in the U.S.A., by Mr. Bruce Springsteen, goes out to a Mr. Saddam Hussein. We all know who you are, but do you know who we are?"

Ship's PA tweaked. Captain Sammy called out, "Crew, Pilot, you know the words, so sing along!" The lyrics to Born in the U.S.A. screamed over the PA. I began screaming the lyrics into my headset microphone. We were just finishing up an especially tense combat sortie so Captain Sammy was letting us blow off a little steam.

"Pilot, Navigator, Gypsy's cleared us off stations in five mike."

"Roger, Nav."

Before the pilot brought the Lady off orbit, we went through one final combat turn, a crisp turn that dipped the wing nearly sixty degrees and left me once more staring straight down at the desert floor. For a moment, I listened to the Lady's hum—the four turbo propellers of our venerable EC-130 churning in the wind—then chatter filled my headset.

"Pilot, MCC, the last of the packages have egressed. Gypsy's pulling out and Phantom left us five minutes ago. Let's get the hell out of Dodge," Tennessee Jim cried out. Bruce Springsteen was just finishing his last rendition on ship's PA when it tweaked out.

"Roger that, MCC. We're coming off orbit."

"Crew, MCC, good job! The package got away safe, and the Buffs really smacked the hell out of Mosul."

"Pilot, Spotter, traffic high, at nine o'clock moving to twelve," I called out.

"Got him, that's Gas Station. The KCs are heading back to base."

"Roger," I responded. This rotation as spotter had gone without a hitch so far, yet I didn't know which was worse—

staring at a bunch of high-tech displays while frantically working the signal environment or watching explosions light up the sky.

"Crew, Pilot, let me remind you that we are still airborne over the sensitive area. Our moment of fun is over. We'll be clear in a few minutes; stay with me until then.

"Spotter, stay alive back there! There's been a lot of activity out there today. That AAA is thick as rain."

You don't have to tell me, I wanted to say. I saw it. The flashes in the view port of the NVG made it seem like the Fourth of July.

Minutes passed. The blood rushing in my ears calmed. The passing of time reverted back to minutes and seconds, and not heartbeats. To my five and six o'clock, I could still see a continuous flurry of artillery bursts flooding the skyline. Soon the guns would fall quiet. We would hopefully be long gone.

"Crew, exiting the combat zone. Post-combat Entry Checklist."

The front-end crew went through their list: pilot, copilot, navigator, engineer, and the air maintenance technician, each calling out in order. The mission control commander said his bit as the mission compartment interior lights turned from combat red to a lusterless white. I shifted from port to starboard and continued my vigil, staring into the night sky. The guns were indeed silent as I turned to look back, but a vast POL storage area was still burning crimson far behind us.

Soon mountains were below us, whitecaps mixed with jagged black outcroppings. Glancing down with my NVG, they seemed to be waiting, taunting me. I was confident that they wouldn't get me today. I tugged at my survival vest and felt the reassuring weight of the government issue .38 revolver within it. I sighed;

having a loaded weapon always seemed to put a part of my mind at ease.

A four-ship of F-15 screamed by. I yelled out, "Traffic low, moving seven to twelve. Four-ship. There goes our support CAP. We're on our own."

"Roger, Spotter. Got them; there they go," responded Ice, our copilot.

I watched the Falcons go, afterburners filling the NVG with green-white fire.

I switched to the port side and saw another pair of afterburners. I was about to call it in when my heart stopped. The green-white fire wasn't coming from afterburners. It was coming from engine number two. A smoke trail was rushing past the window. "Pilot, Spotter, I see smoke and flames coming out of engine two."

At the same time I called out, the copilot spotted the warning lights, "Fire warning, engine two!"

"Roger, Spotter. Roger, Co. Crew shutting down engine two. Spotter, what do you see?"

"We're trailing smoke, lots of smoke; but I don't see any more flames." I had my face pressed up against the plexiglass.

The Lady jerked roughly. My heart jumped into my throat as we lost altitude quickly. It felt as if we'd hit a patch of clear air turbulence.

"What'd we hit? Spotter, check starboard. You see anything?"

"Dear Jesus, engine three warning light just died," cried Ice.

"Crew, we're two engines out. Prepare to begin in-flight emergency procedures," Sammy, the pilot called out. The copilot cut in and began reviewing emergency procedures on Ship's Hot that included contingency plans for bailout, ditching, crash landing, and conditional destruction of our classified equipment. Things the thirteen of us, five in the front and eight in the mission crew had heard, memorized, and reviewed a hundred times.

"Crew attention to brief, crash landing procedures! Don parachutes, helmets and gloves. Remember, six short rings, prepare for impact. Followed by one long ring, brace for impact. In the event of a crash landing, use any available exit to egress as quickly as possible. Formation site will be three hundred feet off the nose."

"Pilot, Spotter, you won't believe this, but we lost the prop on three. There's nothing turning out there!"

Captain Sammy, who had been advising Control, cut in, "Shoulder harnesses fastened and in the locked positions. Gloves on, helmets on, parachutes on." He was following his checklist per procedure.

We'd been supporting a pre-dawn strike and now, of all times, the sun decided to begin its lofty climb. I saw engine two's propellers come to a halt. I held my breath as they did so. I saw a spark of flames and fiery oil spilling out into the shadowy sky. The chute I'd already fitted was in the crew bunk beside me. I strapped it on. "Pilot, Spotter, there's flames coming out of two again!"

The Gray Lady was a great bird. I'd heard tell she could fly with two engines out. We were about to find out. In any event, we still had two working engines. I had my parachute.

"In the event of bailout, remember: three short, prepare. One long, execute. Primary bailout from the aft paratroop doors. Secondary, aft cargo door and ramp. Third is the crew entrance door."

By now, we'd already passed Diyarbakir, which was our alternate recovery point. Instead of turning the plane around, the safest thing to do would be to bring the plane back to our base of origin. This was the plan of action the pilot embarked upon.

We were losing altitude slowly, but the pilot was holding her steady. The bad thing about EC-130s was that with all our equipment and gear we were always heavy. The good thing was we had already used up a good chunk of our fuel, which lightened us a bit. It was this extra bit we were counting on.

Captain Sammy was confident he could safely land the plane; and even though he told us this and we wanted to believe him, there were some worried faces in the back. I was strapped in at the position I had emptied after take-off. Helmet, gloves, and parachute on and ready to go, I double-checked my survival vest and zipped my winter flight up to its highest notch. I was ready for whatever lay ahead; we all were.

A thousand thoughts swam through my mind, only one image in my mind's eye. It was of Katie. I wished to God I could picture her happy, running into my arms. All I could see in my mind's eye was her standing in front of the TV. Her listening to the report of our crash. Her breaking down in tears and a fit of heart-wrenching sobs.

If this was to be the end, I wanted it to be over when we slammed into the ground. I didn't want to freeze to death in the mountains waiting for search and rescue. I'd heard that in such cold, you could just lie down, close your eyes, and let death find you.

Distant in my ears, I heard the pilot calling out. "Crew, Pilot, we're eighty miles out. The field should come into sight soon."

As I had all the radios pulled out, I heard Control's

advisories. For a long time afterward, I just prayed. Then I heard it, the call that sent chills to my bone. "Crew, attempting to restart engine one."

"Engine one?" I wanted to scream.

"She's flaring," responded the Co. "Oil pressure's low, but some power is better than no power. Shit, she cut out again, we're losing oil pressure."

"Crew!" screamed the Pilot, "We're going down. I repeat, we're going down."

I started praying; we all started praying. The copilot was trying frantically to re-start engine one.

"The field's coming into sight. Come on, baby, hold on. Hold on."

I prayed. We all prayed. It was then I noticed I was holding my breath, waiting, hoping for another call. It seemed an eternity that we waited.

As the plane shifted, pictures of Katie and our life together that should have been flashed before my eyes. It was in that moment that I promised myself that if I survived I would live. I mean really live, taking control of my life instead of letting life control me. Then it happened, the one miracle that could save us all. I saw engine one flare just as the copilot called out, "Pilot, engine one's flaring again. There she goes."

I wanted to scream, to shout at the top of my lungs: "I'm not ready to die yet, you sons of bitches," my voiceless whisper giving life to a thought deep in my mind. Surely the enemy was responsible for all that was happening. Surely we'd been hit by a SAM or AAA.

Captain Sammy applied extra pressure to the yoke and tried to hold the Lady level. Over and over in my mind's eye I saw flames pouring out of engine two. Until that moment I'd thought I'd seen it all: the black rain of AAA, SAMs, enemy fighters, all hell-bent on knocking us out of the sky. None of them had succeeded until now. None of it had prepared me for this moment.

I couldn't help thinking, what if we go down in those snowcaps? How many of us will survive? What if we make the runway and go nose first into the tarmac? In the back of my mind, I saw the POL storage area explode to life, the huge flames lapping at the sky.

Seconds ticked by with agonizing slowness. I heard the pilot call out to dump extra fuel. Immediately afterward, I heard Sparrow throwing up her breakfast. I wasn't sure if it were the turbulence or the anxiety that caused it; I only knew the smell was awful. I had a hard time keeping from throwing up, myself. I was definitely a sympathetic puker. Who wouldn't be in such tight quarters?

As we approached for landing it became clear that complications had arisen. The control tower was advising us to go around.

Captain Sammy was angry—I'd never heard him truly angry before. He was screaming, "Tower, Pilot, negative on that go around. We're heading straight in. Repeat, in-flight emergency, two engines out. We're heading straight in. Re-direct that traffic. Get those idiots off the runway. We're not going to make a go around and you're going to be responsible for thirteen corpses."

Tower controller's voice changed, "EC-130, be advised of traffic low and in front of you."

Captain Sammy and the copilot pulled back as fast as they could. Captain Sammy was still screaming, "Tower Pilot, we're heading straight in, tell them to pull out of the pattern. Repeat, in-flight emergency, two engines out. We're trailing smoke. We cannot go around!"

"Pilot, Co, runway's in sight."

"Crew, pilot, I'm taking her in. Brace for impact. It's going to be a rough one."

"What about that KC?" objected the Nav.

"Screw that KC!" Sammy screamed.

I took in a breath. It felt like I hadn't breathed for hours. Suddenly the plane slammed the ground. We went in hard, harder than ever before. The plane skidded. We bounced once, twice, and then came down so hard my head slapped the back of my flight chair like it was a hammer and my head a nail. I accidentally bit my tongue; blood gushed into my mouth.

I braced myself as I was jerked forward, felt my head slam back against the headrest a second time. A moment of uncertainty followed. The world slowed. Everything became clear to me, too clear, almost as if I were seeing the world around me for the first time. I was a nerves-of-steel crewer no more. There were tears in my eyes.

I expected at any moment to feel the runway rip away the landing gear because we'd come in way too fast. I expected to see flames pour in through the crew doors as the plane was torn in half. I expected the breath held in my lungs to be my last. I wasn't okay with it. I'd said my peace, but I didn't have much of a choice in the matter.

I guess I could have been angry, outraged. Twenty-five was too short a life, too little time. There was so much I wanted to do, so much I hadn't done while I had the chance.

Everything slowed.

Everything smoothed.

Everything became real.

I heard the two remaining engines struggle into reverse in an attempt to slow us down. We were racing down the runway, using it up fast.

The plane jerked to a halt as if we'd slammed into a barrier. The interior lights blackened. Someone popped open the crew door. We piled out just as if it were a drill—only it wasn't.

I undid the safety harnesses, bolted out of my seat. I looked back as I ran away from the great Gray Lady that I'd been through so much with. I remember one of the pilots saying once that any landing you can walk away from was a good landing.

I counted myself lucky. We were all lucky.

An array of ambulances and fire trucks began to pull up, their sirens screaming, their lights flashing. A fire team rushed a hose to engine two and drowned away the smoke.

A hundred yards or so away from the plane, the crew gathered. Tammy, Sparrow, and Happy were sitting on the tarmac hugging their knees. Ice hurt his ankle in the egress. Bill and Sammy were helping him to an uneasy seat. Crow, Patrick, Chris, Cowboy, Bad Boy, and I stood staring back at the Gray Lady.

The paramedics gave us the once-over. One of them tended to Ice. Five minutes later, our crew van showed up. I watched the great Gray Lady grow smaller and smaller against the black of the runway.

The sudden frenzy on the flight line ebbed as the rescue vehicles began to disperse.

My thoughts strayed.

It seemed just yesterday that I was home in bed, Katie beside me, and I was watching her sleep. Last summer had been so warm and clear, so very warm and clear—and happy.

Germany and Katie seemed so far away.

Afternoon, Monday, 4 February 1991

Fatigue hit us hard. We were in a slump. The previous flight had been one I almost didn't walk away from. I could still see the fire engines and rescue vehicles lining the runway. Red lights flashing. Sirens screaming.

Sitting in the back of the crew van as it rolled away from the plane, I watched black asphalt fall away to be replaced by the faded markings of an old Turkish road. All I wanted to do was crawl into bed and later wake up with Katie beside me.

This incident coming so close to the AC-130 Gunship shootdown opened a lot of people's eyes. I caught myself wishing I'd gone home with Big John. Yet when the crew van would pull up in a couple of hours, I would pile in, my flight bags in hand; so would Happy, Cowboy, and Bad Boy, who were staying here with me in the PME.

Popcorn was supposed to stop at the commissary and buy steaks for Happy, Bad Boy, Cowboy, and me. He didn't come through. Now the commissary was closed. I would have to wait another day to taste a juicy grilled steak.

Things weren't all bad. We hadn't been alerted yet, so I was trying to get a few more hours of sleep.

Tuesday, 5 February 1991

Leaving the warmth of my sleeping bag was no easy task. As I dragged my tired carcass out of bed to get ready to fly, twelve other crewers were doing the same. Shaving kit in one hand, towel and flashlight in the other, I struggled with the door.

Cold outside air jolted me. Then as my bare feet touched cold concrete, my eyes shot wide open. I'd forgotten to put on my boots, and the ground was colder than the chilly pre-morning air.

Icy cold water from the outhouse sink gave me another rude jolt as I splashed water on my face. Afterward I stared into the dirty mirror, thankful I no longer had hair that needed to be groomed. I ran a wet comb through it and in short order it looked just as it had yesterday. It looked like I had a flat top. I did have a flat top. I glanced at the watch forever strapped to my wrist. 02:10. I hated mornings like this.

After brushing my teeth, I hurried back to the barracks, put on clean socks, and then slipped my flight suit over my cotton long johns. My boots had quick-laces. I pulled the shoe strings taunt, ran the metal cinch back, looped the excess lace around the top of my boot, slapped the velcro over the top, and that was that.

My watch read 02:13.

I grabbed a can of fruit cocktail and an opener then retreated to the rec tent. It would be breakfast while I watched CNN.

At 02:30 the sky seemed especially black. I zipped up my winter flight jacket an extra couple of notches. In a couple of hours we'd be humping the zone and facing a deadly light show of anti-aircraft artillery; yet I could truly say I hated the waiting more than anything else, for it seemed that it never truly ended.

Cosmo, the newlywed, was driving the crew van today. He had returned about fifteen minutes early. As he sat down beside me to watch CNN, he rested his left arm on the chem mask attached to his web belt as if it were his safety blanket. He still had that look in his eyes, the look I had had that first day. The look of wariness and unease, caution and alarm.

"You look so tense!" I finally exclaimed, adding while trying to keep a straight face, "What's wrong, the ball and chain giving you a hard time back on the home front?"

"Not really. Those guys up?"

"I know Happy is. Cowboy and Bad Boy are probably pushing the sleep time. You're early; give 'em a few. This your first day driving?"

"Sixth on MPC."

Right then I understood the look in his eyes. Working mission planning cell was like a mini vacation, relaxed twelve-hour days spent either planning or driving. After six days he was probably going back to flying soon.

Cosmo continued, "I was planning most of the time. Ziggy was driving nights."

"Ziggy's still driving?"

"No, she's flying now. She went up the line before this one." He glanced at his watch. I glanced at mine. "I heard about Monday's mission. What do you think the odds are of that happening again?"

"I'm hoping it's about the same as lightning striking twice in the same place."

"Me, too," Cosmo said dryly.

As he stood and nervously jingled his keys, I knew it was time to load my gear into the van. I hoped the folks at ops would be more cheerful than Cosmo was this morning.

Once in ops, I went straight to the briefing room, which was packed with people waiting for Derrin, our mission briefer. It was a few minutes before the door opened and Derrin entered. "Sorry for the delay," he said, tackling his pointer and slapping it against the map. "SAR codes are listed. By now I hope you've written them down; but if you haven't, we'll take a moment to let you do that."

As he paused, I cast a sideways look at Tennessee Jim. He was in a fire-spitting mood this morning. It looked as if he hadn't shaved or he'd been up all night and hadn't thought about it after alert. Chris looked about the same.

Derrin continued, "There's some interesting reading material in the read files. I hope you all take a couple of minutes to read those over. A lot of new stuff. A lot of new stuff."

The door opened again; Happy and Cowboy entered. An enterprising individual at KC ops had set up a munchies fund. Happy and Cowboy had ambled down for a quick raid on it while the rest of us piled into intel. Derrin looked irritated but continued all the same.

"As you well know, a significant number of Iraqi aircraft have been sneaking into Iran. Clouds are moving in again, along with a strong storm front, which gives them a big window of opportunity. Special emphasis targets won't come as a surprise; our boys are going to hit those airfields again. Hopefully, we can catch them coming out from their bunkers; if not, we'll blow up the bunkers. Either way, aircraft is the key goal.

"The secondary targets won't come as much of a surprise either." Derrin began slapping the board with his pointer, stopping on a single distant target. "That's the farthest target you'll be supporting. Those guys will have a tough time getting in and out. You're job will be to make it easier for them.

"AAA will be thick as rain. Pilots are reporting emplacements continuing to sprout up all over the place. No surprise. Nearly every half-mile along key military roads."

Derrin went on for a couple of more minutes, finishing by showing us a group of glossies with the results of a bombing raid we had supported the day before.

Captain Sammy's briefing was next, followed by Tennessee's standard spiel and pep speech. Both reminded us that weather was a factor today. If the storm front swept in, the packages wouldn't go in and neither would we.

After the briefings, Chris and Jim were the first ones to crash out in the lounge while we waited to go. They looked as if they'd had a really rough night. I sat down and resisted the urge to let my eyes slip closed and the urge to ask Jim and Chris what they'd been up to.

Ops at 05:15 was occupied by a small group of bleary-eyed individuals who were looking forward to getting some sleep when their shift ended at 06:00. As the shift change began, ops began to look alive. The bleary-eyed night crew disappeared one by one, replaced by the bright-eyed day crew. It was right then that Derrin and Quincy did the unthinkable. They started a game of spades in the crew lounge; and since their quarters were directly off the lounge, they brought tunes, an array of munchies, and bravos.

As Quincy sat adjacent to me, I noticed his flat top. "Nice. When you do it?"

"Yesterday," chimed in Derrin at the same time that Quincy did. Derrin held up a pair of clippers.

I started to respond when Captain Sammy burst into the lounge. "Weather's moving in. We got to go now! Time to scramble, folks!"

We scrambled all right. Crow and the Eng, Patrick, hadn't even preflighted the system yet as we prepared for taxi and takeoff. We ran through our checks as fast as we could, racing to beat Mother Nature and already knowing she would probably win in the end.

Fighters had a definite advantage over us. Worst case scenario, they could wait out the weather. It didn't take them long to reach the zone with afterburners. Either way, it'd be close to an hour before they even had to launch. We, on the other hand, had to make the slow turboprop pedal to the zone.

"How's that cloud deck, Co? Vis looks pretty bad and dropping fast. Nav, you got the weather reports over target yet?"

"Cloud decks thickening and dropping in on us, vis down to 1500 meters."

If we got off the ground before the rains hit, we'd be okay.

"Roger, Co, see if we can get taxi clearance from Tower."

"Roger, Pilot."

"I'm checking on the weather over target."

"Roger, Nav, keep a close watch."

The radios were silent for a moment. Just then I realized that I didn't have Tower's channel pulled. I pulled it out.

"Tower just gave us taxi clearance. They're going to put us out there on hold. Weather's coming in thicker than they expected. Vis down to 1200 meters."

"Roger, 1200 meters. Is that acceptable mins, Co? Doesn't look like 1200 any more, though. Double-check that; how low's that cloud deck?"

"A thousand."

"Crew, Pilot, prepare for taxi. Looks like we'll have a delay out there."

"Pilot, MCC, mission crew ready for taxi."

"Roger that, MCC. Crew, we're rollin'. There's the AWACS crew running up also."

"KC's on the left, going to be a back up."

"Roger, Co, I see 'em. You got those weather reports yet from—"

"Tower's advising us to hold," said the copilot.

Bill, the Nav, cut in, "I got those weather reports. They don't look good."

"I got Tower. Co, tell them we'll hold here as advised. I don't think we'll beat that storm front if they make us hold too long.

"Crew, it looks like we made the race for nothing. We're going to have to hold here. Ah, shit, that's thick. Here come's the rain. Shit—one minute, God, that's all I wanted."

"Pilot, Co, Tower's advising—"

"I got him, give him a roger. Tell him we'll wait it out at the stand."

Captain Sammy eased the Lady back to the hard stand. We

knew the rain was whipping down because to back in Crow had to lower the aft ramp and door so he could direct the pilot in.

Hooked to our positions, we waited. The cabin smelled of jet fuel backwash from our prop exhaust kicked in by the strong winds the storm brought with it.

Our scheduled departure time, 07:15, came and went. Still we waited while rain slapped at the Lady. The weather over target began to look grimmer as the storm front moved in and the visibility outside was down to 500 meters.

The decision came at 08:00 to return to ops and wait out the storm there. We all would've preferred flying to waiting but we didn't have much of a choice.

Ops was crowded when we returned. The line after us had been alerted and had just arrived. So now two crews each of KC, AWACS, and EC would wait in the lounge. The late arrivals were the lucky ones; the rest of us had been up since 02:00. Still, none of us had our happy faces on. We all would've preferred flying to waiting.

Quincy and Derrin were still playing spades teamed up against Doc, one of the med techs, and a ground support troop. I watched them play and the morning began to slip away.

I was nearly asleep when someone thumped me on the shoulder. I looked up to see Happy standing over me. "What's up?"

"Steaks today?"

"Cook 'em up even if it rains all day. And Popcorn's not invited. What happened to him yesterday?"

"Maybe he had to fly."

"Probably."

I watched the cards float back and forth for a time as we

waited. Chris and Tennessee Jim were enjoying the reprieve. They'd drifted off to a noisy slumber. The rest of us weren't enjoying the wait much.

A few minutes after 11:00, the word finally came. The area looked as if it'd be sopped in all day. The weather over target was now projected to be overcast for the next two to three days. Two to three days would be an eternity.

It was the kind of weather the Iraqis would like, but we'd grow to hate. By afternoon, the endless day still hadn't ended. Happy and I'd been up since 02:00; and while just about everyone else from our crew had hit the sleeping bags upon return, we hadn't. We'd been busy.

"Slap on some of that seasoning there," I said, "and then some garlic salt and pepper. Where's the aluminum foil you bought? Can I borrow some?"

Happy pointed as he dumped on the different spices.

"Where's that beer you had?"

"What for?" Still he handed it to me.

Without replying I emptied the can over the seasoned meat. "Let them sit while we start the corn and potatoes."

"Good," Happy said. It was fairly clear he'd never seasoned a steak with anything but a sauce from a jar after it had been cooked.

I wrapped two ears of frozen corn in foil while Happy did the same with two large baking potatoes; then we placed them into the hot coals of a ready fire.

The rain had just cleared up, so the air still had a chilly sting to it. We hovered close to the warm grill and waited. My mouth was already watering; and to stop the craving, I snatched up one of Happy's beers. God, my mouth was watering.

Today's celebration would be nothing less than a feast. Neither of us had eaten red meat—other than the stuff in MREs that really didn't pass for meat though it was—for over two weeks. Hot dogs and soy burgers didn't count.

Looking at the seasoned meat in a beer batter, I could have almost eaten it raw. I was tempted to throw it on the grill just so I could hear it sizzling. But that would have defeated the purpose of our long-awaited feast. No, I had waited two weeks too long to taste a well-cooked meal to spoil it.

Popcorn hadn't come through for us yesterday, which was just as well. He would have brought back only steaks whereas we were just hungry enough as we walked down the commissary aisles to grab everything in sight that looked appealing—budgets allowing of course.

I rotated the corncobs and moved them back from the coals. My mouth began watering again. I sipped at the beer in my hand, which no longer had the appeal it had had yesterday or the day before. Happy absently listened to the news announcer's voice coming from the nearby TV.

There were a couple of guys sitting in the rec tent, but they weren't watching the news. They were reading magazines or rather looking at pictures that were in magazines. Smut as I called it. Such magazines had been surfacing in ever-increasing numbers over the past several days. We were, after all, guys.

Happy snatched up one of the more graphic of the group, and I couldn't help watching as he flipped through the pages. Sex is one of the most primal of human instincts and admiring pictures of beautiful naked women was as close to having sex as any of us would come for a long time. Except perhaps for Bad Boy who rather proudly admitted that he used his hand.

I rotated the corncobs again and checked the potatoes. Almost done. I slapped the steaks on and the sizzle broke Happy away from the latest issue of *Juggs*. He slapped on two cans of baked beans.

I plopped a spoonful of butter onto my colossal potato, painted the cob of corn with more of the same, added salt and pepper judiciously, then I was ready for my feast. Happy did likewise. And for a time as we dined, we thought we'd died and gone to heaven. I'd forgotten just how good steak tasted.

About halfway through the mound of food, I came up for a breather. "Is this living or what, Happy?"

Before he could reply, Cowboy lumbered out of his side of the PME. "Well, slap me silly," he said.

"The coals'll still be warm when you get back," I called out as I shoved in a mouthful. Cowboy knew I meant the commissary was still open. Not saying a word, Happy held up the bag of potatoes then turned back to his plate.

"There's corn too," I added.

Momentarily Cowboy disappeared into the barracks, then he was off at a gallop like a Texas race horse, wallet in hand and shoe laces untied, to the commissary two blocks up the street.

I watched him go but didn't stop eating. Soon there was nothing left but half a can of baked beans. Finishing it, I sat back and rubbed my full belly.

As Happy scoured his plate again, gnawing the corn cob perfectly clean, eating the remains of his potato, husk and all, and truly leaving only the well-picked steak bone, I leaned back, snatched up the latest copy of Penthouse and turned the pages. I was on top of the world.

Wednesday, 6 February 1991

I'd been there twenty days. You would think I would've stopped counting by then but I hadn't. It seemed both forever and an instant. Strange.

I kept Katie's picture under my pillow and I looked at it again and again so that I could remember her beautiful smile. It seemed that so much had happened; and truly, a lot had.

The weather was still bad but we were hoping we'd get airborne and not have another endless day. I was still gloating over that steak I had eaten. God, it was good!

There was a rumor flying around that we'd be moving to new quarters soon. I certainly wouldn't miss the old smelly sock of a room.

I went up to ops late the previous night. The big board said today's flight would be short. I really hoped so. Gentleman Bob kindly reemphasized President Bush's speech. "We're here for the long haul," he told us. I believed it.

The time between flights passed quickly, and before I knew it we were humming along at fifteen-thousand feet. When the Gray Lady began her gradual climb, I felt the cabin temperature slowly drop until the air was crisp and icy cool. The situation in the cockpit as we neared the "zone" was calm. The weather had cleared just enough so that after only a two-hour delay, we'd gotten airborne. I was glad. I'd much rather be pushing the zone than pushing a chair.

Today there'd be a time lag before the packages went in-country. Our boys would be coming in fast and low.

As we set up in our orbit and began to work the environment, one thing became strikingly clear—the Iraqis weren't expecting anyone to crash their party. The weather was nearly as poor as it had been the day before and they were taking advantage of it. I'd never seen so much enemy activity.

There was so much activity, in fact, that I punched off Private A so I didn't have to hear the endless target calls. I only pulled it out when I was going to make a call myself and needed to know if anyone else was passing a signal.

Both Tennessee Jim and Chris were having a heck of a time keeping the jamming list current.

For a moment I tuned into the intership radio chatter. "MCC, Nav, thirty mike to first wave ingress. How's it look back there?"

"Gypsy reported anything?"

"Negative, MCC. What you got?"

"Busier than I've ever seen it. There's definitely something going on under that cloud deck. Maybe it'd be a good idea to give them a heads up. What's the latest on weather over target?"

I turned my attention back to the signals filling my screen. Still, I listened in and waited for the response.

"Patchy, scattered clouds, vis is good for a green light."

"Roger."

"And I'll give them that heads up."

Tennessee Jim keyed his mike again, "Roger."

Tammy was in the rear today and I heard her call the pilot on Interphone. "Pilot, Spotter, AAA, four o'clock distant. Not a factor."

AAA already, and we weren't even jamming?

I'd sent over at least a dozen signals that were possible AAA communications channels. I glanced right. Chris had the MCC's jamming coordination list displayed on his screen and was paging through it. Over a hundred signals.

I tuned up a new signal. Voice. Definitely Arabic. As I listened, I pulled out Private A so I could make the target call.

I smiled. Definitely Iraqi. I keyed my microphone. "MCC, Six, target."

"Go ahead."

Just then the Nav spoke over us on another channel. "MCC, Nav, twenty mike."

Jim quickly switched over to Interphone, said, "Roger, Nav," then back to Private A. "Go ahead, Six."

I passed the target. "Another AAA net. No threat. You should see it coming across."

"I got it, Six."

As I punched off A, I heard some chatter on B. Happy was calling Cowboy, but Cowboy apparently wasn't listening.

"Seven, Two. Seven, Two. Cowboy, you there?" I nudged Cowboy who was in the seat to my left.

"Go ahead, Two."

"I have something you should look at. I'm sending it over. Sounds like an Iraqi tower controller, but this stuff's got to be Memorex. There's no way this is real."

I watched as Cowboy tuned up the new signal then turned

back to my displays, keying in on my spectrum analyzer. There was so much activity across the spectrum that it was almost impossible to tell which signals on the analyzer were new and which were old.

"MCC, Seven, imminent threat. Appears to be a very large formation of Iraqi fighter jets preparing to scramble from their bases."

"Seven, MCC, define very large."

"At least eight. Maybe ten. Sixteen or twenty if they're in pairs."

Jim keyed his mike but said nothing for a moment.

"If this is a joke, Seven, it's in poor taste."

"Sir, this is no joke."

"MCS, MCC."

"MCC, I'm already on radios to Gypsy."

"Pilot, MCC, threat situation."

"Go."

"Possible eight Iraqi fighters scrambling as we speak."

"Have you advised Gypsy?"

Before Jim could respond I heard Gypsy's reply. "Shadow, Gypsy, be advised, we have intermittent contact. Wait. Hold one, Shadow. Appears to be bogies; they're low, distant, could be helos or clutter. MiG Sweep's sucking fumes. They're going to refuel. I'll send in Paladin-3 and -4 for a closer look."

Chris relayed the information to Tennessee Jim.

"Seven, MCC, update. What do you have?"

"MCC, Seven, nothing now. I think one pair launched. Must've switched freqs."

"Crew, MCC, search. We can't let them get away."

I heard Paladin-3 and Paladin-4 acknowledge Gypsy's call,

and now they were headed in-country. No sooner had they sped off, afterburners roaring, than Gypsy called Paladin Leader. Shortly afterward, Paladin Leader and Paladin-2 chased after Paladin-3 and -4. With them went the remainder of our CAP. A two-ship was tied up with Gas Station and it'd be a pair of precious minutes before they'd be ready for action.

"Crew, MCC, you searching or drinking tea?"

"MCC, Nav, ten mike to package ingress."

"Roger."

There was obvious tension among the mission crew. We worked the environment and waited, hoping for the best. I focused my attention on my displays and CRT, while Gypsy directed the two formations of fighters. And, of course, I listened in to the off-ship radios.

"Gypsy, this is Paladin-3. There's nothing out here. You still have them on scope?"

"That's a negative, Paladin-3. What's Paladin Leader finding?"

"Gypsy, this is Paladin Leader, I've got empty air. What do you want me to do?"

"Paladin-3 and -4, assist Rebel's pair. Paladin Leader, come back in for cover."

"Roger, Gypsy," Paladin Leader paused, but left his mike keyed, "Paladin-3, you copy that?"

"I'm afterburners; wish us happy hunting."

"First wave of the package inbound in five mike," said Ice.

"MCC, Four, target."

"Go ahead, Four. Is it air?"

"You know it."

Bad Boy passed the target. As Tennessee Jim put the signal onto the jam list, he called Chris. "MCS, MCC, get us jam clearance. Pronto."

"MCC, MCS, Paladin Leader was just pulled back because they didn't find anything."

"Seven, MCC, you listening to this activity?"

Cowboy keyed his mike once. This meant yes. He was too busy to respond.

"This live?"

Cowboy keyed yes.

"MCS, MCC, they just aren't looking hard enough. Get jam clearance!"

We got clearance immediately and the MCC called out "Crew, MCC, we're jamming."

For a few terrible minutes as we keyed in to off-ship channels and continued to hunt down the ever-changing Iraqi channels, we were sure this was it. This was finally the big air confrontation we had been expecting.

Package ingress was less than five minutes away. Gypsy had just confirmed that a formation of Iraqi fighter jets was scrambling from two key Iraqi airfields. We had their comms channels targeted and were jamming them.

Right after we went into jam, Gypsy spotted additional fighters. I imagined a hornet's nest stirring up.

"Rebel-1, they're headed for Iranian airspace!" warned Gypsy. "Knock 'em out of the sky!"

"Pilot, Spotter, traffic low, headed inbound," said Tammy.

"Nav, MCC, you got that? Spotter's got inbound."

"Roger that, MCC, they're right on time."

"Pilot, MCC, we need more altitude to gain coverage."

We turned our corners sharp, trying to stay wings level and facing target as much as possible. Our thoughts went out to the guys chasing down the enemy fighters. We searched through the signal environment as fast as we could, trying to stay on top of new and changing signals.

I hugged my position close as the Captain, Sammy, brought the Lady through another sharp, swift turn—sweat was already dripping along the contours of my face. I worked through the turn, fighting gravity.

Rebel-1 and Rebel-2 had just caught up with the group of fighters attempting to flee to Iran. Paladin-3 and -4 were only seconds behind.

Rebel-1 keyed weapons.

"Locked on target," he said. I heard oxygen flowing through his mask. "Fire one!"

An explosion erupted as he broke off.

Rebel-2 was in hot pursuit while Paladin-3 and -4 engaged separate targets. All four American fighters were getting hazardously close to Iranian airspace. Gypsy advised that they should be prepared to break off, but they were so close.

An instant later Paladin-4 exclaimed, "Splash two!" He broke off hard left to avoid the debris.

"Splash two confirmed!"

"Rebel, be advised," Gypsy said, "you're approaching Iranian airspace!"

Rebel-2 was still in hot pursuit of his quarry and he wasn't about to break off just yet. Rebel-1 and Paladin's pair faithfully followed him.

He launched. "Fire one." Missed.

"Fire two!" he screamed.

The second missile clipped the enemy fighter's wing but didn't destroy it.

Gypsy called out a distance warning again but Rebel-2 didn't want to break off just yet. Rebel-1 was screaming, "Gypsy, position? Gypsy, position? What's that, you're breaking up?"

He wanted Rebel-2 to splash the Iraqi MiG and nothing else was going to satisfy him.

"Ten nautical miles inside Iraqi airspace."

"I got the bandit in my sights; he's mine." responded Rebel-2.

"Rebel-2. Rebel-2, this is Gypsy, turn back now!"

"Rebel-2, this is Paladin-3, we have to turn back. We'll get him another day!"

"Fire three!" shouted Rebel-2 as he grabbed the yoke and turned a hard one-eighty.

I held my breath and waited for confirmation of a kill, and waited, and waited. A few seconds seemed like forever. My heart was pumping so fast I thought I'd never come down from the high. The Lady would get two more assists for sure, but we wanted a third.

"No third splash," reported Rebel-1.

Suddenly everything seemed to become sedate. Now we could only wait for package egress. The chase would surely be the highlight of our day, yet it wasn't the final bit of action we'd see. Before long, Gypsy was directing Paladin Leader against the elusive ghosts that seemed to be popping up with increasing frequency.

For us, the next one hundred and twenty minutes dragged by. When package egress finally started, though, our hearts were racing once more.

We left orbit that day with a lot to think about. Some had flashbacks of home. Some thought about tomorrow and war's end that seemed so very distant. Others just reveled in the moment. The song that played out over ship's PA as we headed back was Rebel Yell by Billy Idol. It seemed rather appropriate.

We all wished Rebel-2 had gotten that last splash, but as Paladin-3 had said, there'd be another day.

Thursday, 7 February 1991

Another terrorist attack—an American worker at Incirlik airbase was gunned down by terrorists opposed to the Persian Gulf War. He was shot four times in the chest and stomach. The Dev Sol, a terrorist group, claimed responsibility. They'd been planting bombs all over Turkey. They had assassinated an adviser to the Prime Minister. Then an American worker. The question was, who's next?

A mortar shell was fired at No. 10 Downing Street. A few more feet, and they would've killed Britain's Prime Minister.

Although I knew that security around the base was tight, I couldn't help but wonder. I knew a lot of people were wondering what would happen next. Meanwhile, Saddam Hussein was calling for the Mother of all Battles.

I had a day off, and the unofficial word was that we were finally moving to different quarters. I really hoped so; everything I owned smelled like the pair of socks I wore yesterday.

The weather outside was warm and sunny. A lot of people were outside and I could hear music from a boom box.

Fabulous, the man of a thousand silk suits, was leaving. His retirement papers had finally come through. The orders had been held up for a couple of months. He was one very happy individual. He was on a plane headed for Germany in a couple of hours.

I knew I would miss Fabulous. I remember his telling me once that "One war is enough for any military career." He'd been in Nam, two tours. He'd been decorated in Nam. I was glad that he was going home. He'd served his time. Yet I could only wonder when the rest of us would be going home, too.

I joined the gang outside playing hacky sack; it sounded like they were having a good time. Happy had been going on and on about the Wagon Wheel, an enlisted club that played mostly country music, and something about a game of "Dead Bug." I thought I might find out what it was all about—and that's what I set out to do.

At dusk, a small group of crew dogs saddled up and made the long trek to Tennessee Jim's quarters across base. Happy, Cowboy, Bad Boy, and I found Jim and Chris already sauced. They'd been drinking since early afternoon. I didn't blame them; sometimes there was a lot you just wanted to forget. We were going to barbecue hot dogs and hamburgers.

The rest of the crew started showing up after a few minutes. Charlotte and Sandy tagged along with Sparrow and Tammy. Ice was the last to arrive.

We ate burgers and hot dogs until we were bloated then played several rounds of the name game. Our beer of choice for the evening was Michelob—it was Crow's favorite, and today was Crow's birthday. Happy and Cowboy had toted along a case of Michelob dark, and Tennessee Jim had a refrigerator chuck-full of Michelob light.

Burgers and beer were fine, but our ultimate destination was the Wagon Wheel where Crow was buying the first round for everyone who showed.

The skyline was totally dark and the stars were out in full when we staggered to the Wagon Wheel with Happy leading the way. Most of the other crewmembers had gone on ahead of us; a few of us had stayed to watch TV. Tennessee Jim had a VCR in his room, of all things! We were all a bit envious of his private room. We'd watched the first hour of Firefox, and then headed out.

The Wagon Wheel was crowded when we arrived. We had to push our way inside. It didn't take us long to find the group of crew dogs amidst the crowd; our guys and gals were the ones whooping and hollering near the bar. They'd commandeered a string of tables and set up camp.

As they spotted us, Crow and Bad Boy let out a whoop that rang in my ears. Crow had just ordered twenty-six tequilas and they were lined up on the table waiting. We were just in time. Lime in one hand, tequila in the other, we joined in.

"To Crow on his birthday!" we screamed.

The shot of tequila went down like a white-hot fuse.

"Another round," yelled Crow. "Barkeep, a round of tequilas!"

The Wagon Wheel didn't exactly have instant service. As a matter of fact, they didn't have table service at all. PBJ and Thomas made the alcohol run. Crow still paid—thirty-nine bucks for twenty-six tequilas.

When tequilas were lined up in front of us again, we shouted out, "To Crow on his birthday!" just before we downed the shots.

That white-hot fuse ran down my throat again, and I needed something other than a lime to quench it. I slipped around the table and asked, "What you drinking, Crow?"

"Bacardi and Coke, triple."

"Triple?" I asked. Crow wasn't normally a big drinker.

"Rum with a splash of coke!" Crow smiled.

I grinned and left to order a triple rum and coke and a six-pack. I returned just in time for the infamous game of Dead Bug. I'd hardly settled into my chair, when Happy screamed out, "DEAD BUG!" in a shrill voice.

The twenty-plus crew dogs seated around the long string of tables dropped to the floor on their backs, their legs and arms flailing. Around us, the music quieted and the cacophony of voices came to a halt. The onlookers were just as amazed as I was. It was right about then that I realized there must be a catch to this game, so I dropped down onto my back like the rest of my fellow crew dogs, arms and legs flailing.

A few moments later everyone got off the floor and sat back in their chairs as if nothing had happened. The discord of music and voices returned.

"Last one down buys," said Happy, patting me on the back.

"I didn't know the rules," I complained, but I bought the next round just the same: rules were rules. After I plopped down two twelve-packs of Bud on the center table, I cracked my first beer, drank it down about half way then screamed at the top of my lungs, "DEAD BUG!"

I was the first one to the floor this time and I'd discovered the secret of the game: if you call out before anyone else does, you're easily the first one to the floor. Still, the game was much more than that; it was zany fun, crew-dog style. No one stopped to think about how stupid we looked as we lay on the floor, arms and legs flailing, but then drinking games weren't meant to be intellectually stimulating.

I crawled back into my chair, turned to Happy and said proudly, "A bit slow to the floor, weren't we, Happy?"

Friday, 8 February 1991

This was a day of headlines. Most of the news was grim. I wondered what damage the heavy winter storm had done in Germany. And if Katie was all right.

I hoped to be able to call her, another five-minute morale call. I could use the Turkish public telephones at the base rec center, but the prices were exorbitant—around $14.00 for a little plastic phone card that would let me make one five-minute phone call to Germany.

The official word had come: we were moving to different quarters. I couldn't wait. The only bad thing was that we'd be flying when everyone else was making the move. We'd likely come back to find our belongings spread out on the ground at our new site. We were advised to pack our things before we went to fly.

That flight promised to be interesting, though. We were supposed to make sure we looked sharp. Sounded to me like they were expecting a "dog and pony" show.

Saturday, 9 February 1991

I had tried to talk to Katie on Friday, but the phone lines were tied up. I hoped to find some time to try again on Saturday. I missed her; I truly did.

I worried more about her than me. She was all alone there. I was the reason she was in Germany away from family and friends. I also knew how much she worried about me.

The only good thing about Friday's flight was that after it, we moved to new quarters. I spent Saturday morning helping to set up beds. They'd moved us into billeting quarters, of all places. The rooms were small, and we enlisted folks were crammed in three to a room. Still, I felt as if I'd moved into a luxury suite of a palace.

The rooms had heaters! There was a sink in the room with hot and cold running water. Two rooms shared a common bathroom, which sported a shower. No more walking three blocks to stand in line to take a shower and then find out there's no more hot water. We even had a television set.

With the heater cranked up, I got my first good night's sleep in over three weeks. No one woke me up in the middle of the night by mistake; no one turned on the lights over my bed; no one slammed the door; and neither Chris nor Cowboy snored loud enough to shake the walls. I felt like I'd just come home from Mars. There was only one problem—I was not really home.

It wasn't long before I was sitting in the briefing room once more, listening to Derrin.

"As you well know from the close call your crew had yesterday, there's been a significant increase in SAM activity from these regions," Derrin said. With his pointer, he drew several lines along the northern part of the map. "They're forming kill rings and it's going to be the mission of a group of F-111s to take them out. Another group will be going after POL storage areas, here and here."

Derrin paused to take a swig from a jug of water.

"Buffs will be striking this key airfield here." Derrin slapped the map hard with his pointer and wove the tip in a circle. "We took out most of the aircraft in hardened bunkers here yesterday. The Buffs will make sure they can't use the runway or facilities for a while. So far, the Iraqis have been pretty quick to make repairs. But this should slow them down a bit."

A lieutenant colonel stood to my right. He was with special operations. I noticed that Derrin's last remark brought a grin.

"AAA has been thick, so watch your distances carefully. That's about all I have for today. Have a safe flight." There was something about the way Derrin said safe that made me want to cringe.

I knew today's flight would be interesting. I also knew the special operations officer wasn't in the briefing for nothing. He'd be going up with us for sure.

The AC's brief was next. It was short and sweet and ended on the same note as always, a synchronization of watches.

"The time on my mark will be 16:02," said Captain Sammy. "Ready."

I double-checked my watch and prepared to adjust it if need be. The rest of the crew did the same.

"Mark, 16:02."

I reset my watch; it was a few seconds off.

After Tennessee Jim's final briefing, we settled down in the crew lounge. The TV was blaring. The USS Wisconsin was pulverizing the Iraqi coast with two-thousand-pound shells.

The special ops officer disappeared and we wouldn't see him again until we boarded the plane. He seemed unduly nervous for some reason; perhaps he knew something we didn't.

Briefly, I keyed into the news announcer's voice. He was talking about the gigantic oil slick in the Persian Gulf. Northerly winds had held it up for about a week, but now it was on the move again.

I was on my way to the head when Jim called out, "Time to saddle up, boys and girls! The van just pulled up; let's move it!"

By the time the Lady lifted off the runway, the sun was starting to set. With all the new activity in the area, Tennessee Jim directed a spotter aft right after takeoff. I'd have the watch until we turned on orbit, then Bad Boy would take over.

As I stared out the portside portal, clinging to the paratroop door, the special ops officer stared out the starboard portal. On the ground he had seemed unduly nervous; now he seemed akin to a caged tiger that wanted to be set free. As I looked down, I saw the air base grow smaller and smaller. Then for a time, as I looked on, we raced for the mountains; and the terrain beneath us was flat and clean.

Soon the snowcapped mountains were beneath us, extending

ever downward, jagged black rocks beneath white caps. And soon after that, the mountains were gone and I was left staring out into a rolling landscape that looked deceivingly serene.

The sun was just beginning to dip below the horizon, and slowly the land below turned black and lifeless. The temperature in the far aft was icy cold. I could see whispers of white when I exhaled. I slipped on nomex gloves and fitted my winter flight jacket over the top of my survival vest.

I waited for the land to become darker still, and then I reached for a pair of night-vision goggles and switched them on. The landscape below folded out in shades of green.

I heard Bill announce that we were coming on orbit and that ETA to first-wave ingress was twelve mike. The dark landscape sprang to sudden life. In the NVG, I watched tiny fiery green objects lift from the earth by the thousands. It seemed that someone had just turned on all the lights of a city; only I knew it wasn't a city, and those weren't lights from someone's kitchen. It was AAA.

"Pilot, Spotter, AAA's coming up all over the place!"

"Roger that, Spotter. We see it; they're giving us one hell of a light show tonight!"

We started to make a turn; I went to switch windows, and that's when I slammed into Bad Boy. I don't know how long he'd been standing behind me. His face was rather pale and his eyes were wide as saucers. I patted him on the back and handed him the NVG.

"Nice light show tonight!" I shouted above the roar of the engine. I unplugged my headset from the auxiliary cord and plugged Bad Boy up.

I walked forward into the mission compartment. I looked

back just once to see Bad Boy standing there still as could be, face pale and eyes wide. I knew right then that this was his first time as Spotter at night. There was a tremendous difference between the day and the night light show, for only at night did the closeness of the threat seem so very real; and it was only at night that you could see just how much of the horizon it filled. It was raining AAA everywhere, as far as the eye could see.

In short order, the first wave came in screaming, low to the deck. Bad Boy called out their ingress as Tennessee Jim slammed the system into jam. We'd reached our window.

Below us, I knew the Iraqi AAA and SAM sites had lost their communications channels just when they needed them the most. I knew this because I'd targeted most of them and was quite proud of that fact—I was having a good day.

The first wave of fighters raced in-country, while a second wave marshaled outside and below radar range.

I heard Gypsy squawking in the background, and a few seconds later we began precautionary evasive actions. Only this time we didn't dive, we climbed. Smoke trails had been seen by one of our CAP fighters—surface-to-air missiles had been launched. We had to gain altitude to save our necks.

For an instant, my eyes glazed over; and then I continued my search for new signals. I hoped the missiles had been fired blindly, and more importantly, not at us. Fighters could launch chaff and other countermeasures—we could only climb or dive. Yet I couldn't help noticing the ticking by of the seconds on the tiny clock in the corner of my screen. From the ground to our altitude by way of a missile was only a few seconds, no more. I waited. Nothing.

The second wave had finished marshaling and they started to

trickle in; the first wave had come in low. These boys were scraping treetops.

I continued to poke away at my keyboard and watch the displays. The next few minutes were critical. We had to make sure the enemy had no idea that second wave was coming in. They were less than a minute from the target area when the first wave kicked in afterburners and made crisp ninety-degree turns. And then both waves were converging on the same area, hell bent on total destruction.

So far, everything seemed to be going according to plan, for which we were all glad. I knew when the packages began their strike because suddenly everything I was watching sprang to life. Now, we'd have to work extra hard to make sure the packages made it out safely. With so many aircraft in-country it wouldn't be an easy task, but we aimed to do it.

The minutes that followed were, as always, extremely tense. We knew the time the first fighter was due to head out; still, our breaths stifled with anticipation when the radios keyed.

Tennessee Jim keyed in on Private. "Stay at it; it's almost over!"

True to form, we stayed at it just a few more minutes. Soon we'd be heading back to base and it would all be over. Then I heard words from the copilot that I'd relive in solitary moments late at night, "Smoke trail, one o'clock!"

Captain Sammy came up on Ship's Hot and screamed into his mike, "Crew beginning evasive maneuvers!"

There was a heart-sized lump in my throat. My heart pounded in my ears. A few seconds later, I heard Gypsy advise that we move to the back of our orbit box. We did, no questions asked. Captain Sammy brought the Lady around hard. Gravity thrust me into my chair, my neck tensed under the strain, my arms, lead weights, wouldn't move.

Moments earlier we had been played-out and more than ready for the end of the mission. Now we just wanted to feel the Lady level off; for if she did, hopefully it meant the sky was clear.

The wing dipped, my head bobbed, my stomach churned. Then suddenly I was slipping out of my seat as gravity reversed—we were falling or so it seemed. Immediately afterward, everything became smooth, as if we were floating. I noticed then that I could move my arms, and everything had stopped jumping—we had finally leveled off.

Yet we were given no breathing space because just then the egress began. We tallied the outgoing fighters one by precious one. Gypsy was squawking, and in the background I heard Phantom. It seemed like it'd been a while since I'd heard good old Phantom, our friends on the RC. But then again, this last week had been so hellish that maybe I had lost their squawk in the frenzy of it all.

There were no better words to hear than Gypsy's final confirmation. "The packages have safely egressed and are headed back to base! Shadow, you're cleared off stations!"

"Roger, Gypsy, we're coming around and going back to base."

The crew's cheer echoed throughout the whole of the Lady, but privately we also sighed.

My blood pressure slowly returned to normal. Soon I could no longer hear the dull thump-thump of my heart in my ears. With it went the surge of adrenaline that had sustained me for the last few hours, and weariness swept over me like a storm. I closed my eyes and momentarily let my thoughts take me.

Outbound pilots reported to Gypsy that they'd never seen the AAA so thick and that there was plenty of new SAM activity in the area—things we knew firsthand. In the coming days those nests would have to be targeted and destroyed or they'd start doing serious damage.

Someone walked by my position, and I opened my eyes long enough to see that it was our visitor. I was sure he had seen quite a bit more than he bargained for. For a moment in my mind's eye I saw Bad Boy's face, his eyes wide, his expression something that wasn't so much awe as shock.

I knew a day was coming when we'd be closer still, a day when we'd be jamming the eye of the storm. The flack would be so close it would seem as if I could reach out and grab it, just as it could reach out and grab us.

Morning,
Monday, 11 February 1991

Saturday's night flight spilled over into Sunday and I got back to the barracks early Sunday morning. Mehmet, a Turkish gentleman who took care of our building, had a surprise for us Sunday, a home-cooked meal. He served up a steaming plate of roast chicken, potatoes and onions, and several loaves of fresh-baked hard bread. It was certainly the best food I'd eaten in a long while, and it made my duty a little warmer and brighter.

Also, I realized something that a few others seemed to realize just then—the Turkish people were really grateful that we were there doing what we are doing. I had had apprehensions about the Turks because of the initial unrest when NATO forces began arriving, but those soon evaporated.

We were settling into our new quarters. Everything seemed promising. It's surprising how much the new quarters had changed people's attitudes. There was renewed excitement even among the habitual mopers. I was confident that in a few days, everyone would have forgotten the PME except me. I wanted to remember it, so I could truly know how fortunate we all were when we finally got to go home.

I was supposed to start mission planning cell the next day, so Monday's morning flight should be my last for at least eight days. I could really use the break; twelve-hour days and a set routine would seem a breeze compared to flying a mission in the combat zone and ever changing schedules. Yet I wasn't sure things would be the same if I were not flying.

I've saved the best news for last. Late Sunday night I finally got a chance to talk to Katie. She sounded worried and sweet. The phone call went much better than last time. And yes, I told her I loved her several times.

She told me she sent me a Valentine's day surprise. I felt bad; I'd forgotten all about Valentine's day. I looked at the Base Exchange for a card, but they were all sold out. So I made a valentine of my own—a hundred hand-drawn hearts and then a hundred more—I hoped Katie would get it by Thursday.

Katie's picture sat on the nightstand beside my bed. In it she was wearing a ruffled red dress pulled loosely about the shoulders. I had taken that picture on Christmas eve.

I had gotten another voice tape from her a few days previously. I now had four. I'd grown accustomed to putting on headphones and going to sleep to the sound of her voice. She always mixed in a few of our favorite songs and she would sing the words in the background—she has such a beautiful voice.

Katie told me that she had called my mother. I still hadn't told Mom I was in the Gulf. Mom took the news hard. She and Katie talked for more than an hour.

Mom said she had known something was wrong when I called the night before the war, but she hadn't known what. Katie gave her my address, and she said she would write.

I'm not sure why I hadn't written her yet. I suppose it was because I didn't want her to worry. I had tried to start a letter several times. It was just that nothing sounded right. And mom isn't the sort of person who takes this kind of news easily.

Tuesday, 12 February 1991

Monday's early morning Go went well, and I was home by early afternoon. I was supposed to start MPC on Tuesday; but as they hadn't pulled me yet, I would be flying again today. Tennessee Jim asked if I'd mind flying again. I told him straight up, "Wouldn't miss it for the world!"

Since the gym was so close, I no longer had an excuse to skip workouts. After almost four weeks without hitting the weights, I felt like Silly Putty. I was sore as hell, and every inch of my body ached. But I determined to go again the next day without giving the pain a second thought. I'm no monster, but as I gradually worked my way up to 275 on the bench, I felt good! When you can't have sex, you might as well hit the weights; you have to vent aggression somewhere, and a good workout takes my mind off other things.

I was pleased when the day's flight went smoothly as well. The Gray Lady touched down just as dusk covered the Turkish landscape. As I and ten other tired souls piled out the crew entrance door, a westerly wind was blowing strong across the runway and as it raced to the mountains across the flat land it took with it what remained of the day's warmth. The crew van still hadn't arrived, but it wasn't all that unusual to wait fifteen to thirty minutes for it to pull up.

I used my A-bags as a seat and sat down for the long wait. Soon the sky overhead was black as coal. Crow and Patrick had already finished up their postflight checks, which included the final powering down and sealing of the plane, and joined us on the tarmac. It'd been a long day and a long flight. We'd had problems with the system the entire time. It'd been up and down so many times I'd lost count. Oddly, when it had mattered most, the Lady's systems had purred; and we were thankful for that much.

Tennessee Jim glanced at his watch and cussed loudly under his breath. Forty-five minutes had passed.

Patrick was about to break the seals and head back into the plane when a pair of headlights approached along the darkened runway. I stood and stretched, then picked up my bags.

"What the hell took you so long?" screamed Jim as we piled into the back of the van. "Click up the rear heaters; we're freezing!"

"I was supposed to get off at 18:00," said Charlotte.

"Boo-hoo!" responded Ice. "We could have been back in the barracks by now ourselves."

"Who's your replacement?" asked Captain Sammy.

Charlotte didn't respond, she just cast her eyes toward the rear of the cabin and then put the van into drive.

We'd already missed most of the post-brief with the other players, so we headed straight for ops. Captain Sammy was nice enough to give us his postflight briefing in the back of the van. "Good job today," he said, and that was about it.

At ops, we had only to turn in our additional gear, which included our .38s and bullets, then check in with intel. I was headed out the door and back to the van when I heard someone calling my name. I turned about on my heel, and saw trouble: Major James standing next to Tennessee Jim.

I started toward them. Charlotte handed me the crew van keys. "Sorry," she said in a subdued, yet relieved tone.

"We need you to work MPC this evening," Major James said, "You have any problems with that?"

I looked Tennessee square in the eye. He knew I was pissed, but I knew better than to complain. "No, not really."

"Good," Major James said, "you weren't supposed to fly today, but it seems there was a mix-up. You were supposed to be on the night crew this evening, and the person you're replacing is already in crew rest to fly. When you come back from dropping off the crew, see the duty officer. I'll explain the situation to him. I'm sure after the next line comes back, you'll be able to go get some rest."

Major James paused then added, "And thanks."

"No problem, sir," I called back, and then, keys in hand, I headed to the van.

I dropped part of the crew off at the new quarters, and then dropped everyone but Charlotte off at their quarters. Charlotte was in the main billeting building; so after she gave me directions, I headed off.

"Sorry," she said again when I dropped her off.

"Hey, it's not your fault," I replied, then sped off.

As directed, I checked in with the duty officer first thing. He gave me a list of names: people I needed to alert for the next Go. In a few minutes, I'd have to head out; but before that, I took a moment to catch my breath. My head was still spinning from the flight, and the adrenaline pump I'd felt during the flight was completely gone.

Almost everyone on the list was in the new quarters, so I stopped there first. On the way, I went by my room to grab something to eat. Cowboy and Chris were already asleep.

The next couple of hours went by quickly. An hour after alerting the crew, I had to go back and pick everyone up. A few hours later I had to drive them out to the plane, and in between I had a number of other things to do. I found out Ray, my office chief from Sembach, was temporarily working the night shift also. He showed me the ropes.

It was after 06:00 the next morning before I finally got to get some sleep—nothing like working a twelve-hour night after a twelve-hour day. By the time I reached my room, I could've slept standing up. Even so, upon reflection, had I the chance to do it again, I still would've flown. Who knows, maybe I was on that flight for a reason; if I hadn't been there, things could have gone differently.

Wednesday, 13 February 1991

It was 17:45 when Charlotte pulled up in front of the barracks. I was waiting outside and she tossed me the keys. She had alerted Captain Hillman's crew nearly an hour ago. By the time I dropped her off at the main billeting quarters, where I picked up Candid the crew's copilot; Karen, aka Mellow Yellow; and Sandy, part of the mission crew, and then returned to the new quarters, everyone else was waiting to head down to ops.

I checked off the names on my list as the remainder of the crew boarded: Rollin, the AMT; Darwin, the Eng; Captain Hillman, the Pilot; Beebop, the Nav; Stopwatch, the MCC; and the rest of the mission crew: Topper, Able, Max, Tommy, and Steve.

I was sure glad I wasn't on this crew. They looked downright glum. It was most likely due to Stopwatch's presence. He was a definite anal-retentive SOB. He was the type of person that made flying a miserable chore just because he was in a sour mood. And since it was fairly safe to say he hadn't gotten laid in the past four weeks unless it was by Madam and her five queens, he was surely in a fire-pissing mood.

The drive to ops went quickly. "Cheer up!" I told Tommy and Able as they piled out of the van. "Things could be worse; you could find out you have to work MPC after flying all day."

The ops center was quiet when I entered. The duty officer was playing Tetris on a Gameboy. He didn't even look up when I put the keys to the van on the key rack.

"Get with Ray," he said when I was about to sit down. "He'll show you how to break out the ATO for tomorrow's lines."

I shot him a hard glance. I was still a little bitter about having to work twelve full hours yesterday after a flight. He didn't even see it. He was still playing Tetris. I asked, "Where is he?"

"Lounge, I'd expect."

I glanced at the big board. "There's a preflight crew that has to go out to the plane in thirty."

"Well, you got thirty minutes, don't you?"

I left the room and found Ray in the lounge quickly afterward. He was watching CNN. "You want to help me break out the ATO?" I asked.

"Relax," Ray said, "we got all evening."

"The LT said—"

"Sisco's got some problems back home; just stay out of his way. Take a break when you can get it. Daytime MPC's hell sometimes. No reason night MPC should be unless you want it that way."

He'd just shown me how to wind my gears down from the high intensity and high anxiety of flying to a low gear and a calmer pace. "Hey, thanks, Ray. That's good advice."

"That's what I'm here for."

I sat down and tried to relax. The couch against my backside felt good when I wasn't all tensed up waiting to go fly.

Thirty minutes sped by and soon it was time to take the Eng and the AMT out to the plane for preflight. Rollin and Darwin gave me a better flight line orientation than I'd gotten yesterday; riding in the back was different from riding up front.

When I returned, Ray and I broke out the Air Tasking Orders for the next day's lines. The tasking orders contained the pertinent information for the flights, including the packages they'd be supporting. They were highly accountable items and they never left the ops center. After we finished with the ATO, we updated the mission plans, the files, and the big board.

"That's the routine," Ray said. "On MPC you drive and you plan; and if we're lucky, Sisco there'll let one of us go early."

Sisco looked up from his Gameboy briefly and smirked. I frowned.

It was time to take Captain Hillman's crew out to the plane, so I ambled to the lounge and yelled, "Time to saddle up, boys and girls!"

The emotions I felt as I drove up in front of the Lady were different than usual. I wasn't all charged up, but I desperately wanted to go. Instinctively, I put the van in park, dropped the keys into my pocket, and prepared to head out, but then I remembered I was the driver today and not the flyer.

I watched the crew go while I stayed; and as an afterthought, I yelled after them, "Have a good flight. I'll be here to pick you up when you return."

Valentine's Day, Thursday, 14 February 1991

I used to love holidays, Christmas and New Year's Eve, and those special days like Valentine's Day. I'd wait for their approach, just as I had when I was a small boy. There was always a special splash of magic in a holiday. But all the magic was gone.

The sun hadn't even begun its slow descent in the western sky when I started the short trek to ops. Several companies of Turkish troops were marching along the side of the road. I regarded them as they passed, and they me. They eyed my flight suit the same way I eyed the weapons they shouldered. I was fairly resolved that this evening's shift would eke by counted by seconds, minutes and hours until morning arrived. I carried with me a flight bag containing supper, lunch, and breakfast, and a manual can opener to open it all.

Thursday had been an interesting day. I'd slept through most of it. I'd slept eight hours and was still tired. Suddenly flopping to straight nights was hell on my already-traumatized system. I still made it to the gym today, squashing my quadriceps so many times that my legs felt like lead weights. I needed the slow amble to stretch out more than I knew.

The Turkish troops were gone now. I was alone, or at least I felt alone. When military vehicles weren't driving by on the long straight road, it was so quiet I could hear my breath, the sound of stones beneath my feet, and the chirping of birds. Everything seemed calm and serene, almost as if I were not a part of the war effort anymore. As I walked, I imagined that it was out there somewhere beyond the mountains and that for a few more days it wasn't going to touch me. Five more days like this was something to look forward to.

The shift began as the previous two had. I checked when the lines would go, wrote out the lists of whom I needed to pick up when, broke out what remained of the air tasking orders—the day shift had already started them. Popcorn and Ray arrived at the top of the hour. Sisco had also been early. He was already waging his private war against Gameboy and Tetris.

No crews needed to be picked up or alerted until 19:45, and as I'd already finished up the mission plans, there wasn't much else to do but sit back and relax. I thought it was a good time to make supper, and so I did. I cracked open a can of refried beans, plopped them onto a paper plate, then opened a can of cream style corn and poured it on top—a gourmet dinner, as usual. I had a few wieners left from yesterday that I'd put in the fridge, so I stuck them deep into the goo. Five minutes in the microwave and it would all come out steaming.

When the microwave dinged, I was ready to eat. I went to work shoveling food into my mouth spoonful by gooey spoonful while staring at the TV. We didn't have much selection on channels. It was either CNN or AFN. CNN was usually on at ops. The big news of the day was still the Baghdad shelter that had been bombed yesterday. There was also a small bit on the burning oilfields in Kuwait that were mucking up the skies over the battlefield. An estimated fifty fields were churning up black smoke.

Eventually, 19:45 arrived. I looked at Popcorn. He didn't look like he was going to move from his relaxed crouch in front of the TV for another five or six hours. I was itching to do something anyway, so I made the run. With a hint of rain in it, the evening air was fresh and rather invigorating. I swept through the barracks rather quickly, alerting ten of the twelve crewers in about fifteen minutes. All the while I did this, the smell of barbecue chicken and beer assaulted my nostrils; a group of crew dogs were having a little get together. I carried that scent of chicken and beer along with me back to ops. Having eaten or not, I still wished I could join in.

When I returned to ops, Popcorn was already trying to talk Sisco into letting him go early. That was Popcorn. "It'll be a slow night. You don't need all of us here."

"I know what you're driving at; I'm not sure I should let you go again, Popcorn."

"He's probably right," I added, putting the van keys back in their place, "it does look to be a slow night."

"All right, all right," Sisco finally said, "you two decide which one of you goes and which stays."

Popcorn pulled a quarter out of his pocket, "Heads or tails?"

I stared Popcorn dead in the eye. He stared back unwaveringly. He had no idea that anyone other than him deserved some relief time. That was Popcorn, always thinking of himself first. "Ah hell, take off. I don't mind staying. Isn't tonight your last night anyway?"

"That's what they keep telling me." Popcorn paused, then repeated what he'd just said, "That's what they keep telling me."

Popcorn stood there a moment eyeing me. "You going to give me a ride back to the barracks or what?"

"Legs broke?"

"Naw, just lazy," he replied.

"I knew that," I said, grabbing the key ring again. When I dropped him off, I just stayed at the barracks. I saw no point in driving back to ops and then returning fifteen minutes later. The smell of chicken and beer drew me to the patio. I was itching to join in, and that's when Tommy found me.

"Have a beer!" he screamed out, seeing me in my flight suit looking like I'd just returned from a flight.

"Can't man, MPC."

"Have one anyway," said Cosmo, who'd just come up behind me.

I glanced at him. His nose and cheeks were rosy red, and his eyes weren't focusing properly. Drunk, Cosmo looked calm as can be.

"No, really I can't, I'm waiting to drive a crew to ops."

"Which crew?" cut in Tommy.

"Three, I think."

"Captain Gandis is the AC? She's a fox. Man, what I wouldn't give for a piece of."

"Wait a minute. You're on Hillman's crew aren't you?"

"Yeah."

"Didn't Able tell you that you're flying? He told me you were in the shower when I came to alert you guys."

"I was. Guess that means I can't finish this beer. Good thing it's my first."

He handed the mostly full bottle to Cosmo and raced into the barracks.

"When you see Able thank him for me, will you?" I screamed after him.

I turned back to Cosmo. "You know your alert time for tomorrow, yet?"

"No, is it an O'dark thirty again?"

"How'd you guess? 03:00 alert, sorry."

Cosmo got that look in his eyes again. "Thanks," he said as he ambled off.

I waited a few more minutes for the crew to start making their way out to the van, then checked their names off as they boarded.

Ops was indeed quiet when I returned. Three hours later, I took the crew out to the Lady and longingly watched them go. "Have a good flight," I shouted after the retreating forms, "I'll be here when you get back!"

It was nearly midnight when I pulled back up in front of ops, and inside the ops center, Sisco wasn't fiddling with Gameboy anymore. We had company. Major James had arrived about five minutes before I had returned; but Sisco was safe, the major wasn't looking for an AC.

"I need you to do something for me," said the major, putting his hand on my shoulder and looking me in the eye. "What I'm about to tell you stays between these four walls. And it's not definite yet by any means." He paused and I looked at him expectantly.

"Who's down there in intel?"

"I don't think anyone is now," I replied, "Derrin's probably asleep, and I don't know where the lieutenant is."

"Well, here's the scoop. There's a major initiative tomorrow, and we need to be able to support packages striking Baghdad."

"Baghdad?" I replied, even though I already knew what he meant by the statement; but I wasn't quite sure that it equated to the start of the ground war.

"Yes, it'll free up forces to start hitting the front lines even harder. They're going to go after troop concentrations and the Republican Guard hard. If we get the green light, we're going to be giving them everything we got tomorrow, and then some. Find Derrin or the lieutenant, and I'll outline the mission on the map. I suppose you know this means some re-planning."

Now I knew what he meant; the ground war wasn't going to kick off, but they were getting ready for it, or so it seemed. "I'm not doing anything else, and a little more planning won't bother me at all."

I didn't find Derrin, but I found the lieutenant. He'd been catching some shuteye, but he snapped awake when I quietly explained that the major wanted to see him. The lieutenant was a tall, lanky guy that we called Elmer Fudd. Not because he looked like him, but because he could mimic the voice fairly well.

Major James outlined the plans and where we'd be flying on the big map. I drew the lines in with an erasable marker. The front edge of the box was right on top of a group of AAA sites.

"See," Major James began, "that's why I need you two to head over to the tactical division and see exactly where the threats are currently located. I'll be here when you get back. We can finish up. You have your badges, don't you?"

"Wouldn't leave home without it," I replied, "wouldn't leave home without it."

I grabbed the van keys, and then the Lieutenant and I drove over to where the TAC guys were. We gave our badges to the armed sentries and they looked them over, asked for our military identification cards, and then waved us through. Neither the lieutenant nor I was sure how much we were to say to anyone about the mission, so we started out cautiously reviewing their current intelligence reports and read files. Then we turned to the Map—I outlined the orbit box with my finger.

"Can I help you?" asked a woman clad in BDUs.

I turned to the lieutenant, and he just sort of looked at me. I was sure they already knew about the mission since that was, in a sense, their job; but neither of us was sure of the level of distribution on this sort of thing. Finally, I admitted, "We're flying a mission into Iraq tomorrow. We were just double-checking the current threat environment."

I saw a number of eyes rise from the planning table and heads turn. The lieutenant was wearing a BDU uniform also and so the not-so-subtle stares were directed at me in my flight suit. Mostly I think they were expecting to see bars on my shoulders, but I had no bars, and the blue-trimmed hat in my pocket somewhat gave me away as enlisted. Right then, I sure wished I was going on the mission, but when I had said we, I meant the unit.

The woman I was speaking to had six stripes below her shoulders. She was a technical sergeant. She looked at my flight suit and then the clipped on badge. She knew I was enlisted too and suddenly she seemed more interested in me. "What you flying on?"

"EC."

Her eyes lit up. "Show me where the orbit'll be, and let me see if I can help you."

I outlined the orbit area on the map again, and she gave me a rundown of the immediate threats. While she talked, I took careful notes.

"Good luck," she later whispered after us.

"Thanks," I told her, "I think we'll need it."

Afterward, we took another look at the intelligence logs. I took some more notes. The Lieutenant collected our unit's classified dispatches from the distro pile. Then we departed.

Back at ops, Major James was eagerly awaiting our return. We held the briefing in the intel room, going over the details with a fine-toothed comb. I had my list of notes, but as I began to explain the threat situation, I recounted it mostly from memory. I'd always had a knack for numbers.

The Lieutenant and I were finishing up; I'd said my adieu and was just about to leave the room when Major James turned to me. "How'd you like to be on that mission tomorrow?"

"You kidding?"

"No. You've done a good job tonight; you deserve to be there more than anyone else. Besides, we could use an extra spotter."

I smiled and replied, "Wouldn't miss it for the world; wouldn't miss it for the world!"

"Good, that's what I was hoping you'd say." Major James looked at his watch. "It's 03:15; you're in crew rest. Go back, get some sleep. It'll be a long one tomorrow."

Friday, 15 February 1991

I awoke to the sound of screaming voices and loud music. The room Cowboy, Chris and I shared was directly across from the day room, and the noise was coming from there. Sleepily, I stuck my head out the door, not even realizing I wasn't wearing anything but a pair of jockey shorts. The room was crowded with crewers, guys and gals, and they were celebrating something.

"What's going on?" I asked a passerby.

"Iraq said they'd withdraw from Kuwait!"

"No shit?"

"No shit."

I staggered back into the room and sat down. I stared into the mirror across from the bed. My eyes said I was still exhausted. And I was. I clicked on the TV, and then lay back on the bed. I listened to the news, waiting to hear what had actually transpired, and somewhere along the course, I fell asleep.

I didn't awake until hours later, and by that time, no one was celebrating anymore. The situation had changed. Iraq had attached so many conditions to the offer that it was little more than a cruel hoax. I quickly found that cynicism had replaced enthusiasm, but I had to push all this out of my mind and prepare for what was potentially the most dangerous mission to date.

The alert came later than I had expected, and by the time Popcorn alerted me, I was pacing like a caged animal. I couldn't tell anyone what I knew, so I had said nothing and stayed mostly in my room. I wasn't surprised to find that the front-end had been alerted an hour before the mission crew or that Gentleman Bob would be flying the plane.

Everything was smooth sailing until we entered intel for our preflight briefing. I watched faces full of life and color, faces that had been lit up with smiles, turn pale and then grow ashen. The small briefing room had been filled with voices, but now it was absolutely silent. An overwhelming measure of unknown had returned. The unknown that had been there that very first day and those first few flights. Here I held an advantage; I knew what we'd face out there, but I didn't know exactly what to expect. You can never know exactly what to expect.

Derrin gave the brief, but after he'd finished, I added a few notes. I had, after all, helped plan the mission, and I knew its every facet.

As the AC, Gentleman Bob gave his brief next, and it wasn't a normal preflight brief. "Gentlemen and Ladies, you heard the briefer; this is a combat flight into enemy territory, genuine O-1 time for those of you who care. I'm not going to kid you about the possible dangers; you just heard what we're facing and what our mission is. I want everyone looking sharp and staying alert! If you feel drained or tired, this is not the time to be sleeping out there! Go see the med techs; they can give you something.

"We'll brief emergency procedures here and on the plane. If anything happens out there, I want you to be prepared for it. As

Derrin here said, today's the day to update your SAR cards if you haven't. We're going to review some stuff; and I don't mean to upset anyone, but the danger is more real than ever. In case of emergency, you know the alarm bells for emergencies. Prepare for bailout is three short, followed by one long bell for execution. Crash landing is six short for preparations, and one long to brace for impact. In the event we have to ditch the aircraft, we will try our damnedest not to put the plane down in enemy territory, but in the event this happens, we basically have only two options. Look at the map and you'll know what they are.

"Again, I don't anticipate this happening, but we need to be prepared, each and every one of us. You can't count on your buddy, only on yourself out there. On the plane, review your checklist for emergency equipment destruction; know where you're sitting and what your tasks are.

"Our two spotters, who are they going to be?"

Stopwatch pointed at Able and me.

"I want crisp clear calls out there. You see something, anything, including ground fire, I want to know the position of it, and if it's a threat.

"And a friendly reminder about things you already know, but may have become lax in doing. Ensure you sanitize: that means combat wallets. You're not going to need your credit cards out there. If you've got that shit back in your wallets, then pull your finger out of your ass; this thing's a long way from over. You know what should be in your pockets and what shouldn't be. Those unnecessary items could be used against you.

"Do not, and I repeat, do not leave this room today without signing out blood chits and evasion maps. And .38s will be loaded today. I know some crews don't load 'em, but it'd be a good idea today. Check the chutes in your seat good; and if you're at your position, I want you strapped in. That's it, and remember, I want two hundred percent out there, not one hundred percent, because that's not going to cut it! I'm counting on you, so don't let me down!"

Stopwatch gave his brief next. We took a closer than normal look at the packages we'd be supporting. Stopwatch was visibly tense but also excited. He kept repeating himself and he said several times, "All the way to Baghdad."

I noticed right then that he was definitely a different guy than the anal-retentive SOB that had left Germany. I just couldn't help wondering if he'd changed for the better or for the worse.

The mood in the crew lounge as we waited to go was extremely tense. Both Able and Tommy were surprisingly quiet.

I was surprised when Steve sat down beside me. He was the mission crew supervisor, and he wasn't much on casual conversation. "We've thought it over, and we want you in the seat."

I wasn't quite sure who he meant by we, but I'd signed on to spot and that's what I aimed to do. "No, I'd prefer a seat with a view. I don't want to kick someone out of their seat. I'm not part of your crew."

"I don't think anyone would mind," countered Stopwatch, joining in.

"No, I'm an extra. It wouldn't be right."

"Well, maybe tomorrow then."

"Tomorrow?"

"The word is that you're flying with us until further notice."

"What about MPC?"

"I guess they'll have to be short or find someone to replace you."

I didn't complain, and when I was riding out to the flight line later I smiled. This is what it was all about.

This night, we had an unusually large crew, sixteen in all, and we clambered up into the belly of the Lady as quickly as possible. I strolled along the narrow aisle past position six, touching a hand to the headrest, to the rear bunk in the stark darkness. I fitted my chute, performed my checks, and was up on headset before the interior lights were raised to a cheerless white.

I watched the others go about their checks and heard them check in one by one. They certainly didn't seem a happy bunch, and Stopwatch already seemed to be riding them unnecessarily hard.

"Three, you're taking too damn long fitting that chute!" he complained. "Two and Four get the hell off Private if you're going to chatter."

"MCS, MCC, checks complete yet?"

"Crew, you know by now that after you complete checks I want you strapped in and facing forward. Gloves on, ready to go. Checks complete, MCC.

"Three, get in your seat!"

Rollin, who'd just pulled the chocks, rolled his eyes as he passed me.

I stretched out on the bunk and listened to the engines wind up. Gentleman Bob checked forward and reverse thrust, and then the Lady began the crawl to the hold line where we'd wait for Tower's final takeoff clearance.

"Cleared for takeoff, EC-130," called out Tower Control at last.

"Roger that, Tower," confirmed Gentleman Bob.

As we began to roll along the runway building up speed, I thought about what was ahead. I started rationalizing and downplaying the situation. What was there to worry about? We'd surely have ample support out there. Gypsy would be providing the air picture and threat calls. Phantom would be there. The Combat Air Patrol team was, as always, top notch. We'd have a two-ship of dedicated HVAA CAP, and four other F-15s would form the MiG Sweep and Alpha CAP.

As we leveled out, I readied the NVG and checked them out. Stopwatch was screaming at Three again, and I tried to tune him out as I stared out the window.

"Is Stopwatch always like this?" I asked Able as he joined me.

"Usually, but you should see some of the stuff that goes on. Three is asking for it. Watch her; you'll see what I mean." He spoke aloud over the roar of the engines as I had.

"Where is she?"

"Up in the cockpit. Probably batting her eyelashes at the AC. She's a prick tease; just stay away from her."

I looked up into the cabin. The lights were combat red. Stopwatch was clearing everyone into the system.

Able tapped me on the shoulder. "He's really not that bad anymore. A lot mellower than when we first got here."

Able and I began our vigil out the windows.

"Crew, attention to brief!" called out Gentleman Bob, "We're going to review emergency procedures one more time, but I'll make it quick."

I keyed into my headset as Bob ran through the spiel, and soon the snowcapped mountains were below us.

A short while later, Beebop's voice tweaked into my headset. "MCC, Nav, ten minutes till we enter the sensitive area."

"Roger, Nav, we're green back here so far. You set in Gypsy's squawk?"

"You're good to go."

"Roger."

"MCS, MCC, see if you can raise Gypsy."

"MCC, already trying."

"Spotters, Pilot, look alive back there!"

I didn't hear Steve calling Gypsy, so I double-checked my switches.

"MCC, MCS, Gypsy's having some minor problems; they say they'll be cleared up in a few."

"Roger, you got Phantom yet?"

"Phantom's not up."

"When they coming up?"

"Check the plan; they aren't."

"Shit, MCS, you're right; there it is right in front of me. Sorry."

I glanced at my watch. Five minutes remaining before we entered the sensitive area.

"MCC, Pilot, how's the picture look?"

"Pilot, we're green, and Gypsy's up. First packages should arrive on schedule."

There was a slight pause. "MCC, Pilot, do we have the go-ahead?"

"We have the green light!"

"Roger, MCC."

The radios began to fill with chatter. It was clear the anxiety level had just doubled again.

"Nav, Pilot, ETA to border cross?"

"Five mike."

"Spotters, you see anything back there, remember, I want to hear about it."

I pressed the NVG closer to my face.

"Remember, crew, we're vulnerable out here. And goddammit, I want nothing less than two-hundred percent when the packages start to ingress!"

I heard Steve calling Gypsy again. "The zone is clear!"

"Pilot, Nav, one mike till border crossing."

"This is it, crew!"

I spotted a thin trail of light spreading upward. It gradually grew thicker, and then I saw aerial explosions. The enemy gunners must've heard our engines. "Pilot, Spotter, AAA coming up, ten o'clock."

"Roger, Spotter, got it."

"Pilot, Nav, border crossing in five—four—three—two—one!"

"Crew, we're headed in-country!" announced Gentleman Bob, and right then, the pucker factor jumped off the scale.

"Pilot, Spotter, AAA bursts from two-thirty," cried out Able.

"Roger, Spotter."

The heavy trail of anti-aircraft artillery I was monitoring became more dominant as we approached. In a slow trickle, other sites joined in. I saw trails of fire rising into the sky in a long line in front of us.

Gypsy was having problems again, and temporarily they couldn't provide us with support again. Things didn't look good. A shiver ran down my spine as I thought about this. We had dedicated CAP, but without Gypsy directing them.

Briefly, I thought about the package we were supporting. The radar jammers would roll in at about the time we kicked in our jammers, and then the first wave would begin to roll in. Three groups would be going in long, all the way to Baghdad. Many others were part of a contingent headed to Kirkuk. A few others were part of a deception. The players this night were Strike Eagles, Fighting Falcons, the Buffs, F-111, F-117, and many others.

While some of them would be in-country an hour or less, we'd have to hang over enemy territory for the next five hours. It'd be a living hell. I knew the gang in the back-end was busily working the environment, but so were Able and I in our own way. "Pilot, Spotter, AAA ten o'clock. Not a factor yet."

"Roger, Spotter. I've got it."

I pushed in the Privates, so I didn't have the clutter of voices from the mission crew calling in targets.

"Crew, we've reached the orbit area; we'll be turned onto orbit facing left in thirty seconds. Stations, environment is left. Co, watch the AAA in the forward edge of the box. We'll have to tighten the orbit a bit to stay clear."

"Roger that, Pilot. I've got my eye on it."

"First wave ingress in one mike," hissed Beebop.

"MCC, Pilot, what's the status on Gypsy?"

"They're still having difficulties. They say they'll be up, and it's too late to back out now. The packages are headed in."

"Crew, we're going into jam!"

"Pilot, Spotter."

"I see it—that's the infamous wall. It's safe to say they know we're here now."

As I watched, the hornet's nest began to stir. Where I'd seen a thin line of AAA before, I now saw what appeared to be endless stretches of it forming a virtual wall. With the arrival of nightfall, I knew the enemy ground forces out there had been expecting strikes, but they hadn't known when or if they would come. Even with our presence, they still didn't know for sure. It was part of the guessing game, only we guessed better than they did.

Some gunners fired immediately and incessantly as they had in previous days as soon as we switched on our jammers, but they couldn't waste ammo forever. That was part of the game, too; if you knew where the enemy was, you could avoid or target him with ease. In the end, with communications cut, only the sound of jet engines or the sight of blasts would give our forces away.

In the fourth week of the war, the enemy was probably running desperately low on ammo, especially in the hard-to-supply areas. Taking out bridges, supply depots, railheads, and other such targets was an ongoing effort. The more they wasted, the less they had when it really counted.

It looked as if I could reach out and touch the fiery bursts in front of us, or worse yet, that they could reach out and touch us. I knew they were firing blind and without critical communications; still, I'd never seen the air literally alive with artillery before. And so close, God so close, I could almost touch it.

"Pilot, Spotter, traffic low moving toward three o'clock."

"Roger, Spotter."

"Pilot, MCC, I've got bad news. Gypsy's bugging out, and they're bent. They've advised that we do the same, head home."

I gulped for air. I knew Gypsy was having trouble, but I didn't think they'd be going home. I recalled what had happened the last time we'd lost their support. Only this time, they were leaving us alone and over enemy territory. "We can't leave now.

The packages are in-bound. Who's going to support them? This mission is too important!" I screamed on Interphone without thinking.

"Thank you, Spotter, I'm with you, but I need to hear the general consensus. Either we're together in this, or we pull out now. You know the dangers, crew; if we turn around now, someone in that package is as good as dead. Yet if we hang around without support, it could just as well be us. We have dedicated CAP, but they can only do so much. Gypsy advised we head home; the final say is ours."

An unsettling silence followed. We made a crisp combat turn, and my face pressed tight against cold plexiglass briefly. As we leveled out, I no longer faced the terrible line, but I still looked out over enemy territory. Enemy jets could come at us from any side they wanted. I made sure I watched with a hawk's eye, turning from high to low, left to right. Suddenly I saw the white hot glow of multiple afterburners. "Pilot, Spotter, two four-ship formations mid-level headed in. One's moving toward two, the other to four."

I keyed into radios, and one by one, I heard the calls to the MCC. "I vote we stay." "I'm with two." "Me too." "We're here to do a job, aren't we?" "Give us your best shot, Saddam." "I say we stay."

"You know my vote, MCC," I called out.

"Let's give 'em hell!" I finally heard Gentleman Bob reply.

Able flagged me down with a thumbs up, which I returned. I was suddenly proud of the crew I had had some serious reservations about. The shit had hit the fan, and they were willing to stick it out.

The mission was far from over. We had dozens of fighters

racing in country and dozens more ready to come in. Buffs laden with heavy bombs would soon be over target. I hugged the plexiglass again as we swung around hard and fast; for a moment, I'd stared straight down at the ground and at artillery bursts not far off. As we leveled out, I saw small clusters of explosions—at first small and then growing exponentially as secondary explosions followed. The first group had surely reached Kirkuk and had started their run.

"Pilot, Spotter, traffic low, moving toward three, looks like two groups inbound."

The fighters raced in. I saw a ground flash then an unusually large explosion. The Iraqis had just launched a SAM. An instant later, I saw another flash and then another. I was sure glad they were firing blindly. The AAA started up heavy again as this new wave came in. I saw the wall form again, up close and personal. God, it was frightening.

We turned again. The wings leveled just in time for me to see another group marshaling to head in. I counted them off on Interphone as they went in.

Able called out more explosions at two and three o'clock.

My heart raced faster and faster; for surely if the Iraqis were going to launch aircraft at us, this was the time. I glanced at my watch. It was after midnight; a new day had arrived, and we still had hours of hanging over enemy territory to look forward to. Able's voice was hissing into my headset describing the myriad of explosions he saw as orange-red fireballs shooting from the ground into the heavens. Another group had found their targets.

The wing dipped sixty degrees; to me it looked like ninety as I stared downward. I saw a trace of afterburners, low and screaming, headed our way. "Pilot, Spotter, two possibly one, headed outbound direct at three o'clock."

A terrible moment of not knowing passed. I was confident this was the first group returning, but until they were identified no one could be sure.

"Pilot, Spotter, they're coming up mid-level."

"Roger, Spotter." Bob paused, unkeyed his mike then re-keyed it. "Nav, Pilot, get someone on radios with Paladin Leader now! Does he see that group coming outbound or not? I don't hear a damn thing!"

"Paladin Leader, Paladin Leader, this is Shadow, do you read? We have outbound traffic. We do not show first package egress at this time. Over."

I waited to hear a response, but none came. I hugged the window closer and braced myself as Gentleman Bob turned the Lady sharply, ninety degrees. "Crew, this is the copilot; we're following emergency evasive maneuvers at this time. Seats forward, safety harnesses in the locked positions. Brace yourselves, and wait for those alarm bells. In case of bailout, the rear paratroops doors remain the primary exit."

The first alarm bell sounded. Right then, most of us prepared to kiss our asses goodbye. There wasn't a whole hell of a lot the Lady could do to outpace a jet fighter. One missile, and we'd be so much debris.

The heartbeats that followed were filled with frenzy. I remember finding my parachute, putting it on and waiting. It's frightening to record the passage of time to the pace of your breaths: inhale, exhale, inhale, exhale. Or to the pace of excited heartbeats.

We keyed to our headsets, waiting for what seemed a lifetime, our thoughts spinning out of control, waiting for someone to say something, anything. Or to hear another alarm bell. We dreaded the sounding of the next alarm bell, but we would have welcomed it to end the silence.

I stared out at the horizon and a night sky filled with artillery bursts and distant explosions. Looking, always vigilantly looking, my head turning, craning in every direction possible. I gripped the night vision goggles so tightly that my hands ached with a dull sting that went almost unnoticed.

Where those approaching fighters were, I had no idea now. The Lady was twisting and turning; it was all I could do to keep upright and attempt to stare out the window. Behind me, Able wasn't having much luck either.

"Spotters, status on those unidentified?" screamed Bob on Hot.

I wish I knew, I wanted to reply. "I lost visual," I said. Able said much the same thing.

At the same time, we all heard it, a weak carrier coming out over Paladin's channel. "Shadow, this is Paladin Leader, the area is clear, repeat clear. Are you going to follow through with the mission abort? Repeat, are you aborting the mission?"

"Paladin, Shadow, what's the status on our CAP?"

"You've got a two-ship dedicated screaming over your heads right now. Two more went inbound for intercept. Paladin-2 and -1 are pedaling off to gas up."

"Negative on that abort. We're coming around."

I stopped listening to what Paladin Leader said after that and returned my attention to the window. It was hard to believe that barely a minute had elapsed from threat call to now.

"Crew, Pilot, we'll be environment right in thirty seconds!"

"Confirm, environment right," said Stopwatch.

The Lady turned. "Crew, environment is right."

"Roger," said Stopwatch. "Crew, we're in jam!"

As I watched, fighters started pouring out, and I counted them two by two. Sixteen F-16s in all. They had started to come out low, then they soared upward, eventually racing past a hundred feet above us. What a rush! I could hear their engines scream. The final two-ship raced over us, upside down. I caught a glimpse of a pilot giving us the thumbs up.

I saw it then, a massive fireball forming in front of us. And then another, and another. Northern Baghdad had never looked so close. Buffs were pounding the hell out of the place. They were not alone in this endeavor. Several fighter groups had gone deep; and a moment later, I started to see fiery flashes that told me they were also over target.

I knew if they were just now coming in over Baghdad, the mission was only half over. I never wished so hard for anything in my life as I did right then for Gypsy's return. But Gypsy wasn't coming back.

Saturday, 16 February 1991

Rain greeted us as we departed ops and somewhere within the murk a new day had already arrived. The big board had said that we'd have another late evening Go tonight, so we were all eager to return to our rooms and get some sleep. The mission had been exceptionally long and trying. My eyes felt like two round saucers still attached to a pair of night-vision goggles.

The line after us was a double Go, but with inclement weather moving in and getting thicker by the minute the mission would be cancelled for sure.

After pulling the shades tight, I crawled into bed and attempted sleep. But I couldn't sleep right away. It wasn't that I wasn't tired, but that I was over tired and still wound up.

Every time I closed my eyes, in the pink haze on the back of my eyelids I saw it: the anti-aircraft artillery fire, the explosions, all of it. My mind was like those afterburners I'd seen racing in and screaming out except I couldn't find the switch to flick them off.

It wasn't until many tortured hours later that I finally did find sleep. I remember waking up and trembling. The room was cold and dark though it was early afternoon. I went to the window and peered out into the gloom. The room was empty; I was alone. The sky was overcast and an uncomforting deluge was drenching the land and splashing up against the window as it was beaten by strong winds.

Even as I looked out at the rain hammering the land, kicking up dark mud and pounding against the window, I saw it: unrelenting flashes of AAA, explosions, jets passing by, and not far off, aerial bursts. In the back of my mind, I heard screams, terrible, horror-filled screams. Screams that until now I had blocked completely from my mind. Screams I'd heard all too often. Screams that numbed my mind and sent shivers up and down my spine. Screams that left me staring into the darkness in the dead of night. Screams of the damned and the dying coming from a keyed microphone. We heard it all—that was part of the job—it had taken last night to stir it all up.

It's odd how you block things like that out of your mind because you don't want to feel the pain and how because of that, a part of you becomes numb. On that last flight with Tennessee Jim's crew, I'd heard such a scream: an Iraqi radio operator screaming to Allah, the merciful; Allah, the benevolent; Allah, the forgiving, his last sound a muffled screamed mixed with an explosion followed by a silent and empty carrier.

The rain continued its onslaught outside my window. I watched it fall relentlessly. I listened to it slap at the land and at the windowsill. I listened to the howling of the wind, realizing something right then that had been a long time in coming: war was not always glorious though it was immersed in death, devastation, and destruction.

Instead of turning away from the window—away from the

pain—I continued to watch the downpour. After a time, it cleansed my mind as it cleansed the earth. I couldn't turn back now. I'd come too far. I'd endured days and weeks, some just this side of living hell, but I'd weathered them just the same. The same way the earth weathered a violent storm. Someday the storm would end and the sun would shine. I was waiting for the sun to shine.

Sunday, 17 February 1991

The bad weather remained throughout the day and late into the evening. By 18:00, all the day's lines had been cancelled. It looked as if the clouds were here to stay for a while. Instead of time off, the rainy weather meant it's back to plan A. I had to report at 19:00. I didn't mind, though; that's the breaks.

Word spread quickly that we'd flown into Iraq supporting missions that had flown "all the way to Baghdad," and everyone wanted to know what it was like. I told Cowboy and Chris, "It was even better than that very first mission. I saw explosions you wouldn't believe! The AAA was so close I could've reached out and touched it."

Something good did happen on Sunday. I got a care package from home from Katie. A Valentine's Day present. Even though it was late in arriving, the timing couldn't have been better. I really needed something to boost my spirits. She sent me all kinds of things. More clothes, another pair of jeans—still not the ones with the worn-out knees—a few shirts, socks, underwear and underneath it all was a heart-shaped box of candy filled with two-pounds of chocolates, a loaf of her delicious banana-nut bread and another tape.

I put on my headphones, listened to Katie's voice, ate, and blocked out the world for a time. Eventually I did share the banana-nut bread and candy with my roomies but not right away.

Monday, 18 February 1991

Sunday night dragged by. There weren't any crews to drive to the plane or pick up, so it was hours of sitting around. Yet morning found ops buzzing. I'd noticed when I arrived for my shift that the walls were covered in fresh, vanilla-colored paint. Signs reading Wet Paint were all over the building. Paper was spread out on all the floors to protect the freshly-waxed and shiny finishes. I knew then without a doubt that a very important guest must be coming to visit real soon. I had no idea who the special guest was, but even so, I never expected so much fuss.

Turkish troops were taking up positions all along the street. A special detachment had set up outside ops outfitted in dress uniforms—I never saw so much white and navy blue in all my life. Soon armed guards were posted throughout the building. Stacks of red carpets were being readied, and everything throughout the building was getting special attention.

Cleaning crews were spot-shining the floors again. The fresh paint was getting touch-ups and then getting air-dried. Clean carpets were getting re-cleaned and vacuumed. Everything to white-glove satisfaction.

Around 07:00, I was finally able to leave ops. I'd gotten four hours of sleep when Stopwatch roused me. "The weather's clearing—we got a 14:00 alert."

"What time is it?"

"It's 12:30."

"Thanks," I replied through a heavy yawn. I dropped back into bed without realizing that I was flying again. When the alert came at 14:00, I'd be elated, but not now. Now I only wanted more sleep.

A few minutes later, Chris knocked on the door. "Who is it?" I barked.

"Chris, I forgot my key. Were you sleeping?"

"No. Well, maybe."

"What you sleeping for? We're planning a barbecue at Tennessee Jim's. He says he's buying if we bring the beer."

"No shit," I replied without thinking. "Wait, I can't, I think I have to fly. I think. I had to work MPC last night."

"Ah shit, sorry, let me just tiptoe in. I'll be out in a minute. You won't even know I was here."

Chris disappeared into the bathroom and I dropped back onto the bed. I'd just pulled the blankets up tight and fluffed the pillow, when Cowboy sprang into the room. "You're missing the game. I don't believe it! Turn on the TV!"

"What game?" shouted Chris from the bathroom, "Who's playing?"

Bleary eyed, I sat up, and then made my way to the sink. After splashing my face with water, I brushed my teeth and shaved, then headed for the shower.

The alert came right at 14:00. "I'm flying again," I told myself.

Outside, the sky had cleared. The rain was gone, so I ambled down to ops early to find that it was still hopping. Captain Gandis and her crew were just finishing up their post-mission briefings. The MPC folks were preparing for the next line's arrival. The Turkish troops were preparing to greet the group of dignitaries. In all the confusion, I'd forgotten about the special visitors: Turkish President Ozal, the Turkish Armed Forces Chief of Staff, and the Turkish Air Force Chief of Staff.

I moved through the ops center quickly, checking the mail bin, though I'd just received mail yesterday. No mail, much as I expected. Captain Gandis stood directly across from me. I remembered what Tommy'd said about her, "Man what I wouldn't give for a piece of that." I'd never paid much attention to her looks before; to me she was just another face—blond hair, brown eyes, and slim figure, mostly indistinguishable.

In fact, her only distinguishing feature was that she was an AC, our only female AC. She was also an instructor pilot and from what I'd heard, a good pilot.

As far as crews went, in the current order of things her crew flew before Captain Hillman's and after Captain Willie's.

I left the ops center and headed over to intel. Derrin wasn't doing anything, so I queried his memory for current events. There were a few developments of interest, but nothing spectacular. I also found out that we'd again fly into Iraq to support packages enroute to Baghdad, and we were still the only crew to go that far into enemy territory—a distinction that would soon be lost; but while it remained, I'd revel in it. I was bound for my second official O-1 mission.

The mission plan itself wasn't much different from our previous mission. Buffs would be carpet bombing. Falcons and

Eagles would be hitting hardened bunkers, targets of opportunity, railheads, and bridges. Several packages would be headed in deep. I could only hope Gypsy wouldn't leave us hanging again when we needed her the most.

When I left intel, I just hung out, watching the troops laboring over the red carpets and making sure everything was still to white-glove satisfaction. Armored personnel carriers were rolling up and down the street, which in itself wasn't a spectacular event; they always rolled up and down the streets. It was the frequency and the number of troops assembling that was significant. I also noticed for the first time that the units setting up were trying to remain inconspicuous, as if they thought no one would notice groups of armed men.

The crew van arrived a short time later carrying Captain Hillman, Stopwatch, and the rest of the crew. There was a moment of frenzy in front of ops as two men clad in charcoal gray suits told the duty driver to pull the van away from the front of the building. After that, things quieted down.

The intel briefing went smoothly; and afterward we checked out weapons, holstered them as usual, then went on with our normal procedures. About an hour later, we were ready to go. The lounge was too clean; and since it was a sunny and warm day, we waited outside.

A large group of armed individuals quickly sent the Turkish security agents back into an uproar. We were discreetly told to head out to the plane early. I'd just run back in to tell Stopwatch and Captain Hillman they had better leave now, or we'd get stuck here for a while. We had just started out the front door when the first shiny Mercedes pulled up.

I had a good view of the spectacle from where I was

positioned. Red carpets were now stretched across the front walkway. Lines of Turkish soldiers clad in white metal caps, white gloves, and bloused boots revealing white cuffs, snapped sharply to attention. They held weapons in outstretched hands straight and true. Attendants opened car doors and a number of men in suits stepped out. Turkish President Ozal emerged next, quickly followed by his chiefs of staff and a number of generals.

We waited until the main group passed before we made a quick exit. The driver started the van, and we drove away.

Through the crew van rear doors, I looked back, watching the guards still standing at attention. It all seemed much needless fuss, but then I thought about how much we'd fuss if President Bush had been visiting and then it all seemed to make sense.

It was now mid-afternoon; by the time we'd be airborne and headed toward enemy territory, the sky would be gathered in dusk. Again, I could only hope that everything would go according to plan. That Gypsy wouldn't leave us when we needed her most. That the Lady would hold true, her systems up and running. That no Iraqi MiG would decide to pop up, say hello, and ruin our day.

During those few quick minutes as we lumbered toward the runway, I thought about Turkish President Ozal. I wondered what it would've been like if President Bush had been visiting instead. The flight had progressed well so far. Our anxiety levels were peaked off the scale. We couldn't wait to come off stations and head back to base. Hanging over enemy territory for endless hours was nerve-racking business.

The spotters were calling out the initial formation egress. I knew it wouldn't be long now; soon it'd all be over. Captain Hillman brought the Lady through a crisp combat turn. Gravity threw me into the seat and held my arms tight. I had my gloves on; still my fingers were cold, icy cold. I rubbed my hands together to warm them up.

"AMT, Six, turn up the heat. I have icicles forming on the insides of my boots."

"Give me a minute, Six," replied Rollin. He wasn't cold. He was wearing winter thermals, his winter flight jacket and winter-weight flight boots. Me, I had grabbed my summer flight jacket by mistake today, and I had no winter-weight flight boots.

The mission compartment was always like that: cold to the point where it was icy or hot to the point where you were sweating, never in between. Some AMTs kept it hot, some kept it cold. I'd learned that Rollin preferred to keep it cold.

"Pilot, Spotter, traffic low, two o'clock," called out Mellow Yellow.

"Roger, Spotter."

Soon hot air started rolling through the mission compartment and my feet and hands began to thaw out.

For a handful of heartbeats, it seemed we had hit a lull. I had cottonmouth and my face was greasy and grimy from the boxed-up interior air. The cabin seemed tight and I noticed the odor then, the airborne odor, the smell you usually don't notice until you are wheels down and the first blast of fresh and clean outside air is hitting you. The odor was a ripe mixture of human odors—sweat, bodily functions, deodorants, and propeller backwash. I took a long swig of bottled water for the cottonmouth, but the smell I'd have to live with. I double-checked times; the main package was over target north of Baghdad, and that was the reason for the perceived lull.

Momentarily, I looked down at the keyboard and the complex

array of color-coded keys. I brought up the system control page, made a few adjustments to my position settings, and then went back to my search.

An anxiety-filled hour passed. I worked the environment feverishly along with my fellow crewers. Able and Mellow Yellow in the rear were having a hellish time; the night skyline was filled with scattered explosions and ground fire. I knew what it was like to stare into the eye of the storm and have it glare back at you.

I vaguely heard Mellow Yellow's voice through the blast of static in my ears as I brought up a new signal. My heart stopped cold. "Pilot, Spotter, I see AAA coming up at two. No—it's coming—Jesus, we're in it. We're in it!"

"Pilot, Co, I got artillery fire off the nose at our altitude!"

"Crew, Pilot, emergency evasive maneuvers." As Captain Hillman was saying this he was already pulling the Lady through a hard ninety-degree turn.

I swallowed the lump in my throat and glanced at Steve to my right. His eyes were wide as saucers, nearly as large as I supposed my own eyes were right then. I went back to the signal I'd brought up earlier. I was in the middle of running identification checks on it when the full-of-static carrier-signal I was listening to and watching on my displays peaked off the scale. Soon after the carrier keyed, a heavily accented voice filled my ears. I ran through the ID checks as quickly as I could, already certain the voice I listened to was Iraqi. The problem with the Arabic language was that there were as many dialects of it as there were states in the union, or so it seemed.

Captain Hillman was still fighting the Lady hard, trying to gain altitude. Able and Mellow Yellow had their eyes glued to the windows watching the artillery explosions. They were so near, especially through a pair of NVG.

"Co, Pilot, you still got you're eyes peeled? You believe this shit?" He paused. "Nav, get a call through to Gypsy pronto!"

"Pilot, Co, I can still see it coming up."

"Crew, Pilot, we're not out of it yet. Bear with me here; we'll pull through."

"MCC, Six, I have a live one here, a ground artillery unit!" I called out as I passed Stopwatch the signal information.

The wonderful sound of jammers filled my ears at the same time Stopwatch returned, "Roger, Six, I've added it to the jam list."

"MCS, MCC, you on that call to Gypsy?"

"I'm on it."

We'd made a second ninety-degree turn and were just coming out of it, wings level, when Mellow Yellow called out again, "Pilot, Spotter, triple A remains at our five o'clock, but it's no longer a factor!"

Her voice was still strong with emotion and still shaking. I said a silent yes, and went back to work. Right then, the call I'd been waiting to hear came. "Pilot, MCC, we've hit our station's time. Gypsy's clearing us out, the last wave's outbound; let's get the hell out of here!"

"MCC, Pilot, I'm with you, no point hanging around now."

"Crew, we're turning off stations and heading back to base. Spotters, we're not out of this yet. We're still in enemy territory and it's a short but long road out. Look alive, back there!"

Stopwatch almost cracked a smile as he replied, "Roger, Pilot."

Sitting in my home away from home, away from home—position Six—I glanced over at Stopwatch, convinced now that he was no Tennessee Jim. He lacked style and confidence in his fellow crewers, but we'd done it. The mission was undoubtedly a success.

"Crew, Pilot, stay buckled up."

Even though the radios were still boisterous, everything seemed to become calm. I was no longer searching for communications channels, and I no longer heard targets being passed to the MCC.

Gypsy'd stayed with us, for which we were all glad. Things were hell without an air picture, though I had learned for the second time that my fellow crewers were performers and if given the opportunity they could rise to any occasion. I only wished Stopwatch could see things through our eyes. No crew was perfect, but you made do with what you had. When you throw thirteen-plus crewers into an aircraft, assault them with AAA, SAMs, fighters armed with air-air missiles and machine guns, you'll quickly find you have thirteen survivors.

That's what we all were, survivors, living another day, another hour, another minute, another heartbeat, each in our own way. If you weren't careful you could get pushed over the edge easily. I knew. I'd been riding the edge since Friday night one step away from no return; yet I waited it out, telling myself we'd be wheels down in no time and then no enemy MiG, SAM, or artillery shell could knock us out of the sky.

Nervous minutes passed. We all waited for the pilot to tell us we were out of country. Outside the Lady, the sky was shrouded in darkness. Able and Mellow Yellow had seen the greatest light-show of their entire lives. The Buffs had smacked the hell out of their targets, leaving roaring fireballs in their wake. The deadly spray of artillery fire, called the wall, was at last growing farther and farther away.

Rollin and Tommy were keyed up Select with me and were yapping away. They wanted to play basketball at the gym after the flight. Me, I just wanted to get some sleep. "I haven't shot hoops since high school; and even then, it was street ball."

"Come on out and play anyway. It's the only chance you'll ever get to whomp on Stopwatch."

"The whole crew's going to be there?"

"Probably."

"Okay, I'll do it. I'll do it. Stop by the room and get me."

For several handfuls of heartbeats, silence prevailed. We waited for confirmation that we were clear; then finally Captain Hillman's voice tweaked Interphone, "Crew, Pilot, we're out! Congratulations! Good job back there. Spotters, I'd prefer you to stay till we pass Diyarbakir. Let's bring the Lady back to base."

It'd be another forty-five minutes or so before we'd be wheels down, but I took a deep breath and relaxed in my seat anyway.

We did play basketball at the gym after the flight, half court, four on four, the best of three. I played quite poorly and was mostly a ruffian on defense. Sandy and Mellow Yellow were there cheering us on.

Tuesday, 19 February 1991

I headed down to ops immediately after waking. I'd found a note on my door that said I needed to check in ASAP. To me, that could only mean one thing. I was probably going back to MPC. The only thing I was sure of as I trudged along the roadside was that today would either be my next to last day of MPC, which I hadn't really done much of, or a day of rest with an early morning Go the next day.

I seemed to be running around in circles, chasing my tail as it were. I wasn't entirely in a pleasant mood. I could've chewed iron spikes and spit out nails. It wasn't that I was really angry, just irritated. The mixed up schedule didn't bother me. When we flew, the schedule was always topsy-turvy. I'd been looking forward to that third O-1, yet what I really wanted was just to get back to Tennessee Jim's crew. More than anything else, I wanted to hear Martha screaming, "There's nowhere to run!" as we climbed out of five thousand feet.

I entered ops and headed into the ops center without giving any thought to the closed door. The door was always closed. I knew immediately something was wrong. Gentleman Bob was in heated conversation with Captain Gandis. He was screaming and she was listening, her downturned brown eyes filled with tears. I did an about face, turning on my heel, and went back into the hall.

Although the door was closed, as I stood in the hall waiting, I could hear the voices clearly.

"I still won't accept the mission," she was saying, "I won't! I don't care if I'm just the Co today or not, and I won't fly in there."

I knew at once what the two were talking about. Her crew had the evening mission, and they were to support packages enroute to northern Baghdad. The mission itself was classified as combat vice combat support. O-2 was every bit as dangerous as O-1; it was just that during an O-1 the threat was that much closer. One of the key topics here and on the news of late was women in combat and women on the front line.

Many of the crew I served with were women, and I had nothing but respect for those that I served with. In my mind there was no question as to whether a woman should or shouldn't serve in combat. But you cannot make up the mind of an individual. Everyone sees things differently. I'd already seen Big John go home with a defeated look in his eyes. In the end, the war had beaten him and he had gone home to a family that desperately needed him to help pick up the pieces of shattered lives. I would find out much later that his marriage fell apart and that his wife eventually took the kids and went home to the states.

As the conversation continued, Captain Gandis' position became very clear. "Here's my badge and my wings if you want them," she said, "but I still won't fly in there."

"What the hell are you saying to me?" screamed Bob. "You're

an AC, aircrew commander, and an instructor pilot, for chrissakes. What the hell am I supposed to tell your crew? Your pilot's yellow and I'm yanking the line?"

Captain Gandis didn't reply although I heard her sobs very clearly.

"What about the crew after you, would it be fair to them? They haven't even been down twelve hours yet? You got an answer for me, captain?"

"You've already heard what I have to say. It is my option."

"Option? What the heck does that mean? Option, my ass. If you're going to stand here in front of me and profess truths, holier-than-thou shit, you'd better come squeaky clean. What do you mean you don't belong out there? Look around. I've half-a-dozen female troops who've already been in combat. You'd better tell me the whole truth, the whole truth!"

"I—I—don't—I'm supposed to get married this fall, you know. Married. Shit, I don't want to die. I don't want to die here."

Her sobs were heart-wrenching. Finally, I just had to walk away. I went into the lounge, sat down in front of the TV but stared at the wall behind it.

I was angry, nearly as angry as Gentleman Bob sounded. We'd all signed up for the same thing: to fly wherever and whenever we were told. Being afraid was natural. Hell, being scared to the point of pissing your pants was all right. We were all afraid of the unknown, afraid of paying with our lives; but we handled it, each in our own way. Some joked about it, attempting to diminish the fear in their own minds. Some sulked and brooded and silently let it slip away. Some found the nerve to talk about it. A few stared at it head on with their eyes wide open.

We all eventually had to face it and overcome it. Captain Gandis wasn't facing it. She was copping out. Right then, I wondered what Sandy and Karen would say, especially Karen. She'd stared straight into the eye of the storm last night and hadn't twitched. I knew for a fact that if I'd said what Captain Gandis had just said, I'd be facing a court-martial tribunal. Those were the rules.

As I stared at the wall, I saw Captain Gandis leave. Her face was red and wet, her eyes swollen, mascara running in dark streams along the contours of her cheeks. Gentleman Bob had a hand on her shoulder, his voice soft and understanding now. "You think about it. I want you on our team. We are a team, always a team." His voice trailed away as they moved down the hall.

I watched them disappear down the long hall. It was hard for me to deny that I felt for her, but war was not sunny days and rainbows. This day, Captain Gandis wouldn't fly; in fact, she was switched to MPC for an indefinite term. Captain Hillman's crew took the line, and by the time I left ops I had just enough time to grab a bite to eat before I needed to gather up flight bags and head out. I never did find out why I was supposed to head down to ops that morning and I never did ask.

As I boarded the Lady some hours later, I tried to forget about the sobs that played in the back of my mind and gnawed at me. The voices my mind wouldn't let me forget. Mixed in with the sobs, I heard the whisper, "I don't want to die." I didn't either. With luck, I'd pull through. We'd all pull through. Someday, perhaps, I could look back on this day and laugh about it, but not just yet.

Wednesday, 20 February 1991

I survived. I'm not sure why I felt I needed to write that, but I did. Perhaps it had something to do with the incident with Captain Gandis.

On this day we had another basketball match: five on five, half court, best of three. Darwin, Beebop, Able, Topper and me. Against Tommy, Max, Stopwatch, Steve, and Rollin. We had fun, burned off some excess steam. Afterward, Tommy, Able and I grabbed some eats, and then drank some beers.

Darwin talked me into playing spades. We played against Tommy and Allen. I hadn't seen Allen in a while. He was doing all right, still with Captain Willie's crew.

Thursday, 21 February 1991

Everything seemed to be gaining momentum as we moved toward the start of the ground conflict. I'd come to terms with some of my demons, thanks in part to Captain Gandis. I found out that I was back with Tennessee Jim's crew—so much for mission planning cell, so much for a leisurely eight days.

I looked forward to the flight as I looked forward to few other things. It represented a return to normalcy and I was pleased when the hours of planning slipped by, more pleased to be up in the air enroute to the mission. This flight was my fourth official O-1 and my twenty-fifth wartime flight to date.

"Shit, Six, it's good to have ya back," hissed Tennessee Jim's voice into my headset.

"Thanks, MCC, it's good to be back!"

Jim keyed his mike then paused for a moment. "You know, of course, that bravos are on you after the flight."

I started to reply then stopped as Captain Sammy called out over ship's interphone. "Crew, it's going to be awhile. We got a red light. Tower's telling us to hold. We could be here awhile."

"This morning flight looks like it's going to be an afternoon flight," tweaked a familiar voice into my headset.

"Seems like it, Cowboy," I replied on Select.

"Just like old times," cut in Happy.

I turned around in my seat and flagged Happy down with a thumbs up. Tammy was on One. Happy on Two. Sparrow on Three. Cowboy on Four. Chris on Five—the MCS position. Me on Six. Popcorn on Seven. Tennessee Jim on Eight—the MCC position. Everything back the way I remembered it.

The engines began to wind down and as the last one came to a halt, we knew the delay could be a long one.

Crow put the chocks back under the wheels, which was a bad sign.

"Crew, Pilot, Tower says the delay could be anywhere from thirty to sixty minutes. Enjoy."

The interior lights came down briefly as we hooked up to external power.

"MCC, MCS, we cleared up?"

"Crew, you're clear; stay close."

I followed Chris, Cowboy and Popcorn out the crew entrance door. I glanced heavenward; the sky was overcast, but the visibility was still good. Cowboy lit up a cigarette and was soon blowing out white puffs of smoke. A preflight team was out at Eighty-five, putting her through the tests. She'd be going up later this evening laden with Captain Smily's crew.

I eyed my watch as the minutes ticked away. We were getting used to delays. A delay caused by Tower wasn't bad because the orders probably came from a higher authority, which ultimately meant the other package components would also be delayed and the entire package scenario would have to be adjusted. Yet it would still equate to a scramble once we were airborne. To get in place on time, we'd have to make a number of adjustments. We'd have to adjust all mission times: station time, ingress and egress, our jam windows, time over target for the packages we'd be supporting, and so on.

The only thing that could make matters worse now would be system problems as we raced toward our orbit—our combat mission. I chased across the barren landscape with my eyes and stared at the distant mountains. My thoughts turned to the mission and the packages we'd eventually—hopefully—be supporting. A group of fighters would be dropping psy-ops leaflets over troop concentrations, telling them to rise up and flood the streets, to lay down their weapons, to return to their homes and loved ones. As we raced toward the ground war, destroying the remnants of the Iraqi nonconventional warfare capability became a key goal and in this our forces were playing a decisive role, for all of these facilities that weren't scattered around Baghdad were in northern Iraq.

I heard a high-pitched whistle and turned. Jim was hailing us. It was finally time to go.

"Before Engine Starting Checklist!" called out Captain Sammy.

Crow pulled the chocks and tossed them in the back end, and we waited for the checks to be completed and the engines to wind up. I followed the voices on interphone, but not too closely. Momentarily, I let my eyes slip closed and pressed my head against the seat cushions. In truth, I was exhausted, for it seemed I was running non-stop, headlong, trying to outrun an imagined freight train that could not be beaten.

"Stop/start three."

"Roger, Pilot, stop/start three."

My eyes snapped open.

"Restart three."

"Roger, restarting three, no-go. Stop/start."

"AMT, flag down that maintenance troop. Tell him we have problems with engine three."

"Roger, Pilot."

The minor maintenance problems we'd been having lately didn't surprise me. The planes were being driven virtually nonstop like us.

"AMT, Pilot, what's he doing out there?"

"Turning the prop."

"I can see that. I mean, I want him in here."

"Roger that. He says to try to restart the engine now."

"Engine three, clear!"

"Engine three is clear," replied Crow.

"No, stop/start. No-go."

I heard heavy footsteps coming from the rear, then saw the maintenance tech pass by. Silence seemed to follow in his wake. He and the pilot were conferring off headset.

"Crew, engines one and two coming down. Gather up your gear, bag drag to eight-five. She's just been preflighted and ready to go. AMT, we'll send them over ASAP and let them go through the checks over here."

"Crew, internal power is coming down." Everything became black as our eyes fought to adjust to the darkness.

I cleared my station, punched off radios, gathered up my gear, and then piled out behind the rest of the crew.

The mission crew was the first to get set back up, and then we waited for the front-end crew. Out on the taxiway, I'd seen Gypsy and Gas Station already heading for takeoff. As I saw it, we were wasting precious time.

Ship's PA came alive as we leveled off, and a few minutes later, the Little River Band was screaming out, "Hang on, help is on its way. I'll be there as fast as I can."

"Attention to brief," called out Tennessee Jim, "Gypsy confirms that we're X plus one-forty. All times listed will need to be adjusted accordingly. And the way I see it, we're behind schedule. You know the drill. So when I clear you in, you're green all the way."

I glanced at my watch. X plus one-forty meant we had to push all mission times forward an hour and forty minutes; that's how long everyone had been held up on the pad. At present, we were behind that schedule due to our additional delays.

Crow was powering up the system as fast as humanly possible. We were over the snowcapped mountains now, and soon we'd be heading in-country. I was glad it was light outside because in the light of day everything seemed less ominous. AAA was reduced to ground flashes and black aerial bursts. SAMs became smokers: smoke trails with aerial bursts. Enemy fighters were usually highly visible.

The music on ship's PA was winding down now; the last song to play out before it was silenced was Tom Sawyer by Rush.

"Roger that, system looks good. Border crossing in five mike. Look alive back there, spotters!"

I watched as faces turned pale. While this was my fourth such flight, this was only the second for the rest of the crew except for Popcorn; this was his first. I wanted to tell him the extra mileage didn't really make that much difference; and whether we were hugging the border or within enemy territory, the dangers remained the same. We were a large flying target. It was us against them; it had always been us against them.

We'd been set up and busily working the system for some time now, and the five minutes burned away all too quickly. "Crew, we have the green light; we're heading in."

"Do we get bonus air mileage points for this? And where do I cash them in at?" asked Happy over Private.

I held back a chuckle and prepared for the frenzy I knew would eventually come. It was good to be back.

The first wave was marshaling and in fifteen mike they'd be heading in, afterburners aglow. I concentrated on my position, waiting for the station's call. The radios were already filled with a tumult of voices. I heard Gypsy, Paladin, and Phantom squawking away. Gypsy was passing the current air picture and sending a two-ship from Paladin's group to investigate a possible pair of bogies. Paladin-3 and Paladin-4 obliged, racing off. Phantom was hailing Shadow; Chris responded.

"Pilot, Spotter, AAA at two o'clock, not a factor on current course."

"Roger, Spotter. I see it." Captain Sammy paused, then said, "Co, you see that flash over there at eleven o'clock."

"Got it."

"Keep an eye on it."

"Roger."

I was still scratching down the list that Phantom was passing when Captain Sammy finally called out, "Crew, stations, environment is right!"

"Environment right," confirmed Jim. "Nav, confirm time to jam."

"Two mike, right on schedule."

I quartered the list from Phantom and passed it out. Two

minutes later when we hit our window, Tennessee Jim slammed the Lady into jam. The spotters began calling out ingressing traffic left and right, and the hornet's nest began to stir. The infamous wall appeared less forbidding in daylight; however, it was still austere.

I counted time to the cadence of combat turns, waiting for word that the first wave was outbound.

The frenzy had come just as I'd predicted and it seemed I didn't come up for air for hours. Then, just when I thought the day would never end, the spotters began to tally the first wave's egress. Twenty F-16s screaming out, their bellies clean, was a magnificent sight. F-111s followed in their wake. Soon the Buffs were over target dropping two-thousand-pound bombs. A group of RF-4s would soon be heading in to survey troop concentrations along the Turkish-Iraqi border and after them the psy-ops boys would disperse their propaganda payload.

The perceived lull between waves became stifling. My heart pounded in my ears as I waited, my fingers trembling as I pounded at the keyboard and worked the controls at my position. I heard the report that the Buffs were over target, "giving 'em hell," and I sighed. That's when a startling call broke through the calm. "Mayday, mayday, this is Falcon-12. Engine's vibrating. Coming apart."

Silence seemed to follow. We were still in the lull between waves, and so the pause was heartrending. "Engine's gone. I'm going down. This is Falcon-12."

Not everyone had the extra radio channels pulled, so for a few awful minutes a group of us shared the terrible news. We didn't say a word. We knew Search and Rescue would be launched. We could only hope the pilot went down in friendly territory and that his ejection seat had functioned properly.

The spotters began calling out the next ingress and Tennessee Jim slammed the Lady back into jam. The second wave had begun, and I had to block the thoughts from my mind.

Minutes began to tick away. I tried to remain focused, but it was a difficult chore. I knew Search and Rescue had scrambled by now and were undoubtedly searching for the downed pilot. I didn't envy them; for wherever the plane went down, they'd have to attempt rescue if possible even if that meant going behind enemy lines. Somewhere near a smoldering heap of multimillion-dollar machinery, they'd find either a corpse or a survivor—I hoped it'd be a survivor.

"MCC, MCS, is the system slowing down?"

"MCC, Six, my position just locked up, and I lost my displays."

"MCC, Four, me too."

Jim's face flushed red as he gritted his teeth. "AMT, the system just died—what's wrong?"

Crow raced back to his position. "MCC, AMT. Looks like we lost a controller; the backup should've got it. Let me see what's wrong."

"Can that, are we still throwing out trons or not?"

"Hold on, I'm checking." Crow was up on Hot; I heard him breathing heavily into his mike. "Yeah, yeah, we are. Do you want me to cycle power or not?"

Jim switched his comm selector to ship's Interphone, "Nav, MCC, time to package egress?"

"First group three mike," replied Ice.

The wing dipped hard and we started into a turn; a moment later the pilot called out. "Environment right."

"Right," confirmed Jim on ship's Interphone before switching to Private. "Can you do it in three minutes, AMT?"

"You know I can't. If you want a miracle, dial 1-800-MIRACLE." Crow knew he'd picked the wrong time to make a joke almost as soon as he said it. The brief pause that followed spoke volumes.

"Keep a close eye on the status of the jammers, AMT."

Crow switched off Hot. "Roger, MCC."

There wasn't anything any of us could do now except pray the system didn't shut down completely. As long as we were still jamming, "Throwing out trons," as Jim sometimes called it, we were all right.

From my position, I had only to look left and up to see a panel of blinking lights. In theory, if we were jamming, the rows of green lights blinked on and off rapidly; if we weren't jamming, the lights were solid green; and if there was trouble, a row of red lights should come on and stay on. The lights were happily blinking green.

I started to wonder what else could go wrong today but stopped myself. I didn't want to think about it.

"Pilot, MCC, system controller is down, but we're still green. I'll keep you advised."

"Roger, MCC."

Frustration levels soared as we waited. The beginning of the egress couldn't have come at a better time.

"Pilot, Spotter, traffic low moving four to ten."

"Roger, Spotter."

I tabulated the totals one by one, two by two. The frustration began to slip away. We'd be heading home soon—only a few more minutes now.

I heard Gypsy squawking weakly and turned up her channel: Phantom was heading home, and a two-ship of our Combat Air Patrol broke off their MiG sweep and were dropping back to refuel. I knew they were eager to start heading home, too.

"Nav, MCC, we've hit the end of our jam window. They should all be out, unless we have some stragglers."

"MCC, Nav, roger. I'll check in with Gypsy to confirm status."

I heard the call go out, "Gypsy, this is Shadow, you read?"

"Go ahead, Shadow."

"We clear?"

"You're clear in two mike, Shadow. The final pair are outbound at this time."

I knew the final two-ship was probably a pair of RF-4 surveying troop concentrations. They liked to straggle.

"Copy, Shadow out. Wait, hold on. You know the status on that Falcon? You got me, Gypsy?"

"Shadow, I'm still here. Looks like his wing man saw the ejection, said it looked like the chute deployed well."

"Was he in or out?"

"According to the reports, he had just crossed the border when he started having problems. Engine dropped right out the back end. Hold on a minute, Shadow. Looks like—"

The radio went silent for a moment and tweaked up with a screaming voice. "Rescue spotted the pilot. He appears in good health. They're looking for a place to set down."

I released the breath I was holding and relaxed in my seat.

"Pilot, Spotter, two-ship low at nine o'clock heading toward three."

"Roger, Crew, we're coming off orbit!"

I turned my seat around to face forward and stared blankly at station 247. In a few minutes, we'd be out of Iraq and my twenty-fifth wartime mission would almost be over.

In the KTO, a Falcon had gone down in enemy airspace. Search and Rescue were on their way in when an enemy armored detachment spotted the smoking wreckage. Suddenly, the downed pilot was caught in a deadly race.

Search and Rescue came in fighting, machine guns rattling away. The Iraqi ground troops were closing in fast when the team spotted the pilot and went in for intercept. In the next few seconds the team had to make a critical choice: was the zone too hot to proceed? The armored column was close, too close, but how could they leave the downed pilot behind when they were so close? Their decision was to go in.

Their fight was quick and fierce. They kept the armored units momentarily at bay while one of the choppers went in; then with a rescued Falcon pilot in their midst, Search and Rescue went out fighting.

Friday, 22 February 1991

My fifth week was at an end. In simple terms of days and weeks that's not really very long, but at times when I was counting hours, minutes and seconds, it was an eternity.

Bush's deadline was the definitive precursor to the ground war. The ground war would come now. Even the Iraqis already knew it. They were making the Kuwaiti Theatre of Operations a living, burning hellhole. Black smoke was obscuring the sky and the battlefield as more than 140 oil wells burned out of control.

A special three-page section in the newspaper discussed casualty notifications. The Army, Navy, and the Air Force all have different notification procedures.

Everything seemed to be gaining momentum again. We were racing faster and faster. I heard it said many times, "There's only one road home, and that's the one through Kuwait." I believed the saying was true; there was only one road home, and we were about to find out how few or how many obstacles there were along it. I also thought a few words needed to be added, "There's only one road home, and that's the one through Kuwait direct to Baghdad."

I got a sweet-scented card from Katie. She pressed her rosy-red lips against the page about a dozen times. She seemed to be holding up well although the commissary cut back on hours, so she was spending a lot of time alone at home. With the living room furniture gone, she had been sitting on the floor to watch TV. I bet Schwarzkopf's wife wouldn't have gotten their furniture taken away, no matter the circumstances.

I was going to try to call home, hoping to get through.

Saturday, 23 February 1991

The green light for the land war had finally come. It didn't look as if Saddam Hussein would back down. The final waiting game had begun. Our mission sorties had stepped up. We all knew the ground war was only a few hours away. The mood was rather glum; no one knew what the casualties were going to be like, and no one wanted to guess. If they were going to be light, they'd say we were lucky. On the other hand, if they were heavy, everyone would say, "I told you so."

A number of eleventh-hour diplomacy tactics were under way, but we all knew none of them would succeed. There was only one road home.

I was alerted well before the crack of dawn for the flight. I'd already showered and shaved, and my gear was in a heap next to the door. No one knew for sure if this would be the one, but we were about to find out.

I discovered that the people in ops were marching to the beat of different drummers, all with their own agendas. The first thing the crew did was to check in, signing our names to the flight orders and ogling the big board. The list of names under our line assignment was the same as it had been yesterday. The mission length and orbit times were unusual. I glanced at the times and wrote them down as normal, not giving them much thought.

We were sure the folks in intel had the answers we sought, so we headed down for the preflight intelligence briefing. Derrin was ready to give us the briefing, but it wasn't what we wanted to hear.

"I know you're all eager to hear news about the start of the land war. The green light has been given. The deadline for Iraqi compliance is still 12:00 hours. As soon as we know more, you'll know more.

"I'll start the briefing with the KTO. The skies over the battlefield are growing thick with black smoke. The Iraqis are doing everything they can to obscure the field. They're setting fire to more and more oil wells. It's going to be as dark as Hades down there on the battlefield."

Derrin talked for a few minutes on troop concentrations, movements, and expectations. We listened intently.

"Over the next several days, you can probably expect that we'll be supporting more and more missions headed to Baghdad. This will allow the forces in the South to concentrate on the KTO. It's nothing new, so there's nothing to worry about."

I cringed; I hated it when people said, "There's nothing to worry about."

"The packages you'll be supporting today will also be heading farther south. To these key places—" Derrin started slapping the map with his pointer.

"They'll also be re-striking the nuclear facility, here." He touched the pointer to a familiar target. "There are still several key buildings intact that need to be leveled."

He concluded his briefing with the usual, "Good luck out there today."

The pilot's briefing that followed was short. Our total station time was just under four hours, and in most cases it would have meant a short eleven-hour day if everything went smoothly. Things hadn't gone smoothly, though; we'd been alerted over an hour early, and the wheels-up time was nearly two hours later than we expected. Initial station's time was 11:30, thirty minutes prior to the possible start of the ground war.

Tennessee Jim passed out our individual briefing folders and did a quick review with us while we looked them over. After that, it was to the crew lounge for the long wait. It was still two hours to scramble time, and anything could happen before we walked out the door in two hours.

We followed the news closely and Derrin kept us updated on the incoming reports. We were now five hours into our day, a day that could turn out to be the longest day of our lives.

After a time, it became clear that the newscasters didn't have anything to tell us we didn't already know. We listened anyway.

Chris and Ice, who had just stepped out for a smoke, came bounding back in. I sat up expectantly. "The van's ready."

Tennessee Jim glanced at his watch, "Yep, time to saddle up, boys and girls! Look alive!" It wasn't the news we were expecting, so none of us moved too energetically. "Hey, Cowboy, lollygag on your own time!"

Ship's PA was tweaking; Martha had just wound down, and Happy had just slapped in Pink Floyd's album, the Delicate Sound of Thunder, which had been fast forwarded to Time. It was a day for hard rock. We were singing along. Everything seemed to be running smoothly.

The system was coming up nicely and Crow wasn't mumbling terse words under his breath. My watch read 10:45.

White-capped peaks sprouted beneath us, and then were soon left behind. I was nodding my head to the last few beats of Wish You Were Here. The momentum was building.

Tammy and Popcorn were perched in the rear windows now. The system was up and the panel of lights above Jim's position was solid green. We were good to go.

I heard Gypsy's reassuring squawk mixing in with the tumult of other voices coming into my ears, and in the background Pink Floyd was still playing its heart out. I'd often thought about the words to their songs, but never more so than today.

Then suddenly the music stopped, and Jim cried out in his mixed Tennessee drawl, "Roger, system's ours. Crew, clear to log in!" My watch read 11:08. Twenty-two minutes from station's time, ten minutes till border crossing.

A furious couple of minutes passed as we prepped the system. I noticed then that Phantom wasn't with us today. Gypsy was still holding back; but as soon as we made our move for the border, they'd move up. Gas Station's team was out there somewhere; I knew for sure that they were silently preparing.

"Green light," Captain Smily said a few minutes later. "Crew, we're crossing the border! Spotters, look alive!"

Bill, the Nav, confirmed the crossing a few seconds later.

Somewhere over Turkey, the first few packages were marshaling: Falcons, Eagles, and Weasels. A squadron of Buffs was leveling off near max altitude.

"Stations in five mike!" called out Ice.

By now, blood was rushing in my ears. We'd all been vigorously working the signal environment since we'd been cleared in. The primary target list was ready; all Jim had to do was push the button and throw the Lady into jam.

Those last few minutes passed in a blur. I vaguely heard Captain Smily declare, "Stations, environment left!"

Jim slammed the Lady into jam as soon as we reached our window. The real work began, along with the light show. Tammy and Popcorn started calling out the ingress and the locations of hot spots.

The cabin was hot; sweat was dripping along the contours of my face. If I hadn't been so busy, I would've asked Crow to turn down the heat. Sweat box or ice box, never in between.

The targets began to do the "hop-skip" as I called it, trying desperately to re-establish communications. Thankfully the gang was on top of things as usual, and those below were having little luck.

Somewhere in the frenzy, 12:00 came and went. I didn't glance at my watch again until 15:30 when we were pulling off stations. We were wheels down fifty-five minutes later.

There would be no postflight briefings today; it was straight into crew rest. Exactly why, we didn't know. But we did know that we'd by flying the O'dark thirty the next morning.

Sunday, 24 February 1991

It was a good thing I had gone to bed early the previous evening, for it was barely past midnight when the alert came. Chris, Cowboy and I weren't at all excited about the news. We would've preferred a few more hours of sleep. Hell, another thirty minutes would've seemed akin to heaven.

My watch read 02:45 as the crew poured into ops. The big board said one crew was already airborne and wasn't due back for several hours. We expected someone to tell us the ground war had kicked off, but no one did.

Preflight briefings were rushed, and we were sitting in the crew lounge an hour later awaiting word on our Go time. We didn't know the exact time; we only knew a mission was to be airborne and ready to provide support as necessary every minute from now until we were directed otherwise.

Tired and haggard, we stretched out on the couches of the lounge, some nearly comatose, or so it appeared.

Within minutes, reports began to trickle in. It had finally happened; we had started our journey down the long road home, the one that went through Kuwait and perhaps to Baghdad.

Happy and Cowboy began screaming and hollering, and the rest of us soon joined in. I think we woke just about everyone in the adjacent rooms. We quickly had not a few sleepy-eyed visitors join us. "What's going on? What's going on?"

"The ground war! The ground war!" we responded.

It was perhaps thirty minutes later that we excitedly stormed out of the lounge. I remember watching the black road slip away as I looked out a window. The unknown had returned to haunt the corners of our minds. Again, we didn't know exactly what lay ahead, and it was at the same time exciting and frightening.

As we slipped quietly down the road to the waiting Lady, I watched the scant early-morning traffic pass; the headlights were white—bright white—as they raced toward us. I squinted my eyes but continued the long stare into the blackness. I watched the vehicles pass thus, several humvees, some armored personnel carriers, and two transport trucks; a few were ferrying Turkish troops and I wondered where they were going.

The flight line was alive with activity and congested. We drove past numerous aircraft heavily laden with bombs and air-air missiles. As soon as we were airborne, the mission currently on station would begin the trek home and minutes later we would take their place. Soon afterward the first package would follow. Leading the charge would be a force of fully-loaded Fighting Falcons twenty strong.

As I clambered up the steps of the crew entrance door, I thought about the tremendous force on the ground that had just been unleashed. Under the canopy of darkness, they were just gaining momentum, starting out at a sedate pace, gradually building until they were moving like an unstoppable freight train, its whistle screaming out into the dead of night. Screaming,

screaming, screaming.

Lurking in the Persian Gulf, poised and ready for action near the Kuwaiti coast, was an amphibious assault force that was ready to storm the beaches as the Allies had in Normandy. In anticipation of this assault, the enemy had deployed reinforcements along the coast as a protective measure. But the amphibious assault force didn't hit the beaches. They were a diversion, the first of several.

Forces that had been positioned directly opposite enemy forces had slipped away silently into the night—a last-minute westward shift of a massive force that would go long and show up where the enemy least expected them.

The land was still captured by the blackness of night when the 1st and 2nd U.S. Marine divisions accompanied by the U.S. Army Tiger Brigade began their gallant assault on the dreaded Saddam line: a lethal maze of razor-wire, minefields, and entrenchments designed to slow the progress of attackers to a standstill while the defenders picked them off.

It seemed that the weather couldn't get much worse for the start of the ground war, but it did.

Breaching such elaborate defenses would be no picnic. The Marines, well-prepared for this task and under the canopy of darkness, stormed the barriers. Suddenly the dark and dreary night sparked to life.

The Marines raced into the barrier complex—runners in a steeplechase. The French 6th Armored Division along with U.S. Airborne troopers, with their very first objective in sight, rushed overland. Their first objective: As Salman Airfield. The deadly coast flooded with Iraqi forces awaiting an amphibious assault that would not come became the instant nightmare of two Saudi task forces.

As I performed the standard preflight checks on my position, I wandered back through the many lost days.

More than 90,000 missions flown.

Forty-three killed in action, twenty-four Americans and nineteen Saudis.

Thirty-seven Americans listed as non-combat deaths.

Another one hundred and five non-combat casualties during Desert Shield.

Fifty-one missing in action—thirty American, ten British, one Italian, and ten Saudi.

Thirteen known allied prisoners of war—nine American, two British, one Italian, and one Kuwaiti.

Forty-one allied planes lost. Thirty-two in combat—twenty-three American, six British, one Kuwaiti, one Italian, and one Saudi. Nine non-combat losses—seven American, one British, and one Saudi. Twelve American helicopters to non-hostile causes.

Iraqi losses were staggering by comparison: nearly 30,000 Iraqis taken prisoner, 140 Iraqi planes destroyed, estimated losses in the thousands perhaps even tens of thousands.

We had won the air campaign hands down, but what would the start of the ground conflict bring? What had happened to the standing army of more than one million strong—the fourth largest army in the world—its thousands of tanks, armored vehicles and artillery pieces? We were about to find out for sure, but estimates said well over fifty percent were destroyed.

There was no denying that they had battle-hardened troops, troops that had survived the eight-year Iran-Iraq war, troops like the Elite Republican Guard. At this stage, they had been pounded mercilessly by five weeks of the most intense bombing campaign in history. They were tired and disheveled and had endured catastrophic losses. A number of units along the front lines were on the verge of physical collapse, suffering from malnutrition and lack of medical treatment.

The roar of the engines broke my reverie. I double-checked my straps, fastened the velcro on my flight suit sleeves once my nomex gloves were in place, and then eased my weight against the back of the chair.

The Lady began to rumble slowly along the taxiway. On ship's interphone, I heard the front-end crew finishing up the last of their checks, and then I heard Tower Control give us takeoff clearance.

The whine of the engines rose to a roar as we raced along the runway. Soon the Lady lifted lethargically into the early morning sky. Then I heard gears moan as the landing gear was secured. In a few minutes, we'd enter the combat zone once more: my twenty-ninth flight. At the time, I couldn't know or guess how many would remain. I only knew the ground campaign was finally underway; and perhaps days, weeks, or even months remained.

Evening, Sunday, 24 February 1991

The ground campaign was progressing with unfathomable swiftness, encountering little resistance and receiving thousands of surrendering Iraqis. I believed it was a good sign and represented promise for the days ahead. The Iraqis were tired of daily poundings by bombs and artillery. Many had read the propaganda leaflets describing the treatment of prisoners of war. They were tired and hungry, and they just wanted the war to end. They also got an eyeful of our invasion force and that was just the tip of the iceberg. I couldn't deny that the worst days might be just ahead. No one knew for sure.

Sitting there, staring at four off-white walls, I thought of Katie often. I wondered what she was doing, what she was thinking. Everything was moving so fast. In the KTO, the battlefield was shrouded in a thick black haze. Smoke from hundreds of burning oil wells created a sea of turmoil and destruction. Above the murky canopy of black, flames from the hundreds of fires shone out dully, but amidst the turmoil of the battlefield the flames blazed on, fed by dark rich oil spewing out of the desert sand.

As the allies in the KTO raced forward, we raced on to Baghdad—the great Gray Lady giving us shelter from the storm for a time. I felt at ease for a few heartbeats, but that false sense of security was shattered just before dawn as the copilot spotted a smoke trail rising from the ground. It was an Iraqi SAM intent on knocking us out of the sky. Captain Sammy turned the Lady evasively. My seat restraints pulled taunt, then gravity took over and slapped me hard against the seat.

Ice screamed on the radio. "Did you see it? Where the hell is it?"

Captain Sammy didn't let up. He followed a textbook evasive maneuver for all it was worth. In actuality, though, there wasn't much we could do now but pray. Our lives came down to a few crucial seconds. Blood was rushing in my ears. I felt time stop as if all the world had paused mid-breath. I could feel my heart beat and I counted the beats one by one as I was jerked around in my seat. Then without notice, the Lady leveled off and everything became smooth, as if we were floating on calm seas.

No one paused longer than it took to expel the breaths stifled in our lungs. It was back to work. Somewhere out there, unseen and unheard, the second wave was marshaling.

Tennessee Jim was on the radio with Gypsy. I heard his voice tweaking in my ears and I heard Gypsy's returning squawk. They were talking about aborting the mission. Aborting the mission? Blood was still rushing in my ears. I wouldn't have minded returning to base, but we'd be letting down those that were counting on us for sure.

Shit had hit the fan before and we'd survived it. This incident was just another harsh reminder that we needed to be ever vigilant. We may have embarked upon the journey home, but it was still a long, long road. It only takes an instant; one heartbeat you're alive, the next you're dead.

In my mind's eye I pictured the Lady engulfed in hungry red-orange flames, and for an instant I thought of Captain Gandis in tears. "I don't want to die; I don't want to die," she was screaming.

We didn't abort that day, but for that one solitary instant, I wished to God we had. Our Lady had just circled the airfield and was coming in for a landing when Captain Hillman's crew was beginning their orbit. I didn't envy them. We'd done our job and now it was time for them to do theirs.

Captain Smily touched the wheels down gently, and then I heard the engines flare. Soon the Lady was gliding to a halt. Shortly afterward, Crow lowered the rear ramp and door so he could better direct the backing of the plane, and a burst of air rolled into the cabin. For an instant it swept in fresh and filled with moisture, then the backwash began and engine fumes rushed inward.

I could tell at once that the air was cooler than usual. And once the rear ramp was fully down, I could see that the sky was overcast and somber.

By now, as always, I had cottonmouth; my ears were crackling as pressure equalized in my inner ear, and a thin film of dirt and grime covered my face and hands. Pulling the irritating foam plugs out of my ears, I tried to clear them with little luck. The Lady was no pleasure liner with constant air pressure. The pressure in my ears on the ride down from altitude had been nearly unbearable, a red hot burn that stretched from my inner ear up to my temples and across my eyes—the start of another cold had found me and I'd run out of sinus medication.

The engines began to wind down, and one by one I heard them come to a halt. The cabin blackened, and I heard Tennessee Jim clear us out of the aircraft. I unhooked my helmet and oxygen mask, clearing the regulator, then disconnected my headset; a few seconds after that, I was clambering down the steps outside the crew entrance door.

Solid ground beneath my feet felt good, but I could still feel the vibration of the Lady and hear the hum of the engines. I watched the crew exit one by one, and I saw mostly happy faces. We were always glad to have both feet planted on solid ground and to breathe fresh, clean air.

The quiet moment was interrupted, though, as we at first heard and then watched a group of Fighting Falcons taxi for takeoff.

While we waited for the crew van, we watched the package slowly pass by and then leave, screaming into the overcast sky, afterburners blazing.

I watched them race toward the mountains, soon disappearing from sight.

I remember that the air was slowly growing colder and I was putting on my jacket but not much else after that. Soon we were rumbling along a bumpy road to ops.

Afternoon brought another stage in the ground offensive, which was progressing with unexpected swiftness. Two more massive U.S. forces began their moves: the XVIII Corps and VII Corps. The VII Corps began a wide outflanking operation to the west while the XVIII Corps set out to cut off all reinforcement and escape routes into the KTO.

Diversionary pan-Arab and Saudi assaults began, straight into the Saddam line. Meanwhile, the 24th Infantry Division Mechanized began to stream across the border, moving west of the main Iraqi troop concentrations; and hours ahead of schedule, the massive VII Corps began to rumble across the barren desert. They launched at a full run, making a clean breakthrough. The U.S. 1st Infantry Division and the British 1st Armored Division also made their move, slipping in between Iraqi divisions and either overrunning or destroying everything in their path.

The final stage was at last set.

Monday, 25 February 1991

This was the Kuwaiti New Year. The TV was filled with gruesome images from the ground campaign. Unbelievably, the Marines were already on the move toward the outskirts of Kuwait City.

It could all be over in a matter of days if this pace were maintained. Unbelievable!

Our crews were still supporting mission packages nonstop. The orders were basically to level everything of strategic or tactical value that was left. A tall order.

Already, everyone sensed that the end was perhaps near. We were in a frenzy to destroy what remained of the Iraqi war machine before it was all over. To me this was a clear sign that we wouldn't push on to Baghdad; but one could always hope, for it was the only way to end this thing for sure. If the war were to end in the next few days, I didn't believe it would bring the solutions that everyone thought it would. Pushing Iraq out of Kuwait was not the ultimate solution, but occupying Iraq was not the ultimate solution either.

It had been an unusually long day. I was waiting for Chris and

Cowboy to come back from ops with news, but I didn't think I could hold out any longer. I was going to try to get some sleep.

When Chris and Cowboy got back, they had good news. It looked like the Iraqis were already making a mass exodus from Kuwait City along Highway 6 that leads north to Iraq. I imagined that we had no few surprises in store for them.

A letter also came for me, all sweet-scented.

Tuesday, 26 February 1991

The headlines were changing so fast the newscasters couldn't keep up with them. First, the Iraqis claimed they were withdrawing from Kuwait, which is partially true; but actually they were running from Kuwait trying to salvage what remained of their once-proud fighting machine.

The Iraqis were on the run. We were keying into the news and the dispatches and little else. The air campaign had not stopped though you would think so by the news coverage. I knew the guys on the ground were facing a living hell, but we'd faced it and run smack into it for these past many weeks, and soon I'd face it again. We had an afternoon flight that day. I hoped everything would go well.

The campaign was progressing beyond anyone's expectations, but the Iraqis were not yet defeated. They continued to set oil wells on fire, making the skies over the battlefield ever more obscured and black. This also covered their retreat. The number of Iraqis surrendering was soaring every hour. More than 30,000 so far.

The night before, our forces did find those fleeing Iraqis

along Highway 6. We smacked the hell out of thousands of vehicles, leaving miles of burned and bombed out vehicles smoldering on the ground.

The news was not all good and came with other sobering news. Late the night before, an Iraqi Scud missile hit an Army barracks killing 28 and wounding nearly 100. The reports said it was "dumb luck" that the Scud struck where it did, but it was "dumb luck" that killed 28 U.S. soldiers.

These thoughts and others fell from my mind as I opened the door to find Thomas standing there. "Long time no see. Aren't you early?" I asked.

"No, right on time. Chris and Cowboy here?"

"Chris is in the shitter. Cowboy'll be back in a few. Don't worry. I'll tell him. Rough day? You look like shit."

"Two more hours, man, and then I'm going to hit the bed hard."

"What's the word from ops?"

"Looks good, real good. Bob's been down there all day." Thomas paused, then added "Hey, got to run. Drop by tomorrow. I got some beers."

"Sounds good. Later," I said, closing the door. I glanced in the mirror. I hadn't shaved yet, so I stuck the electric razor to my face. I'd just gotten back from a long workout, so a shower was the next priority.

I stared into the mirror long and hard. Images of all sorts flashed before my eyes. Today was number thirty-one, yet I knew that when I zipped up my flight suit in thirty minutes, grabbed my flight gear in one hand, my chem gear in the other, I'd feel a sudden rush of energy that would carry me through the long mission ahead.

Wednesday, 27 February 1991

Early in the morning, in the twilight hours before dawn, the liberation of Kuwait City began. After that, the day screamed by with increasingly good news flowing from the KTO. The crew was alerted, and a few of us were waiting in front of the barracks for the duty driver to show. My watch read 20:32. At 20:35, the crew van pulled up.

We made two stops. The first to pick up Tennessee Jim and the rest of the gang from their billeting quarters. The second to pick up Tammy and Sparrow.

Among the crew, there was always a high degree of camaraderie, but tonight during the brief ride to ops, I'd never seen so many happy and energetic faces. We all knew the end was near; we just didn't know how near.

The ops center was buzzing; Kuwait City had been liberated hours ago, the Iraqis were retreating, and our fighters, bombers and helicopters were smacking the hell out of dozens of convoys trying desperately to make it back to mother Iraq in one piece.

Down in intel, Derrin and the lieutenant were in exceptionally good spirits. Over the next few minutes, we found out why.

"You're most certainly flying our unit's last combat mission of this war, gentlemen and ladies. I wish I could fly with you this one last time." began Derrin.

"As I'm sure you already know, the allies took Kuwait City earlier today. The Iraqis have definitely found themselves in a rout. There's not much left, but certainly a lot of cleaning up to do before it's all over. The orbit box has been pushed farther south once again, as you can see." Derrin tapped on the big map with his pointer.

It was tight quarters in the little room; even so, we pressed forward as he began to point out the targets. His pointer came down many times on familiar targets: Mosul, Erbil, Kirkuk, Qayyarah and many others, working his way steadily southward to Baghdad. He left the pointer slapped against the big red circle at Baghdad.

Derrin's last words before we headed to the Lady were clear, "The Buffs are going to re-strike the area around the presidential palace. Five-thousand pound bombs; maybe one of them will hit pay dirt."

I always felt a little cocky with my .38 strapped inside my survival vest, and especially so once I loaded it, which I was doing now. I double-checked the parachute in my seat, having already fitted it once before. I knew I didn't want to be careless now; none of us did.

The front-end went through their Before Combat and Before Takeoff Checks with extra care. Soon afterward, I heard the engines begin to crank one by one. I glanced around the half-lit cabin; the expressions were still happy ones. My watch read 23:35 as we taxied down the darkened runway.

I closed my eyes for a moment and let the hum of the engines lull me. I didn't open them again until I felt the landing gear coil up into the Lady's belly. A quiet couple of minutes passed as I listened to the hum of engines and we climbed into the night sky.

That day, I don't remember hearing Martha, but I do recall hearing Lou Gramm. Over the many long weeks, we had adopted many songs. Each had their special meanings. Lou Gramm's song Lost in the Shadows, was one such song. It spoke of sailing into the night, lost in the shadows, and the emptiness inside you. We all had large, empty holes within us. That night, we were hopeful the holes would begin to fill in.

Thursday, 28 February 1991

The flight begun the previous day continued. "Fifteen mike to border crossing," Bill, the Nav, called out.

An unsettling silence followed as the music stopped and the radios seemed to pause with expectancy.

Cowboy was already in the back spotting, and now Tammy joined him. I saw a green glint of light, the glow of NVG, as I glanced toward the rear.

Tennessee Jim was just finishing up with the system, and now he turned it over to us. "Crew, MCC, clear to log in!"

I slapped my fingers against the keyboard and went through the log in sequence. "MCS, Six, logged in, ready to go to work!"

"Roger, Six."

The others were right behind me.

"Roger. Four, Roger. One and Two, Roger. Three, Roger. MCC, MCS, we're all logged in and ready to go to work."

"Well, then, prepare to give 'em hell!"

"Border crossing confirmed," tweaked Bill's voice into my headset.

I heard Gypsy squawking faintly now, and I turned up her channel. Blood was rushing in my ears already and we weren't even on orbit yet.

Searching the spectrum had been old hack for a while now. I knew where to expect activity and where not to, but I still checked everything I came across. You never knew for sure; you just never knew for sure. We had all passed a number of viable targets to the MCC, and he had the jam list loaded and ready to go long before we turned onto orbit, "Environment right."

"Let's give 'em hell," repeated Jim, "this could be the last one; let's make it count!"

The first wave had already been marshaling and was right behind us. Jim slammed the Lady into jam less than a minute after we were turned onto orbit. Tonight, we were going to hit them hard and fast, and keep hitting them nonstop until we turned off orbit. "Crew, we're jammin'!" screamed out Jim, his voice crackling in my headset. Over his position, I saw the reassuring green lights flashing away.

"Traffic low and fast, moving nine to three," called out Cowboy proudly. "Will you look at that!"

As I worked feverishly, I pictured the green flames lighting up Cowboy's and Tammy's NVG. Two by two, three by three, four by four, fighters screamed in-country. The ensuing light show was tremendous. Aerial flashes, bomb bursts, secondary explosions. Somewhere in the darkness of the night, the Buffs were closing in on Baghdad, preparing to deliver their five-thousand-pound burdens.

For a moment, we came out of jam to take an extra close look at the environment around us. I had just keyed into a new frequency, and my heart nearly stopped. I heard gunfire in the background and explosions growing louder and more predominant; and then I heard a scream, a single, tormented wail that seemed as if it would never end. An instant later I heard emptiness and static. A moment afterward, Jim put the Lady back into jam, and the static grew subtly louder. I listened to the emptiness for a moment more, staring blankly at the video display screen in front of me while the scream replayed in my mind.

When I finally broke the deadlock on the display, I realized I was shaking. I steadied one hand on top of the other and touched my fingers back to the keyboard. I don't know why—perhaps I'll never know why—I took it so hard. I'd heard such screams a dozen times. We'd even laughed about them, the morose way people do, because if you don't laugh you might have to think about what you heard and what it really meant.

"Here they come. Will you look at that? Jesus!" Cowboy whistled into his microphone.

Gypsy was squawking again; the area was still clear. No sign of enemy air activity. There was still plenty happening on the ground. AAA gunners were lighting up the sky in a never-ending and ever-spreading bouquet. The wall wasn't what it had been at the height of the war, but disheveled or not, artillery fire was artillery fire.

Part of the first wave was coming out, and the second wave was already heading in. It didn't take long listening to the Cowboy, Tammy, and the front-end crew whoop and holler for the blood to start rushing in my ears again. This was the last one, I told myself, it had to be. We were throwing just about everything we had at them as fast as we could. It was surely the final face off.

I glanced at my watch again. We were nearing the end of our window. One last hour, I told myself, hopeful now, joyous now.

In the back of my mind, I could see the afterburners of dozens of fighters now, racing in and screaming out. God, it was magnificent!

One hour and forty-five minutes later, the Lady was touching down. Captain Sammy put her down so smoothly I didn't even realize we were racing along the runway until the engines slowed and we were braking to taxi speed. A perfect landing. For a moment it felt as though we were floating on a cushion of air across a slick and clear field of ice, then suddenly we stopped. Crow lowered the ramp and door, and briefly I smelled the dampness of early morning, followed immediately by propeller backwash: jet fuel.

We wouldn't understand the irony of leaving the combat zone, leaving Iraqi territory at 04:00 for several hours. At any rate, I was glad the mission was over. My thirtieth mission was mission complete.

Inevitably, as I walked away from the Lady, I looked back as I always did. The morning was cool and the sky was held in the light of dawn. The day promised to be clear or so it appeared.

It was nearly 06:00 when we returned to ops. A crew was headed out the door: Captain Hillman, Stopwatch, Darwin, Sandy, Topper, Able, Mellow Yellow, Max, Candid, Beebop, Steve, and Rollin. They'd be airborne within the hour and racing toward the zone. At 06:00, we should have been finishing up at ops and preparing to return to our quarters, but we weren't.

We had just been told that President Bush had addressed the nation. He had announced an end to offensive operations in the Persian Gulf, an end to the Persian Gulf War, at 04:00 our time, with the cease-fire to take effect in three hours. Finding out two hours after the fact didn't make the news any less emotional; it brought us to the brink of tears, to laughter, and then back to tears.

The announcement had been made at 04:00 our time; the cease-fire was to take effect three hours later. We all knew that anything could happen in the interim between announcements and follow-through, but we couldn't deny that the appointed hour was nearly upon us. I chewed on my thumbnails as I waited for the minutes to tick by.

Emotions were still flowing strongly; and briefly our faces would flush with mirth or sadness, or even a combination of both. It was a feeling akin to when your mother tells you, "The dog died," but you don't want to believe it; so at first you laugh and then you rationalize, your face flushes with confusion, disbelief, and finally sadness. Then you tell yourself, "No it couldn't be," so you smile a sickly half smile again.

Now I was rationalizing again. I didn't want to fully believe it. The news seemed too good to be true. It is what I had wanted, what we had all wanted, but it seemed more a dream than a reality. My thoughts flashed back to January the 15th. It had been the middle of the night when the news had come. The phone rang once and then twice. I didn't want it to wake Katie, so I ran to pick it up, hoping it was one of our relatives who had forgotten the time difference when calling to Germany again, but knowing in my heart that it wasn't. I had known the voice on the other end of the phone the instant I heard it and the significance of the call in that same instant. I remember hanging up the phone and turning to find a sea of sad brown eyes, eyes filled with shock, horror, and finally tears. Was it over? Was it *really* over?

07:00 came and the cease-fire took effect. Captain Hillman's crew wouldn't get their chance for that one last combat flight.

The distinction would go to our crew. We had flown the unit's last combat flight of the Persian Gulf War.

Reports flooded in. News broadcasters heralded the end of the war. I'd been up most of the previous day and all night; each of us had, but we weren't tired, not any more. Hours later, I still found myself asking, "Is it really over?"

Hours after that, I was sitting in my room alone in the dark, alone with my thoughts, which eventually turned back to the war. I was never far away from it, even when both feet were on the ground, even now when it seemed to be over.

I stood and flicked on the dim light over the sink, standing still, staring into the mirror at the stranger in the reflection. It was then that I noticed it was gone—it being the feeling everything was continuously in motion, the feeling you get when you're sitting strapped into a flight seat and the vibration and roar of the engines are lulling you and calling out to you, the same feeling you get after a twenty-hour cross-country drive, the feeling that you are still sitting in your car driving nonstop down the road while the road stretches out endlessly before you even though you had stopped driving hours ago.

I had a sudden flashback to a night several weeks ago, a night after an intense day. The rain had been pounding and cleansing the land, and it had been all I could do to attempt sleep and stop thinking about what I had seen and heard. Outside my window, it was again raining. Again, I attempted sleep as I had that night; but when that didn't work, I went to the window and peered out into the gloom. The sky was overcast and a relentless rain was drenching the land. Beaten by strong winds, it splashed up against the window.

Even as I looked out at the rain hammering the land, kicking up dark mud and pounding against the window, I saw war: unrelenting flashes of AAA, explosions, jets passing by, and not far off aerial bursts. In the back of my mind, I heard screams. Panicked shouts to Allah the merciful, Allah the benevolent, Allah the forgiving.

The rain continued to pound mud outside my window as I watched and listened. I crossed back to the mirror and stared at the stranger again. "I'm still waiting for the sun to shine," I whispered, "a mere ray of sunshine won't do."

Friday, 1 March 1991

Thursday's headlines read, "Allies liberate Kuwait City." Friday's headlines were even better. They read, "All's quiet on the front." That was good news although I knew that cleanup efforts by army ground forces would continue and could last days or even weeks. Our crew was on two-hour alert status all day, which basically means if hostilities start again, it's our job to scramble. They would alert us, and we would go straight to the plane, no questions asked.

I kept asking myself, is it really over? Have we done all we set out to do? At the same time, I told myself, Hell yes! My gut told me no. We'd stirred up a hornet's nest and then buried our heads in the sand because higher-ups said, "End this thing now." We squashed Iraq and kicked them out of Kuwait, a knock-out at the beginning of the second round. The fundamental question now was, "Should we have continued? Should we have stopped only when we reached Baghdad?" Many of my fellow crewers, guys and gals, seemed to think we should have opted for the latter plan: continuing on to Baghdad.

We had hours of idle time to ponder and debate this—the

dreaded endless waiting. It was not that we were unhappy the war was over; it was just that it seemed we were one step away. One tiny step away. But then we also had to ask what it would have cost in anguish and in lives to take that extra step. If it would have really been worth the risk. We also had to remind ourselves that the Iraqi people are not necessarily our enemy. Iraqi field soldiers were following orders just as we were. Subjugating a people would have solved little. We would've been doing to Iraq what they had done to Kuwait.

I find it ironic that I had dark thoughts on such a glorious day. I decided to join the celebrations across the hall even though I couldn't drink any bravos (perhaps the reason for the glum thoughts).

Gentleman Bob called a meeting of all personnel that evening. We expected good news.

Since that day was a day of remembrance, looking backward and forward, I glanced through the pages of my journal. So many pages filled with my scarcely legible scrawl, it was hard to believe that it was weeks' worth of writings and not months'. The journal was nearly full, only a few last pages to fill.

It was the start of my seventh week in the Persian Gulf. So much had happened, it just didn't seem real. That day didn't seem real though I knew it was. I hoped to see Katie soon. I'd know then for sure it was over.

Sunday, 3 March 1991

I didn't make a journal entry Saturday. I didn't know why then and even as I thought about it on Sunday, I still didn't know why. I had just let the journal rest on my night stand with an uncapped pen on top of it the whole of the day. I decided to leave the page blank with only the date written in.

Sunday was a strange and wonderful day. Indeed, even as I wrote in my journal, the cease-fire negotiations were taking place. High-ranking Iraqi officials were meeting our high-ranking officials at Safwan. CNN no longer heralded "The War in the Gulf," and the major newspaper headlines no longer waved the war banner. On Saturday they showed pictures of grief, soldiers mourning the losses of comrades. Pictures of death, destruction, and freedom.

On Sunday, they'd gone on to other issues. One of the major topics in the news was the troop cuts in Europe. Before the build-up in the Gulf, the big news in Europe had been the expected draw-down of forces. A large number of the combat units in the Gulf were there under the stop-loss program, which effectively extended their duty assignments until war's end. I never thought the war's end would bring that nightmare back to life.

I also thought it odd to find an article on the second page of the Stars and Stripes about U.S. Desert Storm troops upset because they hadn't seen combat. My first thought was that I'd trade my memories of war and combat to be in their shoes. I would bundle up all those tormented hours, those minutes where I counted heartbeats and breaths, and hand them out right then. But then after I finished reading the article, I put the paper down and really thought about it. To have come all this way, trained day in and out, and to have seen nothing would've been frustrating as hell. They'll go through the rest of their lives wondering what they'd have done had the shit hit the fan.

Everyone reacts differently when the shit hits the fan. Some like Captain Gandis break and run for cover when they find the stakes are too high. Some like Big John, who's in Germany alone now, are made to break and run for cover. The bravest and the boldest can become the meek, and the meek can become the example for others to follow. It all comes down to that one instant, that one solitary heartbeat when you face uncertainty and the end of your days on this earth. Me, I don't have to wonder; I know, I really know. I didn't freeze up or run scared. I did what I had to do and looked the devil in the eye while I did it.

As I stop again to ponder this, I think perhaps wondering wouldn't be so bad, either, though I still wouldn't give away the memories. I paid for each and every one not in blood, but in a different way—a way that you can't express or touch.

Thinking about all this seems strange. Looking back seems strange. I thought as I wrote this that I could only look forward once I had looked back. I wanted to look forward, so I knew that

I had to look backward first. A handful of pages to go, and this journal would be full. I was not so sure I wanted to begin another. If I did, I hoped to be at home in Germany with Katie beside me when I started that first page.

For then what I had to look forward to was joining the rest of the crew in the lounge of the operations building, which I did. The big meeting hadn't taken place on Friday and now we were all eagerly awaiting the arrival of Gentleman Bob and Major James.

We were roughly congregated by crews. I saw Captain Willie, whom I hadn't seen in days. Beside him were PBJ, Thomas, and Cosmo. On the far side of the room I saw Captain Hillman and Stopwatch. Max, Tommy, Topper, and Sandy were sitting with their backs against the foot of a couch nearby. Tennessee Jim was to my right, jawing his chew, spit cup in hand. Cowboy and Popcorn were fighting for armrest space to my left.

The TV was on, and the voice of a newscaster boomed across the room above the din of voices and other sounds. History was unfolding before our eyes. The cease-fire talks at Safwan progressed swifter than anticipated. In two short hours, the Iraqis agreed to comply with all coalition demands.

Momentarily, the room grew quiet. Bad Boy leaned in close to the TV to turn up the volume. The newscaster was talking about the status of POWs inside Iraq. I turned my head and tuned in closely to the voice. "Sixty-six troops are currently listed as missing in action: 45 Americans, 10 Britons, 10 Saudis, and one Italian. Iraq's UN Ambassador claims that 10 prisoners of war were released in what they term, 'a gesture of good faith.' Among those released are six Americans. The nationalities of the other four are unknown. The names of the six Americans are not known although it is known that one is a female soldier."

Our spirits soared. The din grew out of control and quickly drowned out the announcer. Then just as suddenly, the room went quiet. I turned my attention back to the hall and saw Gentleman Bob and Major James. They entered the room and we snapped sharply to attention. My arms pinned to my sides, the heels of my boots touching, I stood rigidly, eyes front.

No one had called us to attention; the reaction had been an instinctive one. Pride was at the forefront of our thoughts. We were truly proud to be Americans. Proud of what we had accomplished together.

Normally, Gentleman Bob would have put us at ease and told us to take our seats almost immediately, but today was different. He just eyed us for a moment. This was the closest thing to a military formation we'd had since our arrival, and it seemed strange and not strange to be standing silently at attention.

I clasped my cupped hands tighter to my legs, brought my head and shoulders truer, standing tall. For an instant I heard the hiss of a loudspeaker. Right then, I expected one of Bob's cavalry calls or the Charge of the Light Brigade to begin. I never expected the Star-Spangled Banner.

Instinctively, my right hand went to my heart, and even though the speaker played only music, the words echoed in my mind. I added to this the image of Old Glory waving gallantly before my eyes.

As the last note died in the air, Gentleman Bob set us at ease and told us to take our seats.

"Gentlemen and Ladies, the events over the last few days have been historic, historic indeed. While others can say they've witnessed history, you can say you played a role in the making of history," began Gentleman Bob, his voice filled with vigor. "A lot of you have been bombarding me with questions over the last few days, and I told you I'd answer them when I had some answers. Well, today, I'm going to try to answer most of those questions. The question I heard most was, 'When are we going home?' I know you're all eager to return home. Hell, I am too! If it were up to me, hell, I'd say right now, pack and let's go. But it's not up to me. We have to get the okay from higher headquarters first. I expect the word to come within days, so I'd ask each of you to be patient. We are working on it.

"I know a few of you came to me and told me about pressing family matters. I'm working on that, too. The first thing we are going to do is find out exactly the number of folks we need to maintain our readiness and effectiveness. Once that is worked out, we'll start sending some of you home. Personally, I think we can safely cut the number of crews to three and that will also cut the number of support people needed. All I ask is that you hang in there with me."

I didn't hear a word of what he said after that; I could only see Old Glory waving before my eyes and listen to the lingering echoes in my mind. Now I could look forward to the future and to returning home. The sun was about to shine.

Monday, 4 March 1991

The days were slowly eking by. Ground troops in the KTO were still keeping busy cleaning up the battlefield: destroying munitions and equipment strewn about all over the place, caring for the scores of wounded, and disposing of the enemy dead in the field. It was a grim sight, and a grim thing to imagine. We were keeping busy by packing our gear and cleaning our equipment in the hope that soon we would be able to go home. For us the war was over though the waiting continued.

They'd set up a new MPC schedule. They rotated the schedule by crews on a weekly basis. Our crew was to start the following week. I hadn't flown since the last day of the war. It seemed strange, as if everything had suddenly stopped.

True to his word, Gentleman Bob reviewed the number of crews needed to maintain our effectiveness should fighting restart. Three crews was the magic number decided upon. The idea was that three crews could support whatever happened, and if things heated up too much, those that returned home would redeploy. They were counting on two Go's a day, with one crew in crew rest. We didn't know which crews would be cut, which crews would stay. In a way, I was hoping that I would be one of the last to go back. It'd be terrible to go all the way home and then have to return. I was not sure if Katie or I could take it.

I remember someone asking me once if I would have come here so eagerly, knowing what I know now. I remember saying, "No questions asked." Things were different then. Would I go home and then come back again? I could only hope I would never have to make that decision. I missed home. I missed it a lot. I missed Katie more than anything.

It would have been something akin to torture to go home and then have to come back. I didn't want to see Katie's face covered in fear and horror again, her eyes filled with tears. If I didn't see her again, then I wouldn't know, and not knowing was definitely much better than knowing.

The growing civil unrest in Iraq made me certain that if we did go home any time soon, we'd surely be coming back. We had stirred up a giant hornet's nest and now we were unsure what to do about it, yet we couldn't just leave and let innocent people be butchered in the streets.

Tuesday, 5 March 1991

The first U.S. troops were to return on Thursday. As many as 15,000. There was much talk about homecoming celebrations, parades, and parties. TV was showing celebrations already in full swing in the states. People waving American flags and singing songs like "God Bless the USA." That song forever brings tears to my eyes.

Baghdad radio announced that all remaining allied POWs were freed. Thirty-five POWs would be turned over to the Red Cross: fifteen Americans, nine Britons, nine Saudis, one Kuwaiti, and one Italian. I was sure that their families were relieved.

The civil unrest inside Iraq was intensifying, especially in and around Basra where anti-government troops and Republican Guard troops were clashing. The unrest was spreading to city after city. Kurdish rebels had apparently seized Erbil, a city of about 900,000 people, and at least four other northern Iraqi towns.

I was able to go off-post on Tuesday—Happy, Cowboy, Bad Boy, and I. The taxi ride to Incirlik, which was the small city directly outside the gates, cost $1.25 each. We ate lunch at a little diner, a Turkish dive, but the food was good and cost about $5.00 for one of the best meals I'd eaten since I'd been here.

We spent a few hours wandering around the city streets, going from shop to shop. The Turkish are a polite and honorable people, but their poverty strikes me as sad. My meager month's salary, which I think of as just above poverty levels by stateside standards, is a year's wage.

I didn't buy anything other than lunch, though I did look at a pair of gold earrings. I'm sure Katie would've loved them. At $35.00 they were a steal, but out of my price range.

It was quiet in the room. Chris had left, and Cowboy was crashed out from too many bravos. I decided to write Katie another letter before I called it a night, too. I thought I might beat it home if I were lucky.

Wednesday, 6 March 1991

So much idle time was driving me insane. All I could do was think of home and Katie. I tried to keep busy, but I couldn't stay busy all the time.

Mornings were the slowest time; there weren't many duties to do. I passed the afternoons playing spades with Darwin, Tommy, and Allen, evenings wandering about or watching the TV. Who'd believe the war had ended only a week ago?

Four crewers and two support troops departed on a C-5 Tuesday for Sembach, five more to go on Wednesday. Thursday, still more. It was hard to watch them go, and in a way I envied them. I knew my day would come; I just hoped it would be soon.

A lot of the guys were in a financial pinch, me included. I was scraping dimes again. Quite a few were getting advances on their pay and spending it all in the local market—leather, brass, copper, and jewelry were dirt cheap. I didn't want to get another advance on my pay, because I wasn't sure when I'd be going home. If I got another advance, I'd surely spend it; and sooner or later, I knew I'd have to pay the piper.

Bills were piling up at home, and I didn't need to be spending unnecessarily. Especially since the word was that they were going ahead with the planned base closures in Europe. Sembach was on the original hit list, and only the war kept it from closing along with dozens of others. The move to Germany was expensive enough. The move back to the states or wherever they would send me next would probably wipe out the last of our savings even if I took a two-month pay advance.

I wrote Katie and told her to sell the car. The only chance we had of getting our money out of it was to sell it before the market was flooded with used cars. I hoped we could sell it for enough money to pay off the bank loan.

I volunteered to clean vehicles. Anything to keep busy and stop thinking about going home.

Thursday, 7 March 1991

All I could think about was going home and Katie. I wanted someone to pinch me so I would know it was really over.

Friday, 8 March 1991

This is the next to the last page of my journal. I was hoping to be going home soon. Days were slipping away one by one in tedious succession. Victory celebrations in the states were in full swing. Homecomings, parades and parties were planned or taking place all over the country. Two weeks had passed since the war ended.

I talked to Katie Thursday evening. She was holding up well. She didn't understand why we were still here, especially if the war was actually over. I told her these things take time and with our planes they want to make sure before they send us home. Her voice was sad, and a few times she was in tears—she said it was a cold. I could tell that she was also relieved that the war was over and I was safe, especially when I told her we weren't flying now.

If nothing else, those days gave me a great deal of time to think. I knew I was not the same person who got on a C-5 bound for the Persian Gulf. The person who got on the C-5 didn't wake up in cold sweats, jump at the sound of a car backfiring, or duck for cover when sirens went off. Before, it had always been training, practice for the real thing. Then suddenly it was the real thing, and there I was in the middle of war, flying combat missions.

Would I go back there again? I'd thought about that question a lot. It seemed a simple enough question at first. I was in the military; I go where they tell me to go. After giving the question some more thought, I was not really sure. There were plenty of options; there's always a way out. Captain Gandis found one, Big John found one, and half a dozen others that were here did, too. To me, though, that way out seemed a cop out. I swore an oath to God and my country, and I upheld it. I was filled with nothing but pride for having done that. I'd have given my life if that had been the call, but it wasn't.

I guess the real reason I was thinking about all this was the forms on the nightstand that Major James had given me. Reenlistment paperwork. After I had looked at them, I avoided thinking about them. Six more years, or was it time to get out? I didn't know.

Major James had me pegged as a "lifer." He said I was "ate up." Gung ho. But reenlistment this time would be a serious step. If I were going to stay in over ten, I might as well stay in for twenty, or so the saying goes. Here's where I found myself going back to the first question. I really needed to sit down with Katie and talk about it. It was a serious decision and one I didn't want to make on the spur of the moment or without her input.

I was looking forward to going home like never before. There was just so much to think about, to do—the base closing, reenlistment, selling the car, bills, and money. I was down to a cup of change—dimes, nickels and pennies—and five one-dollar bills.

Saturday, 9 March 1991

The word finally came. What a rush! We could be going home as early as Sunday. I didn't believe it.

I didn't have time to write much; there were so many things we had to do. I doubted that we'd be able to get everything done to leave tomorrow. But I knew we would try. Cleaning out ops was a chore and then some.

Sunday, 10 March 1991

No chance of going home to Germany and Katie on Sunday. I remained hopeful of what Monday might bring. I didn't want to get my hopes up too high, though. Another disappoint would be too much.

Morale was at an all time low.

I was down to my last $2.

Monday, 11 March 1991

It seemed that everything I owned was stacked in a neat pile in the hall beside dozens of other neat and not-so-neat piles. The last thing I had packed was the picture of Katie in her red carnation dress. The picture I'd taken on Christmas Eve—a time that seemed a lifetime ago. We'd worked through the weekend, cleaning out ops, turning in gear, packing, doing all the things that you can only do at the last minute.

02:30 had been a hellish time to wake up, but I had to be ready to go by 04:00. My watch read 03:45—still fifteen minutes to spare. I could have slept fifteen more minutes, or so I told myself, knowing full well that I hadn't really slept at all since daybreak of the previous day.

Sleeping was an impossible wish with a thousand thoughts roaming through my mind, yet all I could think about was that finally we were going home. I'd waited for this day for what seemed an eternity; and now that the day had arrived, I couldn't believe it. My mind kept telling me I was dreaming again, and I'd wake up soon.

God, there was excitement in the halls. I'd be flying home

with Tennessee Jim and the rest of the gang from the crew. Gentleman Bob and Major James would also be on board. The flight home would be a long one; the Nav estimated our flight time at nine hours. We'd be hitting head winds most of the way, or so we expected.

The departure from Incirlik would be to the last man. Three crews on three planes heavily laden with our gear and as many extra passengers as could be accommodated. A C-5 would be taking all remaining personnel and our equipment home. In all, 300 were finally heading home.

Gentleman Bob was orchestrating the event so that we all arrived at Sembach Air Base, Germany, at the same time. The C-5 would touch down in nearby Ramstein and buses would take the personnel to Sembach. Three Gray Ladies would circle the airfield in flight formation then touch down one by one. The lead aircraft, crew one, would fly the Stars and Stripes from the forward hatch as the Lady taxied up the runway. The second, the German flag. The third, our unit colors.

While we knew this, we didn't know what type of reception we'd be getting. Sembach was a small base, so we expected a small reception. Even so, we were eager to be going home. Still, Bob was playing it up. He always played things up.

Other groups were also leaving Incirlik today: a wing of F-15, a wing of F-16, and their accompanying array of support personnel. Thousands were going home. We were going home.

Loading the plane took nearly an hour. My watch read 05:30, thirty minutes till takeoff. While excitement was running rampant, the rush to load the planes was over. It seemed that time had come to a halt whereas before it had whirred by.

We milled around outside the plane like lost sheep. Cowboy

was fiddling with the broad brim of his Texas cowpoke hat. Tennessee Jim was jawing his chew. Chris was pacing. Bad Boy was chain smoking. Sparrow was fussing with her hair. Tammy was blowing bubbles with her gum, one after the other. Pop, pop, pop.

Doc, one of the med techs who'd been itching to fly a mission since arrival but hadn't been able to, was nervously eyeing the Lady. In contrast, Hutch, an engine repair specialist, was crashed out on his knapsack. Gentleman Bob was prancing around with a glitter in his eye, Major James at his side. I glanced back at Tammy who was still blowing bubbles.

I inspected my wallet, one one-dollar bill, two quarters, one dime, and five pennies—$1.65. Yes, I was broke. I felt the weight of papers in the long leg pocket on the left side of my flight suit. I still hadn't selected my options: re-enlist, extend, or good-bye. I didn't want to think about that now, so I turned to look out at the mountains one last time, the land running smooth and clear to the rising ridges.

Beyond the mountains was Iraq. Not much remained of the former fourth largest army in the world. Saddam's mighty army was in shambles. Kuwait was a free nation. Iraq was in turmoil, riddled with violent unrest. Meanwhile, we were going home. It didn't seem right somehow, yet at the same time it felt good.

"Saddle up!" shouted Jim. I broke from my reverie and scrambled to my position.

Strapped in, facing forward, I listened to the pre-flight checks, the spin and then the roar of the engines.

"Crew ready for taxi and takeoff?" tweaked Bob's voice into my headset on ship's Interphone.

I gave a double thumbs up. The entire crew did.

"Pilot, MCC, we're all ready to go back here. Let's get the hell out of Dodge!"

"Roger, MCC. Crew prepare for takeoff."

"Roger."

"Crew, we're homeward bound!"

"Homeward bound," we returned.

I felt the rumble of wheels and engines as we rolled down the runway and then lifted into the sky. Nine hours to go, I told myself, only nine hours to go.

A nine-hour flight with mission is all in a day's work. A nine-hour flight with only expectations is endless.

For the first couple of hours enthusiasm levels remained off the scale. Music boomed out of the PA. Endless conversations were taking place on Select. Everyone was happy.

As time wore on, the enthusiasm wore thin. By the sixth hour the cabin was quiet and seemed lifeless. Most were curled up at their positions near sleep, feigning sleep, or asleep. I couldn't sleep though I tried. My watch kept calling to me. I wandered to the flight deck, to the rear, munched on crackers.

Doc was the only one who still seemed to be somewhat enthusiastic. He was looking out one of the rear portals. Nearby, Hutch was sound asleep, stretched out on the rear bunk.

Then the call came out over Interphone. "Crew, we're about an hour forty-five out. We're making good time and are going to cut back the throttles a bit so we don't get in too early. Our ETA is shortly after 16:00, 15:00 Germany time."

It was as if we'd just been alerted. Everyone stirred, looked at their watches. Frenzy and excitement returned.

I ate a can of soup I'd brought along for lunch. Cold from the can the way I'd grown used to eating—everything in a rush—

even though the ship's small oven would've heated the soup just fine in about five minutes.

Afterward, I brushed my teeth, combed my hair and even washed my face. Around me others were doing much the same. Cowboy was dousing himself in Stetson. Tammy had an array of make-up out. Eyeliner, black. Lipstick, bright red. Chris was grooming every hair on his head.

It was an eternity later that Bob called out, "Crew, we're fifteen minutes out. We'll circle the field twice in formation, then head on in."

Before long, we were circling Sembach Air Base. The commentary from the front-end had us all eager to race forward, but we were strapped in and ready for landing. "Will you look at the crowd?"

"There must be three or four thousand people down there."

"Let's give them a show," called out Bob. "Crew, one more time around the field."

I heard Tower's squawk return clear now as Bob relayed to Tower that we were going to go around once more. I heard Lady-2 and Lady-3. "Roger, breaking formation. Lead heading in."

"Crew, we'll be touching down in a few minutes here. I just want to say a few last words, so as soon as we hit the ground you're free to disperse. I know you're all eager to find your loved ones and some of you will be eager to go off home to find some quiet time alone."

"Do a little motion grinding," cut in Ice.

"Well, that, too." Bob's voice wavered and then took a very serious tone. "This homecoming celebration is for you, so enjoy it. It's something you'll remember for the rest of your life, and something you'll hopefully tell your children about. You have plenty to be proud of, each of you. Plenty to be proud of whether you flew combat or were part of the support team. You all did one hell of a job!

"There'll be plenty of time for quiet moments with your wives, husbands, girlfriends, or boyfriends later. You each will be given a pass, so there's no duty until Wednesday. The only thing you really have to do today after we land is unload your personal gear. But that can stay on the plane until later. I understand the base has donated food: brats, buns, and all the fixings; and the local communities have donated beer and drinks. Find your loved ones, enjoy the celebrations!"

A short pause followed. "Who's got the flag?"

"I do," returned Chris.

"Crow, as soon as we land, crack the hatch. Chris, then you can fly Old Glory. You'll probably need two people to hold it."

"I'm on top of it, sir."

My heart began pounding faster and faster, blood racing in my ears. We touched down on the runway, a small jolt, then everything smoothed out. We slowed to taxi speed. I watched as Crow opened the overhead hatch and as Chris and Cowboy raised Old Glory.

Behind us, Lady-2 and Lady-3 landed. Lady-2 raised the host country flag, the German flag. Lady-3, the unit colors.

In the cabin there was momentary pandemonium. Those of us strapped in couldn't stay strapped in; we had to get out of our seats. We did so almost as if the seats were on fire. We paced back and forth waiting for the sleek Gray Lady to stop so we could pile out the door.

But then when she did stop and Crow opened the crew entrance door and Bob cleared us out, no one moved. It was as if we didn't know what to do. The open door was there, but beyond it?

Then all at the same time, we scrambled for the door. I was there first. Bad Boy and Happy were right behind me. Doc, from all the way in the rear, was right behind them.

"Go ahead," I said.

"No, you."

"No, you first."

"Shit, I'll go," said Doc. He stormed out the door, head high. I followed. American flags, yellow ribbons and people were everywhere.

There was an enormous crowd held back by ropes. I saw video cameras all over the place. I looked into the crowd for the one face I wanted to see but did not see it. My heart skipped. What if Katie wasn't here?

I glanced back at the crew filtering quickly through the crew door now, and then moved into the faceless crowd. I stared and wandered, stared and wandered. Time passed, seconds or minutes I don't know which.

Crew two and crew three were mixing into the crowd of thousands now. I saw couples racing to embrace each other. Men hugging and kissing their wives. Fathers embracing their sons and daughters. Women running into the arms of their waiting husbands. But no Katie.

The buses arrived carrying those that had come in on the C-5. They filtered into the crowd. Everyone racing to find their families, their loved ones.

"You seen Katie?" I asked one couple I knew, interrupting their precious embrace and not meaning to.

"She was waiting over by the rope."

"Thanks." I rushed off, in a panic now. Katie was petite, but how could I miss her? Her long flowing brown hair was easy enough to spot.

I stopped and scanned the crowd then headed toward the roped off area. As I turned around, I spotted Katie, long brown hair and all. She was wearing dark jeans. A white blouse was partially hidden beneath a waist-length leather jacket. She was waving a tiny American flag, and a yellow ribbon was tied to the lapel of her jacket.

Her face was filled with the same confusion and fears mine had held; she hadn't seen me yet. What followed was a scene straight from the end of a Harlequin romance.

She turned and smiled just as I raced toward her. I picked her up and held her in my arms, an embrace I never wanted to relinquish. She was in tears now and so was I. Finally, we kissed and at last I smiled.

"I love you," I whispered in her ear. "I missed you. God, did I miss you!"

"I missed you, too. No, don't let go, hold me."

"I'm back, Katie, I'll never leave you again."

"Shh. Do you hear that?"

"Hear what?"

"Listen, music. There's a band over there. Let's go listen. You hungry? Thirsty? There are brats and drinks."

"I am hungry," I replied.

"I'll get you something."

"No, I don't want to let you go," I whispered, "let's just stand here a while longer. No one will notice."

Katie and I stayed just long enough at the celebrations to hear the band, eat a brat, and gather my belongings, and then we headed home. Katie drove.

It was strange holding her hand, looking at her face, seeing her smile, and smelling her perfume.

The silence between us as she drove to our apartment on the other side of base spoke volumes. We didn't know exactly what to say to each other after the I love you's and the I miss you's. It seemed the months apart had made us strangers, but the fact was my love for Katie soared and my heart raced every time I looked at her. I held her hand tighter and tighter.

I know she was dying to ask me about the war. I hadn't talked about it much in my letters. Actually, I usually avoided the subject even in our phone conversations.

As we drove up the road to the admin side of base, I noticed the mustard fields of last summer were gone. I'd pictured those yellow-green fields often; they represented peace and tranquility. Small mounds of snow still lingered along the sides of the road though it was already early spring.

Katie stopped at the gate, and then handed her ID to the guard.

"Can I see your ID, too, sir?"

"Sure, just a minute."

"Can I see your registration, too?"

Katie pointed to the glove box. "Here you go."

"Okay." The guard handed back the IDs and the registration. "Would you mind opening the trunk and hood?"

"Sure."

Katie opened the trunk and hood. The guard looked in the window at my bags, and then said, "You have a good day now."

"Have a good day, too," I replied, "and thanks."

The guard had a puzzled look on his face as he waved us

through. He didn't understand why I was thanking him, but I was glad to see security was tight. "Been like that since I've been gone?"

"Usually worse."

"That's good, real good."

Katie furrowed her eyebrows; she didn't understand either. "I didn't check the mail today; you want to go down to the post office and check it?"

"Expecting anything?"

"Bills, just bills."

"Let's just go home."

"Good. You look tired anyway. I'll take you home and go later. Was it a long flight?"

"Nine hours. Did you have to wait long?" I asked.

"Since eleven. They said you'd be in around twelve. I didn't want to miss you, so I came early." Katie parked the car in front of the apartment building. I let go of her hand.

"Just leave the bags," she said, "We can get them later."

We lived on the first floor, but the building was on a hill, so we still had to climb a long flight of stairs. Holding my hand, Katie led the way.

The apartment was much the same as I remembered it except for the living room, which was virtually empty. A kitchen chair was pulled up in front of the TV and there were big empty spaces where our living room furniture set had been. I could picture Katie sitting there every night glued to the TV in that rickety chair waiting for news.

The apartment smelled like perfume, Katie's perfume. There was no longer a balanced blend of our odors, hers and mine. I walked past the bathroom to the bedroom, glancing into the spare room as I went past. My computer and desk sat in one corner of it just as I had left it.

I walked into the bedroom. The apartment was the same; Katie and I weren't. We'd never be the same. In time, I hoped that we could heal. We'd heal together; that much was for certain, if nothing else was.

Katie said, "You look tired. Why don't you take a nap? I've got some things to do in the kitchen. I'll wake you later."

"I don't want to."

"Shh." Katie pressed a finger to my lips. "Sleep. I'll wake you later."

I lay back with my arms crossed behind my head, intent on not going to sleep. But the covers were warm, the pillow so soft and fluffy that the last thing I remembered was Katie pulling the blankets snug. What I didn't see was her standing there watching me until long after I fell asleep. My last thought was that I was home, really and truly home.

The storm was over; the sun was shining at last.

Epilogue
Germany, April 1991

Days passed and soon March was over and April was beginning. The week began with April Fool's Day and slowly progressed from there. For Katie and me, the war was behind us. The only thing I ever told her about my ordeal was that I didn't want to go back.

She understood what that meant, so after that we never talked about it. We looked only to the future. The healing had begun but wasn't complete. Both of us knew neither would be exactly the same person we had been before January the sixteenth. We were willing to accept that.

Our marriage that was less than two years old had been severely tested, but it had survived. It was, in fact, stronger than it had ever been. Other couples weren't so fortunate. Marriages were floundering, near divorce. Families that had been united were now broken. Lives had been changed and shattered all at once.

The mission wasn't the same any more. I went to work

Monday to Friday, 07:30 to 16:30. The planes were still down for engine overhauls, inspections, and other long-term repairs, so we weren't flying. The days were slowly passing by. It was good to be home.

We knew for sure that the base was closing, along with dozens of others across Europe. The draw-down under the Conventional Forces Agreement was a reality. The actual date hadn't been set though we expected the closure to take place sometime in June; and June being only two months away, this was what everyone at the unit was preparing for. There was so much for everyone to do, it was unbelievable. Outprocessing, assignments, packing, all of our unit buildings had to be cleaned, all the items within inventoried. The list went on and on.

I still hadn't re-enlisted, so at present I didn't have enough retainability to get an assignment unless, of course, my plan was to get out of the military. The Air Force was also offering early outs. I could be a civilian in a matter of days if I really wanted to. I was unsure. My career was at a turning point and I wasn't sure down which road to turn, though I knew one thing for sure, I couldn't afford to get out nor could I afford to stay in. We needed a steady paycheck to pay the bills if we were going to move again. Moving was expensive whether the government footed part of the bill or not. Katie was tired of moving. I was tired of moving. This would be her fourth move in two years: Washington, Arizona, Germany, and wherever they sent us next. This would be my fifth move in three years.

We had talked about it. She wanted me to stay in, but she also told me the decision was ultimately mine and that she'd stay with me no matter what I decided. Either way, I knew it'd be a hard choice—no road would be easy. Under normal circumstances, I would've re-enlisted in a heartbeat, but things were no longer normal. A week that had started slowly hadn't stayed that way; and by Friday, things were downright hectic.

I'd left home at 07:00, same as usual. I'd already eaten the lunch Katie had packed, and at 12:30, the small scheduling section I worked in was empty. Everyone else had gone home for lunch or was across base running errands. Everyone knew today would be a long day, yet I was still at my desk, staring into space while I waited for the phone to ring.

The manning report Major James had asked for with projections through next week was sitting on my desktop, neatly organized in sections: who was on leave, who was on Duty Not Including Flight, who was TDY, who was available for duty, and who had appointments when and what for. Standard stuff included in the daily manning report I'd given him at 07:30 this morning. But that had only been the projections for Monday, not today and the entire week ahead.

There was also a list of flights for next week. Finally, we were going to fly again and I'd just finished scheduling the crews. Seven flights projected, a good start.

I glanced at the clock on the wall. It read 13:05. I was fairly certain the chief and the major were in their office. I was about to get up when the phone rang. I answered it on the first ring. "Scheduling, can I help you?"

"Chief here. You finish that report? The major wants it ASAP!"

"I'm on it chief; I'll bring it over."

"Bring the scheduling books too."

"You got it. I'll be right over." I started to hang up the phone.

"Did you schedule the flights for next week yet?"

"Just finished them."

"Good, bring those too."

"You got it." I hung up the phone.

"Was that the chief?"

Recognizing the voice, I turned. "Yeah, Ray, that was the chief. You want to bring this stuff over? He wanted the flights for next week, too. I finished them. Here."

"No, you go ahead. Wait. On second thought, I'll go with you. You outlined it, so you go over it with him."

Ray was the section chief. I wasn't going to argue with him if he wanted to go along, and so I said, "Okay." The door to the operations director's office was closed when Ray and I arrived. Ray knocked, and the chief told us to come in. As soon as I stepped in and Ray closed the door behind us, I knew something was wrong.

"Here's the manning report and the crew lists, Chief. Let me go through the projections with you." I went through the report while the chief eyed the copy I'd given him, and then I went quickly through the crew schedule for the following week.

"Good, good. You have the schedule book? Let me see it."

"I need thirty-six names, three full crews. How many did you say were DNIF again?"

"Six."

"Give me the names again. Let me update my board here." I read off the names again. "Any coming off today or Monday?"

"Miller should be coming off today. Should've given me the forms this morning. He probably will go to afternoon sick call, though."

"Soon as he's cleared, I want to know."

"You got it."

"I want three good crews. You know what this is for, don't you?"

"I can guess."

"Good, keep this between us and these four walls. It's not positive yet, though it looks good. We'll know definite by Monday, so anyone that's on these crews shouldn't be flying Monday or probably even Tuesday if you can help it. Take the single people first if you can, then those without kids. And still I want three good crews."

"You'll get them, Chief, you'll get them."

"No, I mean now. Let's go over the names."

I looked at Ray, and Ray looked at me. "It's going to be a long day, isn't it, Chief?"

"You know it is."

And it was. It was nearly 18:00 when I made the cross-base trek home. The table was set, supper was well charred in the oven and Katie was in a panic because I hadn't called. She had expected me an hour earlier. I told her, "I know, I'm sorry. I should have called."

Katie was closing the oven door, and she threw the potholder at me. "Well, why didn't you?"

"I know, I'm sorry. I didn't know I'd be this late," I replied. I wanted to tell her exactly why I had been late, but I didn't see any good in upsetting her further.

"I called the office. There was no answer, so I figured you must be on your way home. That was an hour ago. Where were you?"

"Smell's good, pot roast?"

"Used to be." Katie shot back.

"I'm sorry, I'll call next time." I looked at the table, which was already set and asked, "What do you want to drink?"

"Water's fine. What's wrong? Something's wrong, isn't it?"

I poured two glasses of ice water. "No, nothing. Here. Want some more ice?"

She shook her head and sat down. "I was worried, you know. It's only a ten-minute drive from the other side of base."

"I'm sorry. I'll call next time." I cut a piece of the pot roast using my fork. "Tastes good. You use that soup mix my mother told you about?"

"It doesn't taste good; it's burnt. What's wrong?"

"Nothing, usual Friday. Chief wanted to make sure the flights were scheduled for next week, that's all. I got stuck in his office on the way out."

"You sure?"

"Yeah. Can I have some more potatoes?"

Katie looked at me. "You want me to warm up leftovers from yesterday?"

"No, really, this is fine. Can you grab me a sharp knife though?"

Katie passed me a knife from the silverware drawer. "You said flights. You flying next week?"

"Not Monday or Tuesday."

"Good. You know I have an appointment at the optometrist Monday. I can't drive home with dilated pupils."

"Don't worry, I'll be able to drop you off and pick you up. It's at two-thirty, right?" Katie nodded. "Good. Maybe I can get off work early then."

For a time, we ate quietly. I did my best to clean my plate, but eventually pushed it away.

Later she asked, "You didn't eat much. You sure you don't want me to warm up some of those leftovers from yesterday?"

I touched her hand, and then I grabbed it and pulled her close. "I love you. You know that, don't you?"

"I love you, too." Katie turned; I kissed her, and then held her tight again. She didn't know it, but I was near tears. The past was coming back to haunt me, and I was unsure if I was prepared for it.

We spent a quiet evening, just the two of us. We went for a walk after sunset, just as we used to once upon a time. We watched TV, but with only one channel we didn't have much of a choice. It was the Armed Forces Network or the Armed Forces Network. We still hadn't bought a couch, so we sat on blankets on the floor.

On TV there wasn't anything interesting, so mostly we just talked to each other. We had a lot to talk about, especially with the upcoming move. A hundred times in the course of those two hours, I wanted to tell her what I knew, but I didn't. I knew it would tear her heart apart if I told her there was a possibility I might be going back.

I could only remember the promise I'd made to her that first night after I had returned. She had asked me if I thought I'd ever have to go back, and I had responded with an emphatic no. "I'll never leave you again," I had said. But now I wasn't so sure.

While I waited for the news to come on, Katie readied for bed. She always wore the same silken nightgown with her long brown hair tied back in a french braid. I watched her for a time, then tuned into the news.

The first thing on the late news that evening was a piece on a victory celebration parade. It was a several-days-old piece from a news broadcast in the states. Gulf war heroes returning home.

Katie was crossing from the kitchen to the bathroom when the phone rang.

"I'll get it. It's probably my mother." We had just been talking about my mother. The last time I had called her had been the day after my return three weeks ago. I swallowed hard when I recognized Ray's voice on the other end of the line. "Did I forget something?" I asked

"No," Ray answered, "you didn't forget anything. Be over at the squadron at 04:00 tomorrow morning with your bags."

"This is a joke, right?" April Fool's day had been Monday; I'd gotten old Ray pretty good.

"No, this is real, I'm sorry. The word came down about an hour ago. You know I'll be here if Katie needs anything. You just tell her to call me. You have my number, right?"

"Of course, Ray."

"I gotta go. You know I have to make other calls."

"You need any help?"

"No, I got it. You just spend some time with that wife of yours. See ya."

The receiver went dead. I hung up the phone. I didn't envy Ray having to make all those phone calls. Suddenly, thoughts of Turkey and war flashed before my eyes. I had to sit down. Things had to be serious if they were stepping up the timetable; the jump from a slim possibility to a Go was too quick.

I needed to think. Katie was still in the bathroom. I had to find my A-bags and start packing them.

I was stuffing dark green canvas bags when Katie found me—not what I'd intended. She knew in an instant what it meant: the phone call, the bags.

"You son-of-a-bitch; you knew all this time." She slapped me. Her face was red and tears were streaming in long unbroken lines. "When were you going to tell me?"

"Katie, I didn't know until just now. They said it was only a possibility, and I didn't know any details. We weren't even supposed to find out for sure until Monday or Tuesday. Don't let it tear us apart. Jesus, Katie, don't let it tear us apart."

"I put it all behind us. Damn you! You lied to me. You said, 'Never again.' "

"You know I couldn't make a promise like that and keep it. It's not my fault."

"Then you shouldn't have made the promise." Katie didn't swear, ever. I tried to hold and comfort her, but she pushed me away.

"Katie, calm down. You know I—"

"To hell with your promises! I don't want to calm down. Just once, I want to be mad. I have a right to be mad and I'm going to be mad! I want to be mad. I have to let it all out or I'm going to explode. I can't hold it inside anymore. Do you understand? You expect me to keep it all bottled up inside me. I can't!"

"No one asked you to."

"Do you know what it was like waiting and waiting and waiting? Do you know? I sat in front of that goddamn TV set every day. I didn't move. I watched the TV. I ate in front of it. When I was in the bathroom, I kept it turned up so I could hear it. I woke up to it. When I came home from work, I came home to it. I was afraid that if I missed even a moment, I'd miss hearing about you. I knew something terrible would happen if I wasn't listening. I don't want that again, never again. I don't want it."

"Just because we're going back doesn't mean there's going to be war again. I'm sure it has to do with the civil unrest."

"I don't care what it's about. We're not going back, you're going back. Don't you see? It's the same, no matter what the circumstance. I'll be tied to the phone, to the TV. If you die, I'll never forgive you!"

Teardrops welled up in my eyes. "I'm not going to die, Katie. I'm coming back. I'm a survivor, remember? Survivors pull through. You tie that yellow ribbon, you tie it tight, because I'll be coming home. And you'll wait for me!"

"Damn you!" She brought her fist down on my chest. I pulled her close. She was trembling. I held her as tight as I could. "Damn that I love you," she whispered.

"I love you, too. I'll always love you, Katie."

I looked up at the clock; it was 23:45. Katie and I had about four hours until I had to go. There wasn't much time to mend the pieces of our lives; and while I wished in those ensuing hours that I could hold back time, I couldn't. Our world was changing again. We had no control over tomorrow. Tomorrow controlled us. Such was the life of the duty-and honor-bound. You went when called. Did what was asked.

Sometimes you paid with flesh and bone. Other times you paid with things that no one could see, the scars running inside your mind and etched onto your soul. The scars forever changed you and shaped you. They were the things you really couldn't talk about or express in simple words.

As I looked into Katie's eyes, I could see the scars within her as well. It was the type of thing no one or any thing could prepare you for. No one had ever told me that these things called duty and honor would take hold of my life in such a way or that they would have such effect on those that I loved. These were the things that no one told you when you enlisted. These were the things that only those who had served with you could understand and relate to. Well, Katie had served with me and she understood. She understood all too well.

At 03:30 I left the apartment, closing the door behind me and leaving Katie shivering in the hallway. I stood there quietly on the steps for a few heartbeats. I could see her through the thin drapes in the window, shivering more now before collapsing to the floor in great sobs. I wanted to rush back in and tell her everything would be all right, but how did I know for sure? I didn't. A false promise is an empty promise and some things are better left unsaid than said.

As I walked away and went down the steps, I didn't look back. Everything I had to do was in front of me. I had to have a clear mind to get through it. In a time when divorce had already divided families of fellow crewers, I knew in my heart that Katie would be waiting for me when I returned. I didn't doubt it for an instant. There was a bond between us. We would share it for the rest of our lives.

Katie would wipe the tears from her face and stand strong by the window, watching as I left. She would take control of the thing I couldn't control. Because underneath it all, she was stronger than me. She had to be to get through it, to stand there calmly as everything around her fell apart for the second time.

The trek across base was short—and long. I watched the yellow stripes of the road while the memories of the last few weeks with Katie played in my mind. For an instant, it all seemed a dream and I believed I had never left the Gulf. Then I realized that a part of me hadn't left the Gulf. It was the part of me that was in my past.

After entering the ops building, I went quickly to the briefing room where the commander was about to speak. I sat down quietly to listen, picturing Katie in my thoughts.

"Gentlemen and Ladies, you've each been given a set of orders. Now those orders say we should be home in thirty days; of course, thirty days is just a waggle. Our destination is classified, but it doesn't take a rocket scientist to figure out where we're going. Our mission will be support operations for Operation Provide Comfort, an effort to aid Kurdish refugees. We'll be flying combat missions, most likely over northern Iraq, nothing new." The commander paused for a moment, then concluded with, "You know where to pick up your combat gear, so let's get moving. Good luck, gentlemen and ladies. We leave in two hours. I'll see you on the ground at our destination."

Our planes did leave in two hours, and when they did, I would leave Katie and my world behind for the second time. Some day I would get back and would be able to have dreams. That day wasn't this day.

A week later, at 26,000 feet, during a combat mission over northern Iraq, I re-enlisted in the United States Air Force. It was one of the proudest moments of my entire life because I knew it was something I wanted to do. The proudest moment of my life came in 1994 when the first of my children was born.

Sembach Air Base flight operations closed in early June. Katie and I moved on. Years later I would become a writer. Among the many books I'd write would be this story of a time and place that now seems a distant memory in the fading echoes of my thoughts.

GLOSSARY OF TERMS

AAA Anti-Aircraft Artillery. Most Iraqi AAA ranged from short range 23mm to long range 130mm artillery. Small caliber weapons fire vast amounts of rounds and rely largely on this high number of shells to destroy the target. Large caliber weapons fire large shells, which contain an explosive charge (detonated at altitude) to scatter a great number of fragments. Most AAA systems rely on command and control communications and radar to help target enemy aircraft and are largely mobile.

AAM Air-to-Air Missile. Most fighters are equipped with AAMs, which are used to destroy enemy aircraft.

AIM A type of air-to-air missile. The AIM-7 (radar-seeking missile) and AIM-9 (heat-seeking missile) are widely used by US fighters.

Alarm There are four conditions of alarm associated with possible nuclear, biological, chemical and/or conventional attacks. With the exception of the all clear signal, the alarms require the donning of protective gear and assuming defensive posture. See All Clear, Alarm Black, Alarm Red, Alarm Yellow.

Alarm Black Nuclear, biological or chemical contamination is expected or present.

Alarm Red Alarm condition that means an attack is imminent or in progress.

Alarm Yellow	Alarm condition that means an attack is probable.
All Clear	Alarm condition that means to resume normal wartime activities.
ASM	Air-to-Surface Missile. Smart ASMs launched from fighters are very effective in destroying their targets.
AWACS	Airborne Warning and Control System. Refers to the E3A Sentry aircraft and/or its associated airborne radar system used to detect enemy aircraft and direct friendly aircraft to intercept them.
Bandit	An enemy aircraft. Usually a fighter.
Bogie	An unidentified (possibly hostile) aircraft/fighter.
Buff	Refers to the B-52. A heavy bomber capable of delivering a substantial payload.
C3CM	Command Communications and Control Counter Measures. Tactics for denying enemy command and control communications through jamming and other electronic means.
CAP	Combat Air Patrol. Normally a group of one to four F-15C, which provide air support and are directed to intercept enemy aircraft by AWACS.
Control	The ground controller at the operations center.
Dogfight	Aerial combat with friendly fighters pitted against enemy fighters.

Eagle	Refers primarily to the F-15C, an air superiority fighter used for air support. Could also refer to the F-15E Strike Eagle which can be used for deep interdiction missions. The F-15C and F-15E are very similar and it is difficult to tell the two aircraft apart. However, the F-15E normally carries a payload along with its air-to-air missiles.
EC-130	Electronic Combat configured C-130, the Gray Lady. One of the most capable electronic warfare aircraft in the US inventory, it is primarily a communications jammer. The many different EC-130 configurations are denoted with a suffix. The experimental models flown in the Persian Gulf have since been decommissioned due to budget issues.
Egress	Exiting the sensitive/critical area where enemy activity can be expected.
Environment	The targeted area where most enemy activity can be expected to originate from.
EW	Electronic Warfare. Primarily the use of counter measures (like jamming) and other electronic means to detect and counter enemy communications and radar.
Falcon	F-16. A superior air-to-air/air-to-ground capable aircraft. Excellent for close-in dogfights.
Ingress	Entering the sensitive/critical area where enemy activity can be expected.

Jam	To deny/degrade enemy command and control communications through electronic means. Effective against AAA, SAM sites, and enemy aircraft by blocking communications and/or radar.
Jam window	Refers to times when the EC-130 aircraft must jam to support an inbound wave or package group.
JP-4	Jet fuel.
KC	Refers to the KC-130, KC-135 or KC-10 aerial refueler. US fighters such as the F-15 and F-16 use KC for aerial refueling. Aerial refueling is vital for fighters that provide air support and conduct long-range missions.
Life Support	Group responsible for maintaining aircrew gear, which includes helmets, oxygen masks, and air chemical protection gear.
MCC	Mission Crew Commander/Controller. An officer who controls the mission crew of an aircraft such as the EC-130 or AWACS.
MCS	Mission Crew Supervisor. A senior enlisted crewmember who often coordinates with other EW assets.
MiG Sweep	A forward CAP dedicated to intercept enemy aircraft.
MPC	Mission Planning Cell. Performs auxiliary duties such as planning, coordination and duty driving.

MRE	Meal Ready to Eat. Field or combat rations consisting of packaged and largely dehydrated foods. MREs contain a main item such as barbecued pork, hot dogs, or ham; a vegetable item; and a dessert such as a brownie. Also usually included is instant coffee or hot chocolate and crackers with peanut butter, jelly or cheese.
Nomex	The material flight suits, flight jackets, and flight gloves are made out of. It is designed to resist flames.
NVG	Night Vision Goggles. NVG are very similar to binoculars except they allow you to see in the dark. Small and distant lights can be reflected through the green of the viewer. Afterburners reflected in NVG are normally a very bright green.
Ops	The operations center. A center of control for missions and crews.
Package	A group of friendly aircraft, which usually includes fighters, bombers, and radar jammers projected to enter enemy territory. A package normally refers to more than one wave (or groups) projected inbound into enemy territory.
Pad	An aircraft's hardstand or parking area.
Raven	Refers to the EF-111. A capable radar jamming aircraft.
RC	Refers to the RC-135. A reconnaissance aircraft.

SAM	Surface-to-Air Missile. Iraq's SAMs ranged from handheld Stingers, to mobile SA-13 air defense units, to fixed sites such as SA-2 sites. SAMs are fired at enemy aircraft. SAM sites/units depend on radar and command and control communications for their effectiveness.
SCIF	Sensitive Compartmented Information Facility, a high security, restricted access facility.
SP	Security police. A security police officer.
Splash	Knocking an enemy fighter/aircraft out of the sky (destroying it).
Squawk	Refers to an aircraft's channel or radio frequency.
Thunderbolt	Refers to the A-10, a ground attack aircraft.
Tower	The air traffic controller at base.
Wave	A group of friendly aircraft, which usually includes fighters, bombers, and radar jammers projected to enter enemy territory. Part of a package.
Weasel	Refers to F-4G fighter. A capable fighter that can locate and then destroy enemy electronic emissions. Also used for reconnaissance.
Window	(see Jam window)

Timeline

Start of the Persian Gulf War
Wed., 16 Jan   Alert
Thursday, 17 Jan   Fly to Turkey

First week deployed
Friday, 18 Jan   1st combat flight
Saturday, 19 Jan   2nd combat flight
Sunday, 20 Jan   3rd combat flight
Monday, 21 Jan   4th combat flight
Tuesday, 22 Jan   5th combat flight
Wed., 23 Jan   6th combat flight
Thursday, 24 Jan   7th combat flight

Second week deployed
Friday, 25 Jan   8th combat flight
Saturday, 26 Jan   9th combat flight
Sunday, 27 Jan   10th combat flight
Monday, 28 Jan   11th combat flight
Tuesday, 29 Jan   12th combat flight
Wed., 30 Jan   13th combat flight. First major ground offensive
Thursday, 31 Jan   14th combat flight

Third week deployed
Friday, 1 Feb   No flight
Saturday, 2 Feb   15th combat flight
Sunday, 3 Feb   16th combat flight
Monday, 4 Feb   16th flight ends
Tuesday, 5 Feb   17th combat flight
Wed., 6 Feb   18th combat flight
Thursday, 7 Feb   no flight

Fourth week deployed
Friday, 8 Feb   19th flight
Saturday, 9 Feb   20th combat flight
Sunday, 10 Feb   20th flight ends
Monday, 11 Feb   21st combat flight
Tuesday, 12 Feb   22nd combat flight
Wed., 13 Feb   MPC
Thursday, 14 Feb   MPC

Fifth week deployed
Friday, 15 Feb   23rd flight, Baghdad
Saturday, 16 Feb   Bad weather
Sunday, 17 Feb   Bad weather. MPC
Monday, 18 Feb   25th flight, Baghdad
Tuesday, 19 Feb   26th flight, Baghdad
Wed., 20 Feb   No flight
Thursday, 21 Feb   27th flight, Baghdad

Sixth week deployed
Friday, 22 Feb   No flight
Saturday, 23 Feb   Green light for ground war. 28th flight, Baghdad.
Sunday, 24 Feb   29th flight, Baghdad. Ground campaign starts. Late evening 30th flight, Baghdad.
Monday, 25 Feb   30th flight return. Kuwaiti New Year.
Tuesday, 26 Feb   31st flight, Baghdad
Wed., 27 Feb   32nd flight, Baghdad. Liberation of Kuwait City begins.
Thursday, 28 Feb   32nd combat flight continues. Kuwait City is liberated.

Seventh week deployed
Friday, 1 Mar   On standby. KTO mop up begins.
Saturday, 2 Mar   On standby. KTO mop up continues.
Sunday, 3 Mar   On standby. KTO mop up continues.
Monday, 4 Mar   On standby. KTO mop up cont. Civil unrest growing.
Tuesday, 5 Mar   On standby. Civil unrest continues.
Wed., 6 Mar   On standby. Civil unrest continues.
Thursday, 7 Mar   First troops going home. Readying to go home

Eighth week deployed
Friday, 8 Mar   Readying to go.
Sat., 9 Mar   Waiting to go.
Sun., 10 Mar   Waiting to go.
Mon., 11 Mar   Return to Germany.

1st Crew

According to crews flown with

Front Crew

Position	Aircrew Member
AC	Captain Smily
Co	Lt. Faber
Eng	Jerry
Nav	Captain Wilcox
AMT	Big John

Mission Crew

Position	Aircrew Member
MCC	Captain Willie
MCS (Pos. 5)	Todd (PBJ)
Pos. 1	Robert (Bobby)
Pos. 2	Charlotte
Pos. 3	Thomas
Pos. 4	Craig (Cosmo)
Pos. 6	Author
Pos. 7	Allen

2nd Crew

According to crews flown with

Front Crew

Position	Aircrew Member
AC	Sammy
Co	Ice
Eng	Patrick
Nav	Bill
AMT	Crow

Mission Crew

Position	Aircrew Member
MCC	Tennessee Jim
MCS (Pos. 5)	Chris
Pos. 1	Tammy
Pos. 2	Sparrow
Pos. 3	Ziggy, Happy
Pos. 4	Popcorn, Bad Boy
Pos. 6	Author
Pos. 7	Mike, Cowboy

3rd Crew

According to crews flown with

Front Crew

Position	Aircrew Member
AC	Captain Hillman
Co	Candid
Eng	Darwin
Nav	Beebop
AMT	Rollin

Mission Crew

Position	Aircrew Member
MCC	Stopwatch
MCS (Pos. 5)	Steve
Pos. 1	Sandy
Pos. 2	Topper
Pos. 3	Karen (Mellow Yellow)
Pos. 4	Able
Pos. 6	Author
Pos. 7	Tommy